MANAGING
the BUSINESS OF
SCHOOLS

MANAGING *the* BUSINESS OF SCHOOLS

Edited by
IRIS KEATING
and RAY MOORCROFT

National College for
School Leadership

P·C·P
Paul Chapman
Publishing

Paul Chapman Publishing
SAGE Publications Ltd
1 Oliver's Yard
55 City Road
London EC1Y 1SP

SAGE Publications Inc
2455 Teller Road
Thousand Oaks, California 91320

SAGE Publications India Pvt Ltd
B-42, Panchsheel Enclave
Post Box 4109
New Delhi 110 017

Library of Congress Control Number: 2006901379

A catalogue record for this book is available
from the British Library

ISBN 10 1-4129-2116-3   ISBN 13 978-1-4129-2116-9
ISBN 10 1-4129-2117-1   ISBN 13 978-1-4129-2117-6 (pbk)

Typeset by C&M Digitals (P) Ltd., Chennai, India
Printed in Great Britain by T.J. International, Padstow, Cornwall.
Printed on paper from sustainable resources

Contents

Contents **vii**

Conclusion   55
    Effective management   55
    Realising the possibilities   55
Suggestions for Further Reading   58
Useful Resources   58

Chapter 4   Managing Human Resources   59
            Anne Bryson

Introduction   59
Policies and Procedures in Practice   59
Recruitment and Selection   60
Grievance and Discipline   65
Absence   66
Termination of Employment   67
    Redundancy   67
    Terminating a contract of employment   67
Terms and Conditions of Employment   68
Employee Relations   69
Rewards and Benefits   69
Legal Requirements   71
Equal Opportunities Legislation   72
Developing Staff – Putting Vision and Values into Practice   72
Other issues which impact on Effective Human
Resource Management   74
Conclusion   74
Suggestions for Further Reading   75
Useful resources   75

Chapter 5   Office Systems Management   77
            Jean Blair

Introduction   77
The Background to Office Systems Management   77
The Changing Face of OSM   79
The SBM Today   80
Background to the Developments and Changes of
the Past Two Decades   83
Improved Performance   84
Legal Requirements   86
    Other Issues that Need to be Addressed   87
The SBM of the Future   87
Conclusion   88
Suggestions for Further Reading   88
Useful resources   88

Notes on Contributors

Jean Blair worked in schools for 36 years, spending the final eighteen years of her teaching career as Headteacher of a multi-ethnic comprehensive school. Since autumn 2003 her work has included that of a facilitator on the CSBM and DSBM programmes and she is currently the NW Manager for the Bursar Development Programme.

Anne Bryson has spent most of her working life supporting School Business Management, initially as an officer of Gloucestershire LEA and more recently as a freelance consultant. She supports schools with the appointment of school business staff, leads support staff in-service training, has conducted a number of support team reviews and is a tutor and assessor on both CSBM and DSBM.

Joy Coulbeck is a Senior Lecturer in Education, Leadership and Management at Manchester Metropolitan University and is Programme Leader of the BA (Honours) School Business Management degree. Formerly a Primary Headteacher, she is a tutor on the CSBM and DSBM programmes.

Margaret Dadley My background is Primary School Headship. After leaving headship I went to work for East Midlands Leadership working across all the leadership programmes from the National College for School Leadership. I have been involved with the bursar development programme from the beginning. My main interests outside of education are travel and my grandchildren.

David Evans David Evans gained B Ed (Hons) from St Martin's College, Lancaster. More recently Headteacher at Kirkley Middle School in Lowestoft until 2001. Now Education Facilitator and Tutor, working with several NCSL and TDA programmes, including delivering and assessing the CSBM/DSBM and NPQH. Formerly programme manager for CSBM in East of England.

Dave Grewer Primary Headteacher for 10 years in three schools. Now a tutor for CSBM and DSBM in addition to a wider range of NSCL Leadership programmes for middle leaders, senior leadership teams and headteachers. An accredited Ofsted Team Inspector.

Angela Harnett Angela Harnett has worked in education for the last 27 years. She has worked with a variety of age groups within the school sector. She became a university lecturer in 1999. This role included undergraduate and leadership and management teaching. Through this role she became involved in the School Business Management programme as a tutor and writer. She has recently become the Education Quality and Standards Manager for the Institute of Administrative Management (the awarding body for the programme).

Iris Keating is a principal lecturer at Manchester Metropolitan University where she is the Project Manager of the Schools Business Management Materials Review. She also teaches educational leadership and management on the Open University's Masters programme.

Dittany Matthews After a career in banking, Dittany Matthews became Business Manager of an 11–16 comprehensive school in south west London. After completing the pilot certificate course for school business managers in October 2002, she has been a tutor and assessor on the course.

Jenny Moore Having worked in accountancy in the private sector for a number of years, joined the education service in 1986, working in a number of roles in HR and Finance, latterly as Area Finance Manager. Supported schools across all sectors and extensively involved in training programmes for the delivery of LMS (Local Management of Schools) to governors, headteachers and administrative staff. Currently School Business Manager in a large secondary school in Essex and a CSBM course tutor.

Irene Naftalin has worked as a senior lecturer at MMU lecturing on the Masters programme in Educational Leadership and Management, since 1991. She has worked with the Bursar Development Programme since its first cohort as well as the development teams of other NCSL programmes, New Visions for Early Headship, Leading from the Middle and Strategic Leadership of ICT. Prior to coming to MMU she was involved in national initiatives leading a pilot educational project for young offenders and another for adult unemployed.

Clive Opie is a Deputy Director of the Institute of Education at Manchester Metropolitan University. He is a CSBM tutor and also undertakes NPQH school based assessments. Formerly, he was in the School of Education at the University of Sheffield and Director of the School's MEd programme in Singapore.

Anthony Shallcross Leader for International Education and designated researcher. Over twenty years' experience teaching in schools. Two edited books and several journal papers and chapters in books published in the broad field of education for sustainable development.

Peter Taylor is headteacher of Worth Primary School in Cheshire. In addition to serving as a headteacher for some 20 years Peter works as an associate tutor for Manchester Metropolitan Universtity, as a consultant leader on a variety of programmes for the English National College for School Leadership and as an associate adviser for Cheshire Local Authority. Peter has served as an adviser to the Department for Education and Skills. He serves on several DfES committees as a subject matter expert and is widely published.

Patricia Whittaker is an international Health, Safety and Environment professional and has been employed in the speciality chemicals, health care, port transport and pharmaceutical sectors for more than thirty years. She specialises in developing cost-effective, pragmatic approaches to control health, safety and environmental risks in order to gain management commitment to their implementation.

The National College for School Leadership and its Programmes

Working with school leaders and the wider education community, the college aims to:

–   provide a single national focus for;

  • school leadership development
  • research and innovation;

–   be a driving force for world-class leadership in our schools/wider community;
–   provide support to and be a major resource for school leaders;
–   stimulate national and international debate on leadership issues.

The college has three core areas of activity: leadership development (leadership and strategic programmes, including for example the National Professional Qualification for Headship), research and development and online learning, networks and information.

   The college operates under the direction of a leadership team, with strategic guidance and support provided by a governing council. It is based in a state-of-the-art learning and conference centre in Nottingham, which has dedicated residential and conference facilities.

LEADERSHIP DEVELOPMENT OVERVIEW

All the programmes offered by NCSL are as follows.

Leadership Development Overview
All The Programmes offered by NCSL are as follows:

Emergent leaders	Established leaders	Entry to headship	Advanced leaders	Consultant leaders	Strategic programmes	Team programmes
For teachers who are beginning to take on leadership and management responsibilities, including heads of subject/area and subject co-ordinators	For experienced leaders who are not planning to pursue headship, including assistant and deputy headteachers	For those aspiring to their first headship and for newly appointed first-time headteachers	For experienced headteachers looking to develop their professional qualities, skills and expertise	For experienced headteachers and other school leaders who are ready to further develop their facilitation, mentoring and coaching skills	Focusing on issues within leadership or on particular types of schools	For school Leadership teams who wish to improve their team effectiveness
Leading from the Middle	Established Leaders' Provision	National Professional Qualification for Headship (NPQH)	Leadership Programme for Serving Head-teachers (LPSH)	Development Programme for Consultant Leadership	Certificate of School Business Management (CSBM)	Developing the Capacity for Sustained Improvement (DCSI)
Fast Track Teaching Programme	Leadership pathways	National Professional Qualification in Integrated Centre Leadership (NPQICL)	International Place-ments for Headteachers (IPH)		Diploma of School Business Management (DSBM)	Working Together for Success (WTFS)
		The Trainee Head-teacher Programme	Partners in Leadership		Strategic Leadership of ICT (SLICT)	
		Early Headship Provision	Leading Small Primary Schools		teamsLICT	
					Black Pupil Achievement Programme: Leadership development programme for senior leaders (BPAP)	

BURSAR DEVELOPMENT PROGRAMME

The aim of the programme which is made up of two courses (the Certificate and Diploma of School Business Management) is to deliver professional skills and training to bursars and school business managers (SBMs) in order to increase their level of competence in key areas around the school. This enables SBMs to take a leadership role within the school management team, thus freeing up teachers and headteachers to focus on teaching and curriculum development.

For more information on the college and its programmes visit: www.ncsl.org.uk

Foreword

Trevor Summerson

It is less than four years since the National College for School Leadership was invited to develop a series of training programmes with the aim of improving the skills base of staff involved in business management and administration within their schools. Prior to 2001 there was no national structured training programme for school business management.

Since then remarkable progress has been made:

– over 3000 candidates have completed, or are undertaking the College's school business management training courses;
– the college now has the capability to deliver up to 1,500 certificate places and approximately 300 diploma places across England each year;
– both the Certificate of School Business Management which provides SBMs (school business managers) with the with the skills to undertake the role and the Diploma of School Business Management which provides SBMs the higher level skills to undertake strategic and leadership roles have been designed, delivered and are externally accredited. There is clear evidence that universities are exploring the possibility of developing first degree courses in school business management;
– evaluation consistently shows both high satisfaction rates amongst candidates and the positive impact trained school business managers are having on their schools.

The following chapters, using comments from tutors and candidates as well as quantitative data drawn from our evaluation studies, show clearly the real impact these professional development programmes are having on both the individuals undertaking them and on the schools in which they work. This impact was evident during a series of regional conferences held last year by the college, where many headteachers commented on how positively both the Certificate and Diploma of School Business Management have been received. In particular, participants commented on the significant contribution these courses have already made to improving business decision making in schools and ultimately improving the life chances of our children.

Consequently, I believe that effective school business management lies at the heart of helping schools remodel successfully, reducing bureaucracy in order to free teachers to teach and introducing a business management discipline into both the day-to-day operation and strategic decision making within schools.

Through undertaking these courses, SBMs are now able to increase their involvement in running their schools significantly. They can take on more leadership- and management-oriented roles and show improved confidence and ability to put their views and ideas across and affect the school environment in a positive way.

School Business Management discipline has never had a higher profile. Indeed, the need for sound business management and decision-making skills to be present in all our schools is now widely accepted. It follows that a book which explores through the experiences of tutors and candidates the key themes of the role of the school business manager, whilst providing practical advice on the essential technical aspects of the role, is long overdue.

Introduction

Iris Keating and Ray Moorcroft

Managing the business of schools has always been a hidden and assumed activity. Assumptions have been made that someone will collect the lunch money, manage the buildings, sort the stationery, monitor absence, minimise risk and so on. Questions concerning how or to what standard have been considered irrelevant. However, since 1988 and with the changes arising from the Education Reform Act it has become, and is continuing to be, a major issue for schools today. Changes in legislation, management and funding mean that managing a school as a business is no longer merely an option, but has become essential.

In December, 2001, a PricewaterhouseCoopers (PWC) study commissioned by the DfES argued that better trained, more highly motivated bursars and business managers, acting at a sufficiently senior level, will have a dual role in the school workforce. Firstly, they would free headteachers and others from a wide range of school management and administrative tasks, enabling them to focus on the transformation of teaching and learning. Secondly, by using their expertise in resource management, they would play a pivotal role in the wider remodelling of staff deployment across the whole school. Following extensive piloting and evaluation which confirmed the concept as a reality, the Certificate in School Business Management (CSBM) and the Diploma in School Business Management (DSBM) courses were developed under the umbrella title of the Bursar Development Programme (BDP). The view is now held that successful schools must be well led, with leadership which encompasses competent specialist staff able to manage finances and resources effectively and efficiently. The advantages of such a structure are clear as schools move to a model which offers greater independence.

PWC is, of course, a large international consultancy, and questions may immediately arise as to the transferability of industrial/commercial perspectives:

can a model and approach developed in the industrial/commercial world be applied to an educational context? There are two responses to the question: the first and more generic answer, was provided by Davies and West-Burnham (1990) who noted that there was much to be learned by both sides. The second and more specific response was to examine the features of a successful organisation and ask whether any of these should not be applicable in a school context.

Such a list is suggested in the table below and is compiled by looking at behaviours which authors in the field deem important for effective team-based organisations and then translating these into outcome criteria.

Criteria	*Source*
The organisation has meaning for	Bennis and Nanus,
each of its members	1986
A hotbed of tests of the unconventional	Peters, 1988
Shared knowledge among team members	
Peer-mentoring	
Equitable resource allocation	Kozlowski et al.,
Group-centred decision making	1997
Coaching as a central feature of the process	Temme, 1996
Challenge – people not afraid to take risks	Brown and Ralph, 1994
Objectives not compromised by political issues	Kolb et al., 1995
Effective communication	Wilson, George and
	Wellins, 1994

A comparison of these factors to Sammons et al.'s (1995) or McBeath's (1999) list of factors which make up effective schools indicates some commonality, although this is dependent upon personal interpretation. However, would any school *not* want to have these characteristics?

This book has therefore been written for a number of individuals, including school business managers, school administrative staff, members of school senior management teams, school governors and parents – indeed all those involved, in whatever capacity, in the business of a school. The book is designed not only to encourage the reader to consider the underlying principles of management, but also to provide hands-on and practical ideas on how we might manage our schools as businesses. The chapters also conclude with ideas for further reading and also a range of useful resources.

Throughout the book there are activities in the form of SBM Toolkits. These are designed to encourage the reader to consider what they have read and place this in the context of their own setting. Also throughout there are a number of case studies. These have been written by practising school business managers and many of them provide practical and real illustrations of the issues raised and the key points made in the respective chapter. These school business managers are either currently studying or have successfully completed the Certificate or Diploma in School Business Management.

The certificate covers the core functional areas of activity involved in managing schools: areas such as, Finance, Human Resource Management and Facilities Management. The Diploma focuses on expanding this knowledge and understanding to support participants in exploring and developing their own management and leadership skills together with their professional skills. The diploma enables SBMs to play a full role in schools at a strategic level. Section 1 of the book is concerned with the skills and technical competencies that are considered in the CSBM and Section 2 focuses on DSBM's more strategic issues.

Trevor Summerson, in the Foreword to this book, provides the key statistics and features relating to the impact of these courses. We believe that the CSBM may prove to be a significant development in changing the culture of school leadership. It presents a view of leadership which fits a loose–tight model of organisational management, with less operational control by headteachers: this perspective is labelled 'Leadership at all levels'. The key contention here is that the School Business Manager (SBM) should be part of the leadership of a school and there is evidence, based on the impact evaluation data produced by the NCSL that the Bursar Development Programme (BDP) has been instrumental in bringing about this situation. The conclusions reached are that the programme is instrumental in producing innovations in organisational structure and is leading to attitudinal change with regard to the value of different expertise in schools, both of which reflect implementation of the model of leadership at all levels.

The book is divided into three sections:

Section 1 Skills and technical competencies
Section 2 Thinking strategically
Section 3 Reflection and analysis.

Section 1 is concerned with the competencies identified by the NCSL as the essential technical aspects of the role of the school business manager. Each chapter considers one of these technical competencies and has been written by an expert in that field. In Chapter 1, (Managing Risk) we are concerned to change the emphasis from safety and accident prevention to a more proactive management of risk. In order to achieve this we consider firstly the hazard and risk that are present in today's society and then we go on to examine the specific challenges that are facing our schools. The chapter provides a range of useful and practical ideas concerned with risk assessment and its management that will help the reader to consider this often ignored aspect of school business management.

Chapter 2 (Managing ICT) considers both the importance of ICT to support learning and teaching and also Management Information Systems. Here the links between ICT and the raising of standards are made explicit. Chapter 3 addresses what many would see as the traditional role of the school business manager – 'Facilities Management'. However, in this chapter, we begin by exploring the extent of facilities management including the need for a strategic perspective in effective facilities planning. Issues including building maintenance and transport are addressed as is the highly topical issue of school catering. 'Managing Human Resources' is the focus for Chapter 4 and here there is a considered and comprehensive discussion on the essential aspects of HR including recruitment and selection, grievance and discipline, absence and the termination of employment. The development of staff is also addressed, acknowledging the importance of ensuring that vision and values actually become practice.

Chapter 5 focuses on a key aspect of the role of the school business manager, that of 'Office Systems Management'. This chapter provides a fascinating account of how this has changed and indeed continues to develop with a consideration of the school business manager of the future. In this chapter practising school business managers describe and illustrate how their role has changed almost beyond recognition. Effective and efficient Financial Management is of course of great concern and Chapter 6 provides a detailed account of how this can be achieved. Not only are the practical aspects considered, but also wider issues are addressed including the *professional* role of the school business manager.

In Chapter 7, a more recent but equally important aspect of the school business manager's role is examined, that of 'making sustainable environmental management work in schools'. All those involved in schools need to be aware of the importance of sustainable development and environmental management, and in any whole-school approach the school business manager is key, with the role concerned with school grounds development, sustainable energy and water use in schools and working with site managers and the cleaning team.

Section 2 (Thinking Strategically) addresses the *big* questions. In Chapter 8, 'Strategic Management' is considered from the starting point that over the last three decades there have been unprecedented changes in the responsibilities that schools face. In particular there has been a significant increase in the level of control that they may exercise over their future direction and strategic plans. Thus the chapter concentrates on the kinds of thinking and techniques needed, both by school business managers and the broader school leadership team, to understand strategic activities and make them work most effectively. There is a view that as a result of initiative overload, many schools have become subject to a series of fragmented and episodic changes that have resulted in school leadership being increasingly less focused upon its key function of leading learning.

Chapter 9 (Managing School Improvement and Performance) argues that school leaders, including business managers, must now regain ownership of vision and seize the initiative or they will become functionaries in a system rather than leaders of people and shapers of hearts and minds. Chapter 10 (Change

Management) considers the effective methods that the school business manager can put into place to manage change. This involves seeing educational institutions as organisations which encompass much more than the mechanical systems they contain. Here the culture of the school is seen as an important factor in helping or hindering change management as it impacts on the way people see both themselves and others and also on the way they view innovation and change.

Section 3 provides both reflection and analysis. In the final two chapters there is a backward look at what has gone before and also an analysis of what might be to come. In Chapter 11 reference is made to a wealth of evidence about the impact of the NCSL's Bursar Development Programme upon individuals and on schools. In this chapter the voices of the school business managers are particularly evident. It is especially interesting to note that where the school business manager has completed the BDP, the school has seen a significant improvement in the efficiency and effectiveness of resource management and, in addition, a positive impact on the teaching and learning environment and workload practices of all staff.

Chapter 12 is concerned with future developments. But, paradoxically, the way to think about the future is first to understand the past. The chapter opens with context setting about the nature of futures thinking and it goes on to explore some of the futures thinking that has informed government and shaped educational legislation over the past decade. This final chapter has an unapologetically strong educational focus in order to locate the context of school business management firmly into the vision for education and to help aspiring school business managers make sense of the ways in which they will make an increasingly significant contribution to the vision for teaching and learning.

The future

Part of the CSBM programme encourages candidates to use the widely recognised technique of 'futuring'. The implications of the CSBM programme for innovative school processes have been considered at length by all CSBM candidates. In this respect, Nick Tomlinson of the DfES in 2004 (NBA Conference, Lincoln) provided a government perspective which encompassed new ways of using space, breaking down the one teacher-one class model, and even School Business Managers as Joint Chief Executives. We believe this is a step too far for the foreseeable future (although legitimate as part of a futuring exercise). Until 'superleadership' (Mantz and Sims, 1989) or even its derivative, 'distributed leadership' (Drath, 1998) becomes a widely-accepted concept; the School Business Manager cannot extend much beyond the current role.

The NCSL have already moved towards raising awareness here, in that there is more information sharing and integration of programme content in the NCSL suite of programmes. The CSBM programme seems also to be instrumental in helping this become a reality, but the timescale for full realisation of this reality may lie beyond the currently-projected lifetime of the programme. This does not, however, diminish the importance of the BDP as a catalyst for action. The key question revolves around the extent to which a critical mass of changed school cultures will have been created by the end of the programme's lifetime.

In the interim, evidence of other impact implications is emerging. For example, many groups report that the SBM is beginning to fulfil a valuable role as deputy CEO in leading and managing the *external* stakeholder's input to the school. Given international concerns about the development of education for citizenship and sustainable development, this is a developing role as schools become increasingly central to community development. In turn, this links to the extended school concept. In this book we offer some original insights into possible developments in the role of the SBM as schools themselves change, which, we believe, makes it a pragmatic and illuminating contribution to the growing body of knowledge in this area.

The BDP opened up this area of activity to a wider audience who have since proved that efficient management of schools can improve all aspects of school life. However, school business management is still a young discipline, with a small but growing literature and research base. Therefore, we are particularly pleased to note the differing and contrasting views of the contributors. They provide a very personal look at the new issues which trained SBMs are tackling in schools. The range of material gathered here demonstrates the diversity of this new profession of school business management. There is however a growing view that there exists a 'core' of competencies. These can be discerned in the new, 2006, International Standards. School Business Managers who believe that this new profession needs to be actively supported may wish to compare their achievements and areas of expertise to these Standards and code of Ethics published by the Association of School Business Officials International (ASBO), and the NCSL is working with them to ensure consistency of competencies, so there is a direct relevance.

As the NCSL works with organisations in the USA and Africa to standardise good practice, this book is a timely contribution to futures thinking. It takes all involved a little further along on the journey in search of answers to questions about good – or even ideal – school business management. As editors, we can only endorse this objective and urge others to contribute – even if only as readers.

REFERENCES

Bennis, W. and Nanus, B. (1986) *Leaders: the strategies for taking charge*. London: Harper & Row.
Brown, M. and Ralph, S. (1994) *Managing Stress in Schools*. Plymouth: Northcote House.
Davies, B. and West-Burnham, J. (1990) *Education management for the 1990s*. Harlow: Longman.

Kolb, D.A., Osland, J. and Rubin, I. M. (1995) *The Organizational Behaviour Reader,* (6th ed) Englewood Cliffs, N.J.: Prentice Hall.

Kozlowski, S. W. J. and Ford, J. K. (1997) *Improving training effectiveness in work organization.* Mahway, N.J.: Lawrence Erlbaum Associates.

Macbeath, J. (1998) *Effective School Leadership: responding to change.* London: Paul Chapman Publishing.

Peters, T. J. (1988) *Thriving on Chaos: handbook for a management revolution.* Basingstoke: Macmillan.

Sammons, P., Hillman, J. and Mortimore, P. (1995) Key characteristics of effective schools. Report commissioned by the Office of Standards in Education. London: Ofsted.

Temme, J. (1996) *Team power: how to build and grow successful teams.* Missions, KS: Skillpath publication.

Wilson, J. M., George, J. and Wellins, R. S. (1994) *Leadership Trapeze: strategies for leadership in team-based organizations.* San Francisco, CA: Jossey-Bass.

Section 1

Skills and Technical Competencies

1

Managing Risk

Patricia Whittaker and Dittany Matthews

INTRODUCTION

In this chapter you will find material and discussion focussing on:

- The changing emphasis away from safety and accident prevention to proactive risk management.
- Hazard and risk in present-day society and the challenges facing schools.
- Information about putting the system in place:

  - policy
  - accidents and near-misses
  - the risk assessment process
  - the use of hazardous substances
  - special educational needs and disabilities.

- Fire safety.
- Emergency and contingency planning.

This chapter deals with the principles of risk management. The guidance contained here is considered to be international best practice and specific legislative requirements are not dealt with due to variations from country to country. Local courses are available if you wish to have a detailed knowledge of local laws. Environmental issues are often integrated into the management systems that organisations put in place to deal with other risk issues. A closer examination of these issues can be found in Chapter 7.

A further recent consideration for the UK's schools is the Freedom of Information Act, which requires all organisations, including schools, to provide information to any person on almost any subject. This will include risk assessments and accident records.

The risks facing schools are wide ranging. An examination of newspaper articles over recent months would reveal the following incidents:

- a large tree falling on a playground injuring a pupil which might have been avoided had the trees been regularly surveyed and maintained;
- loss of money through fraud which could have been avoided by adequate financial controls;
- injury to pupils on school activity visits where no risk assessment was done;
- injury to pupils by employees which could have been avoided by proper recruitment and pre-employment checks;
- loss of a school building through fire caused by an electrical fault which might have been avoided by maintenance;
- loss of data because of computer failure and inadequate back up procedures.

Although these incidents are relatively uncommon, school managers will recognise that the possibility exists of similar incidents happening in their schools. No procedures can make our schools entirely risk free, but the risks should be assessed and managed.

THE CHANGING EMPHASIS: AWAY FROM SAFETY AND ACCIDENT PREVENTION TO PROACTIVE RISK MANAGEMENT

Early health and safety legislation which affected children was aimed mainly at the conditions in the factories that they worked in. Restrictions were imposed on hours of work and minimum standards of heating, lighting and ventilation were specified.

As the twentieth century dawned, legislation widened and started to regulate other types of business premises and to make more detailed provisions relating to health, safety and welfare. In the second half of the century, major legislation such as the Health and Safety at Work Act in the UK and the Occupational Safety and Health Act in the USA was passed. These acts covered all types of commerce and industry and enabled further specific legislation to be put in place, changing the focus from merely accident prevention to a risk-based approach.

By the beginning of the twenty first century, the insurance industry was encouraging policyholders to take a wider view of risk and to be more proactive in its management. Effective risk management is of benefit to both the insurer and the insured because premiums are influenced by the claims/cost ratio. In addition to injury or financial loss, schools that fail to implement good risk-management systems will suffer loss of reputation, which can have long-lasting repercussions. The topic of risk in schools extends much further than health and safety issues and includes financial and business continuity risks, including emergency planning, management and recovery.

HAZARD AND RISK, PRESENT-DAY SOCIETY AND THE CHALLENGES FACING SCHOOLS

A hazard is defined as anything which can cause harm, for example chemicals, electricity, radiation. Risk is the chance (high or low) that someone will be harmed by the hazard.

Traditionally, risk management starts by carrying out an assessment exercise that ranks potential events in terms of the likelihood of them happening and how serious the consequences would be if they did come to pass. This is represented by the equation

$$Risk = Severity \times Likelihood$$

In more modern times, a third element seems to be required to be factored in. This is the degree of outrage that would occur if an event happened. The equation now reads

$$Risk = Severity \times Likelihood \times Outrage\ Factor$$

An example of the difference that this factor makes is that the number of people killed or seriously injured on the roads every month does not make the news headlines. In itself it is not a newsworthy item, but it would create huge media attention if the same number of people were killed in a jumbo jet crash. A further example can be found in the difference in reaction between a child falling from a school climbing frame and breaking his wrist and the same accident happening at home. This has meant that schools in several countries have banned playground games for fear of being sued by the parents of injured children.

In industry, risk management has a useful last form of defence – that of personal protective equipment. One school in the UK has followed industry's example by investing in industrial safety goggles for children to wear when playing the ancient game of conkers, where horse chestnuts threaded on string are struck against each other and the winner is the one who ends up with an intact conker. The head of the school says the move is a 'sensible' step to protect children's eyes from pieces of flying horse chestnut. You may or may not agree because the balance between challenge and safety is an important consideration in the development of children.

The best facilities, environments and experiences are those that offer children the maximum developmental value while ensuring that their safety is effectively managed. Playground activities help children learn teamwork, cooperation and organisation, and develop coordination and dexterity while exercising. At the same time, children also get hurt performing these activities, so we have to balance the benefits against risk to the school from (for example) the financial effects of a legal case. If the correct procedures have been followed, there is good evidence for teachers to use to refute accusations of negligence. Other challenges facing schools from this shift of emphasis arise from the management structure and the subsequent chain of responsibility for risk management.

If the proactive approach is to be evidenced, then all staff in schools, including governing bodies, should take their part in managing risk and health and safety. Awareness of this responsibility can be raised in a number of ways:

- by including a reference to health and safety or risk management in all job descriptions/profiles;
- by introducing basic health and safety into the induction process for new staff as early as possible, for example fire evacuation procedures and a risk assessment of their teaching room and work space;
- by inclusion as part of an annual performance review, with targets regarding risk assessment directly relating to a person's role (for example, planning a visit or journey with pupils, use of the school minibus);
- by training for staff in emergency first aid and risk assessment;
- by identifying responsibilities through policies which are regularly reviewed and consulted upon;
- by a committee of the governing body needing to take responsibility for risk assessment and health and safety – this should be identified in the committee's terms of reference and made visible to school staff through the committee undertaking regular risk assessments of selected areas of the school grounds and buildings.

SBM Toolkit – RM:1

A simple practical tool to raise awareness in school would be to use your weekly bulletin or notice-board for regular and timely reminders on basic health and safety matters, for example:

- Keep corridors clear of obstructions.
- Make sure waste bins are emptied regularly.
- Make sure vision panels in doors are not covered with notices.
- Make sure all staff report light bulbs which need replacing, particularly in corridors and stair wells.

This need not be punitive in tone, and indeed, will have more effect if put in the same positive format that the construction industry uses. For example; 'It is now two terms since we've had an accident involving obstructions in corridors. Congratulations to everybody.'

PUTTING THE SYSTEM IN PLACE

Health and safety policy

A school's health and safety policy should consist of three parts.

- The first part is the policy statement itself. This is a general statement of intent which contains the objectives and outlines a school's overall philosophy in relation to the management of health and safety. It should be drawn up by the school and agreed by the school's board of governors, who should keep the policy under annual review. If appropriate, schools can take advice on drawing up this policy from their managing authority. Once written and agreed, the policy should be made available to all staff and introduced to them at a suitable staff meeting.
- The second part of a health and safety policy is the organisation of people and duties for the implementation of the policy. It should show clearly the chain of command and who is responsible for what. This section can also contain the details of how the implementation will be monitored, how a safety committee will function within the line management structure and how individual job descriptions and objectives will contain personal accountabilities.
- The third part will deal with the arrangements needed to reduce risks, and will include such items as safety training, inspections, accident prevention and investigation, dealing with contractors and fire safety. The risk assessment process, including putting control measures in place, should be described here.

The responsibility for determining policy, organisation and arrangements lies with the governing body which has the ultimate responsibility for health and safety within the school, although authority for various issues can be delegated.

Accidents and near-misses

An accident is defined as 'any unplanned event that results in personal injury or damage to property, plant or equipment'. A near-miss is 'an unplanned event which does not cause injury or damage, but could have done so'. Examples would include: items falling near to personnel, incidents involving vehicles and electrical short-circuits. There are many more near-misses than accidents, and if a robust reporting and investigation process is put in place and lessons are learned from its findings, it is possible to eliminate many minor accidents.

The school should have a policy which outlines the procedures that are to be adopted when any pupil, staff member, visitor or contractor experiences an accident, near-miss or dangerous occurrence on the company's premises. These will all be investigated to determine their underlying causes and how a recurrence can be prevented. It is therefore important that all accidents and incidents, irrespective of the resulting injury or damage, be recorded according to the procedures laid down.

These accident records should be reviewed regularly by the governors to establish the nature of those incidents which have occurred in school and to ensure that sufficient resources are available to deal with the causes, with proper action subsequently taken to help prevent an incident being repeated.

SBM Toolkit – RM:2

Schools may find it useful to log accidents and near-misses in a simple data base or spreadsheet. The data could include a column showing the action taken to prevent further incidents. Staff and governors will then be able easily to observe trends and 'accident black spots' and take appropriate action to reduce the risks. Groups of schools could collaborate in sharing and benchmarking their data. The findings resulting from these exercises can then be used to inform and motivate other staff.

The risk assessment process

Performing a risk assessment is a way of formalising a sound, common-sense approach to managing risk. It is a process that is required by statute in Europe, but even when not strictly required by law it is good practice as it documents the risk minimisation precautions taken, and provides proof of carrying out the duty of care owed to pupils, staff members, visitors and anyone else on school premises.

Although the person performing the assessment does not have to be a health and safety expert, short training courses are readily available. More complex situations may necessitate help from a competent source, but these are unlikely to occur in a school environment. There are several models of risk assessment, but they are all variations on the same theme, consisting of five steps.

Step 1 – identify the hazards

The hazards can be identified by walking around the area concerned and looking at what could reasonably be expected to cause harm, ignoring those things which are trivial. Examples of frequently encountered hazards in a school context are slipping/tripping hazards, water (for example in outdoor activities), trapping hazards, or laboratory chemicals. Other people who are familiar with the area should be asked for their opinions. They may have noticed things that are not immediately obvious. Accident records can help with identifying problem areas.

Step 2 – decide who might be harmed, and how

Those who are at potential risk are people who are present all the time, but consideration should also be given to visitors and part-time workers such as cleaners, contractors or maintenance workers.

Step 3 – evaluate the risks and decide whether existing precautions are adequate or more than adequate

The likelihood of whether a hazard could cause harm should be evaluated to determine whether or not more needs to be done to reduce the risk. After all the precautions have been taken, some risk usually remains and the decision has to be made as to whether this remaining risk is 'high', 'medium' or 'low'. The aim is to put all risks into the 'low' category by taking precautions as necessary. An action list should be prioritised dealing with the highest priorities first.

There is a hierarchy of actions suggested by the UK's Health and Safety Executive in the publication *Five Steps to Risk Assessment* (1998) (available at: www.hse.gov.uk/pubns/indg163.pdf) which advocates asking the following questions:

- Can I get rid of the hazard altogether?
- If not, how can I control the risks so that harm is unlikely?

In controlling risks apply the principles below, if possible in the following order:

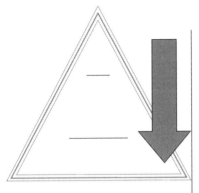

1. Try a less risky option.
2. Prevent access to the hazard (for example by guarding).
3. Organise work to reduce exposure to the hazard.
4. Issue personal protective equipment.
5. Provide welfare facilities (for example, washing facilities for removal of contamination and first aid).

www.hse.gov.uk/pubns/indg163.pdf)

SBM Toolkit – RM:3

Improving health and safety need not cost a lot. For instance, placing a mirror on a corner to help prevent vehicle accidents where pedestrians and vehicles may come into contact or putting some non-slip material on slippery steps are inexpensive precautions. Failure to take these simple precautions can cost a lot more if an accident does happen.

   More, importantly, such remedies can help 'prove' the case for precautions which do have a greater cost implication.

Step 4 – record your findings

Significant findings of the assessment should be recorded. This means writing down the significant hazards and conclusions. Examples might be "Laboratory fume cupboard air flows checked by manufacturer, sashes marked and recorded", or "Handrails on stairs checked and found to be sound". All affected persons must be informed of the findings.

   The written record should be kept for future reference or use; it can help if an inspector asks what precautions have been taken, or if there is any action for civil liability. Many schools have their own forms, or a simple free text document could be sufficient where the assessment is simple and easily repeatable.

Step 5 – review your assessment and revise it if necessary

If there is any significant change, the assessment should be updated. It is also good practice to review assessments from time to time to ensure that the precautions remain sufficient. The date should be set at the time of the original assessment and noted in a calendar, as a review could be overlooked.

   An example of a simple risk assessment for the use of a hedge trimmer in the grounds of your school is shown on the next page.

NAME AND ADDRESS OF SCHOOL:	
ASSESSOR:	
DATE OF ASSESSMENT:	DATE FOR REVIEW:

ACTIVITY:
Hedge Trimming

SIGNIFICANT HAZARDS:
- Operator falling from ladder due to over-reaching or failure to secure ladder
- Items falling from ladder
- Injury to operator from contact with blades
- Flying debris
- Ignition of fuel
- Vibrating tool

PERSONS AT RISK
- Ground maintenance staff
- Staff
- Pupils

EXISTING CONTROLS:
- Training in use of ladders
- Personal protective equipment provided – coveralls, eye and face protection, gauntlets, safety boots
- Training in use of hedge trimmers
- Planned preventative maintenance programme for ladders and hedge trimmers
- Regular breaks and changes of activity
- Work undertaken when staff and pupils offsite (if not possible, working area to be secured)

RISK RATING (SEVERITY X LIKELIHOOD)

Severity of consequences	High (3)	✓	*Likelihood* of consequences occurring	High (3)		*Risk Rating* = 3
	Medium (2)			Medium (2)		
	Low (1)			Low (1)	✓	

RISKS WHICH ARE NOT ADEQUATELY CONTROLLED AND FURTHER ACTION REQUIRED:

None

The use of hazardous substances

The use of hazardous chemicals in cleaning operations or laboratory experiments requires special risk assessments and precautions. The label on the container holding the chemical reagent or cleaning material will carry a safety sign informing the user of its hazards and the precautions to be taken. In addition, a manufacturer's safety data sheet containing more specific details should be available. The information from both of these will be considered along with the activity to determine potential exposure. Control measures will be put in place as with any other type of risk assessment and may include the use of barriers such as fume cupboards and personal protective equipment.

The major area of impact is in the teaching of science, and science inspectors in consultation with health and safety professionals have produced comprehensive guidance for schools in a number of countries. It is necessary for risk assessments to be carried out at a school activity level as the actual circumstances of use must be taken into consideration. This is a continuing process but step-by-step guides are available to help schools carry out the task with the minimum of effort.

Competent persons should monitor dust levels in woodwork rooms and pottery areas, and ensure that the testing of science laboratories' fume cupboards and exhaust extract systems in craft, design and technology areas is undertaken.

The use of personal protective clothing must be considered to protect against dermal or inhalation exposure.

PUPILS WITH SPECIAL EDUCATIONAL NEEDS

In most schools it will already be the usual practice for lesson plans to include provision for pupils with special educational needs. For practical lessons (for example, science, design technology, PE and dance) it will be necessary to include in the plan any arrangements that need to be made for pupils with physical disabilities. Many schools will use a proforma to assist staff with planning lessons – an additional section could be added to cover risk and the special needs of any pupil. This approach would raise awareness among teaching staff, as well as providing an opportunity for recording that this important aspect has been considered.

FIRE SAFETY

Fire is a chemical reaction, which is accompanied by a release of heat – an exothermic reaction.

Three elements are required for combustion – heat, fuel and oxygen. When all three elements are present in the correct proportion, fire will result. This is known as the Triangle of Combustion.

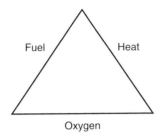

If any one element is removed or reduced, then the fire can be brought under control.

Fires may be classified into the groups below, with their respective preferred extinguishers which are of four types – water, dry powder, foam and carbon dioxide.

Class A

These are fires involving solid materials normally of an organic nature (compounds of carbon), for example wood, cloth, paper and so on. Combustion generally occurs with the formation of glowing embers. Class A fires are the most common and the most effective extinguishing agent is generally water in the form of a jet or spray.

Class B

These are fires involving liquids or liquefiable solids, for example oil, spirit, alcohol, grease and fat. For the purpose of choosing effective extinguishing agents, flammable liquids may be divided into two groups – those that are miscible with water and those that are not. Depending on which group the fire belongs to, the extinguishing agents include water spray, foam, carbon dioxide and dry chemical powders.

Class C

These are fires involving gases or liquefied gases in the form of liquid spillage, or a liquid or gas leak, and these include methane, propane, butane and so on. Foam or dry chemical powder can be used to control fires involving shallow liquid spills. (Water in the form of spray is generally used to cool the containers.)

Class D

These are fires involving metals. Extinguishing agents are ineffective and even dangerous. Carbon dioxide and the bicarbonate classes of dry chemical powders may also be dangerous if applied to most metal fires. Powdered graphite, powdered talc, soda ash, limestone and dry sand are normally suitable for Class D fires. Special fusing powders have been developed for fires involving some metals, especially the radioactive ones.

Electrical fires

It is not considered that electrical fires constitute a class since any fire involving or started by electrical equipment must be a fire included in the above classes. The normal procedure in such circumstances is to cut off the electricity and to use an extinguishing method appropriate to what is burning. Only when this cannot be done with certainty will special extinguishing agents be required which are non-conductors of electricity and non-damaging to equipment. These include dry powders and carbon dioxide, although the latter's cooling and condensing qualities may affect sensitive electronic equipment.

Heat as a danger

Heat transfer in fires may be via conduction, convection or radiation.

Conduction is the transfer of heat through a material. Some materials are better conductors than others, for example metal *vs* brick. Conducted heat will travel walls, floors and ceilings and into adjacent rooms, especially through metal partitions or along pipes and joints. Building regulations and codes pay special note to this fact. If the internal linings of adjacent rooms are combustible, or if combustible materials are stacked close to the adjoining wall, there is a danger that they may become heated to their ignition temperature by conducted heat, thereby spreading the fire.

Convection is the mass movement of a hotter, less dense gas through its cooler, denser surroundings as hot air rises. Convected heat is the primary mode of fire spread; about 75 per cent of the combustion products of a fire are dissipated in the rising convection currents of hot gases, at temperatures ranging from 800–1,000 degrees C, which heat anything in their path. When the upward movement of a convection current is blocked by, for instance, a ceiling, the hot gases spread laterally along the underside of the ceiling (the 'mushroom effect'). Convected air currents can carry smoke and toxic gases for long distances and can smokelog escape routes; they often carry burning brands, which can ignite combustible materials at some distance from the fire.

Radiation is the transfer of heat energy as electromagnetic waves. Radiation does not heat gases it passes through, but does heat solids and liquids it impinges on. Radiant heat is transmitted to buildings not shielded from the fire. The intensity of the radiation decreases with the square of the distance from the flames, but it is often sufficient to ignite combustible materials in nearby buildings, and buildings with many or large windows are most likely to spread the fire to their neighbours. When two areas of combustion are close to one another, mutual radiation between them intensifies the fire.

Fire as a danger

The main causes of fires and fire spread in buildings are as follows:

- open flames;
- spontaneous ignition;
- hot surfaces;
- sparks from mechanical sources;
- electrical equipment overheating, shorting out;
- friction – for example poorly lubricated bearings;
- heating/lighting devices too close to combustibles;
- static electricity;
- flammable liquids incorrectly handled;
- smoking in inappropriate areas;
- hot work without proper safety precautions;
- arson.

Fire creates its own conditions for its continued growth. Once a fire has started, it can grow rapidly with surrounding materials becoming sources of fuel. In an enclosed room or compartment, a stage may be reached where all the combustible materials are heated sufficiently to evolve flammable concentrations of vapour and the fire suddenly spreads very rapidly to give merged flames throughout the compartment – this is known as a 'flashover'.

After the fire's rapid growth, it passes through a development stage during which its temperature increases more slowly. Eventually the fire runs out of fuel or oxygen and burns out. Occasionally, combustion can continue at a reduced rate at very low oxygen concentrations and a fire may smoulder for a long period. If the full oxygen concentration is restored, for example by opening a door or breaking a window, combustion may be re-established with explosive force.

Fire detection in buildings is carried out commonly using either heat detectors, which detect a rise in temperature, or smoke detectors which detect smoke in the area. The former are not as fast-reacting, but the latter may be misled by excessive dust or steam and therefore the activity in the area needs to be considered when selecting a suitable type.

In order to raise the alarm in the event of a fire, manual call points – which are switches with easily-breakable glass covers – must be located on exit routes, especially staircases and near the final exit to a place of safety. The installation must be planned so that all parts of the buildings are within a short distance of a call point, the distance being dictated by local legislation. The wiring must be protected. Once activated, the warning devices may consist of electronic klaxons, bells or sirens. Activation of sprinkler systems will also sound a warning device. The rules for travel distances, exits, fire doors, staircases, notices and emergency lighting will vary according to local legislation. Training courses and advice are available from fire authorities.

Control and indicating equipment should be situated in a central, manned area such as a reception area. It shows faults in the power supply, wiring and general and miscellaneous devices such as fuses. If it fails in any way, an alert is sounded. Sometimes, a secondary or 'mimic' board is provided in an alternative area in case the main board is unstaffed. Connection to the fire brigade can be made automatically via a telephone line, manually by an operator or the alarm can be transferred to a commercial monitoring company who will call the fire brigade.

Evacuation of the building and planning for this are covered in the following section on emergency planning.

FIRE RISK ASSESSMENT

Fire risk assessments are required in the UK to meet legal requirements, but should be carried out as good practice in schools in order to ensure that everyone in a school and its buildings is protected.

The process of carrying out a fire risk assessment is done in a similar way to other risk assessments.

Step 1 – Identify fire hazards
Potential sources of ignition can be identified by looking for possible sources of heat which could get hot enough to ignite material in the workplace. These sources of heat include:

- smoking materials;
- naked flames;
- electrical-, gas- or oil-fired heaters (fixed or portable);
- hot work (such as welding);
- cooking;
- engines or boilers;
- machinery;
- faulty or misused electrical equipment;
- lighting equipment – for example halogen lamps;
- hot surfaces and obstructions of ventilation equipment;
- friction – for example from loose bearings or drive belts;
- static electricity;
- metal impact, such as metal tools striking each other;
- arson.

Indications of 'near-misses' such as scorch marks on furniture or fittings, discoloured or charred plugs and sockets, or cigarette burns can help identify hazards that may not otherwise be noticed.

Anything that burns is fuel for a fire. Things that will burn reasonably easily and are in sufficient quantity to provide fuel for a fire or cause it to spread to another fuel source should be identified. Some of the most common 'fuels' are:

- flammable liquid-based products such as paints;
- flammable liquids and solvents such as cleaning fluids, or solvents in laboratories or workshops;
- paper and card;
- plastics, rubber and foam;
- flammable gases – for example hydrogen;
- furniture, including fittings;
- textiles;
- loose packaging materials;
- waste materials.

Consideration should be given to the construction of the walls, floors and ceilings and how it might contribute to the spread of fire. For example, the construction may include large areas of hardboard, chipboard or block-board, or there may be synthetic ceilings or wall coverings such as polystyrene tiles. If these are present, and there is any uncertainty about the dangers they may pose, advice may be sought from a safety advisor or surveyor.

The main source of oxygen for a fire is the air around it. In enclosed buildings this can be provided by the ventilation system. Additional sources of oxygen can sometimes be found in materials which are used or stored, such as some chemicals (oxidising materials) which can provide a fire with additional oxygen and so assist it to burn.

Step 2 – decide who could be harmed

As part of the assessment, it should be identified who may be at risk if there is a fire, as well as how they will be warned and how they will escape. To do this, it is necessary to know where people are working and consider who else might be at risk.

People who may be affected are students, staff, maintenance staff, contractors, cleaners and members of the public. Special attention should be paid to people with disabilities who must be considered separately, and evacuation drills should include practising the arrangements for their evacuation.

Arrangements should also be made so that the school can establish, at any time, who is on site and that someone is responsible for taking with them the school's registers and visitors list when there is an emergency evacuation.

Step 3 – evaluate the risks

Steps 1 and 2 will have helped identify what the hazards are and who may be at risk because of them. The risks need to be evaluated and decisions made as to whether enough has been done to reduce them or whether more needs to be done by considering:

- the chances of a fire occurring and whether it is possible to reduce the sources of ignition or minimise the potential fuel for a fire;
- the fire precautions that are in place and whether they are sufficient for the remaining risks and will ensure everyone is warned in case of a fire;
- the means people can use to make their escape safely.

Where potential ignition sources, fuel and oxygen have been identified in Step 1 an assessment should be made as to whether they can be reduced or eliminated, and if so, how.

The fire detection and alarm system should be capable of detecting an outbreak of fire and warning people quickly enough so that they can escape to a safe place before the fire is likely to make escape routes unusable.

Once a fire has been detected and a warning given, everyone must be capable of being evacuated without being placed at risk.

The means of fighting a fire must be provided.

All people on site must know what they should do in the event of discovering a fire or hearing the fire alarm.

The overall assessment of risk

Once the process has been completed, the question should be asked as to whether the risks from fire are adequately controlled, and if not, what improvements should be made.

The most common causes of fire in schools are arson and electrical faults. When a fire is started deliberately in a school it is commonly done by intruders lighting fires (in skips or by using other waste) after school hours. Schools can control this risk by ensuring that contractors' skips are placed as far away from the building as possible, and that waste is cleared from bins regularly and stored in a lockable compound away from the building.

EMERGENCY PLANNING

It is important to have an emergency plan even when the chances of an emergency are low, because without a plan a relatively minor incident may escalate into a serious situation.

It is in a school's interest that emergencies are dealt with as quickly and successfully as possible with the minimum fuss. In order to respond to an incident effectively and rapidly, the emergency services need information, advice, assistance and direct action from the school involved. Prior discussion with the emergency services is essential.

One of a major challenges for schools in contingency planning is keeping the plan up to date. Schools need to have an up-to-date list of pupils and their parents, staff and other contacts available to key staff at all times, preferably also off site. This can be managed as part of a school's arrangements for securing back-up data from its computer system which should include all of the required information. A school should check, however, that their back-up system is reliable, that it is possible to restore the information from this back-up off site, and that key staff know where the information is stored.

Experience has shown that emergencies develop and alter rapidly. People will have to react in a difficult, fast-moving situation and are vulnerable unless properly prepared. Candidates who have studied this area of risk are often concerned to find that even basic emergency plans for fire evacuation are not sufficiently rehearsed.

Planning for involvement will give opportunities for minimising the following:

- the death and injury of pupils, staff, emergency services personnel and members of the general public;
- damage to neighbouring property and the environment;
- damage to buildings and equipment;
- the possibility of criminal prosecution and civil action against the governing body.

The plan should cover the stages before, during and after the event.

Before the event, there should be an assessment of hazards; the type and scale of consequences; what resources will be required; the allocation of duties to specific personnel; training; and liaison with external interests.

The section of the plan covering the event itself should focus on site action – alarm warnings, evacuation of the area, accounting for students and staff. Once the emergency services arrive, there will need to be provision of information, advice and direct assistance. Collection of information will be required to be communicated to others. Medical and first aid aspects should be considered.

Afterwards, post-incident activities must be detailed.

A detailed, up-to-date knowledge of the school is necessary. This includes its layout, and its hazardous areas such as labs and workshops. The plan should cover all arrangements made to protect people, property, equipment and the environment.

SBM Toolkit – RM:4

The contacts requiring information will be unique to the school concerned but a list should be prepared beforehand which is likely to include: parents; governors (who may be asked to give statements to the media); neighbouring schools (whose pupils may be affected because they are siblings); the police; the media; neighbours; and insurers.

Training and exercising turn the plan into a practical system. Regular practice and updating of procedures are the only ways to ensure that when the real thing happens a plan will work. It is particularly valuable if the local emergency services can be included. 'Table-top' exercises cause little disruption to lessons; they are relatively easy to control and can be used to test parts of the plan. They cannot simulate the real emergency situation fully, and in particular do not test communications which are often a weak point. On-site exercises give the best test of the physical practicalities of the plan and make people work from the locations they would have to use in an emergency.

All exercises, whether full scale or restricted, demand detailed preparation if they are to be successful.

It is important to manage the media in the event of an emergency situation arising. Dealing with reporters can be intimidating but training is available from many sources to help become more comfortable with this. It is helpful to nominate one person to deal with the press, and to agree a written statement on which communications can be based. The key point to remember when in this situation is to be as open as possible and to answer all questions as accurately as possible. If the answer to a question is not known, the best option is to say so, and then find out and let them know.

You might now like to consider how you would set up a risk management system for your own school, including all the documentation you will require. The responsibility might seem daunting, but staff should remind themselves that all school personnel share responsibility for their own safety and that of others. In addition, many schools will be supported by specialist staff in their local authorities and specialist consultants. One of the first tasks to be tackled by staff assuming responsibility for risk assessment might be to assess the level of awareness among their colleagues and managers. You can do this with a generic audit sheet such as the audit proforma which follows.

ORGANISATIONAL STATE OF AWARENESS

Audit Proforma

	Senior Management	Middle Management	Staff
1 Policy inc. reviews and updates			
2 Responsibilities and Structure			
3 Target			

Processes

1 Health and Safety
  a Training
  b Inspections
  c Fire Safety
2 Risk Management
  a Responsibilities
  b Procedures
  c Business continuity plan

The proforma can be used at a number of levels. The most basic is simply to assess whether or not (for example) health and safety training has taken place; in which case a simple 'tick' in the box will suffice.

At a more advanced level, a percentage estimate of awareness of staff at different levels could be made.

CONCLUSION

This chapter has discussed the way that proactive risk management is replacing safety/accident prevention in a climate where both hazard and risk are problems facing schools. Means of implementation of a suitable system have been described, as well as the specifics of fire safety and emergency and contingency planning. This chapter is an international overview but clearly local legislations also apply and must be incorporated into any system. These include environmental issues and in the UK the Freedom of Information Act.

USEFUL RESOURCES

Health and Safety Executive A wide variety of online resources and publications is available from the HSE website, covering all aspects of health and safety and risk. This can be accessed at: www.hse.gov.uk/services/education.

First Aid Training Including advice on school first aid and training resources. This can be accessed at: www.firstaidtraining.org.uk.

Accident Prevention The Royal Society for the Prevention of Accidents (ROSPA) website has a huge bank of resources and leaflets to download. This can be accessed at: www.rospa.com.

Electricity Safety This site includes resources about electricity safety for teachers. This can be accessed at: www.efdenergy.com/powerup/.

Health and Safety in Schools A wealth of resources and online tools covering all aspects of risk management and health and safety relating to schools. This can be accessed at: www.teachernet.gov.uk/wholeschool/healthandsafety.

2

Managing ICT

Margaret Dadley

INTRODUCTION

The School Business Manager (SBM) is a key element in managing Information and Communication Technology (ICT) provision in a school and throughout this chapter this will be highlighted in relation to two main areas of ICT development. First is the use of ICT to support and raise standards in learning and teaching and second is how Management Information Systems (MIS) support and enhance the successful leadership of a school. The discussion will consider how the SBM can support developments in these important areas.

In the world of education, change is rapid and nowhere is this more pronounced than in the field of ICT. The ICT agenda is one of the most exciting aspects of school development and it pervades all aspects of school life. Central government has invested heavily in ICT provision and continues to do so, but there has not always been a coherent policy and development has often been piecemeal. As schools implement the Every Child Matters agenda, the Department for Education and Skills has recognised the need to have common systems across children's services for electronic learning and administration and for all organisations to benefit from a collaborative approach to purchasing ICT equipment and services. Children's services must collaborate under the Extended Schools agenda, so there is a need for an integration of information to support the personalised needs of each individual child. The government's vision for ICT presented in *Fulfilling the Potential* DfES, 2003) states that 'We want every school leader and governor, every teacher and member of support staff and every pupil to become e-confident' (available at http://publications.teacher net.gov.uk/eOrderingDownload/FulfillingthePotential.pdf).

ICT is now a key factor in the effective delivery of learning and teaching as well as supporting successful school leadership. It is essential for schools to keep abreast of new developments as the technology improves and to become e-confident, providing exciting lessons with more choice about how and where to learn.

ICT TO SUPPORT LEARNING AND TEACHING

Since 1997 central government has encouraged, through its ICT strategy, the use of ICT to support learning and teaching in schools. Curriculum Online provided schools with funding and a scheme of approved learning materials. Schools were given earmarked funding to purchase hardware and other initiatives were implemented such as laptops for teachers, with the Strategic Leadership in ICT (SLICT) programme also providing opportunities for headteachers to develop their knowledge and understanding of key issues and to appreciate the potential of ICT for their schools. The majority of (but by no means all) schools now have broadband and have improved their infrastructure.

The impact of these initiatives has been significant but despite this ICT still compares unfavourably with other national curriculum subjects, especially in primary schools, and significant weaknesses remain. In addition, there is no consistent pattern across the country and the strategy has created a digital divide between the best and worst provision.

ICT is not yet embedded in the work of many schools and it is important to bridge this digital gap to enable ICT to make an important contribution to raising standards across the curriculum and to ensure that all schools are maximising their potential for good practice in e-learning. ICT needs to be used for planning and assessing lessons, creating and delivering them and identifying pupils' needs, progress and achievements.

The Ofsted Report, *CT in Schools: the impact of government initiatives five years on* (2004, Section 24, p.12) notes:

> The vision and understanding of senior managers are crucial in setting a context in which ICT can flourish. In the schools that are further forward with ICT, senior managers have been involved in planning whole school provision with a clear understanding of how ICT can enhance teaching and learning.

The e-status of a school

An e-confident school is crucial to this development. The National College for School Leadership has defined the following features of an e-confident school:

- high levels of staff confidence, competence and leadership;
- redesigned teaching, learning and assessment, integrating effective use;

- leading and managing distributed and concurrent learning;
- effective application within organisational and management processes;
- secure, informed professional judgement;
- coherent personal learning development, support and access – for all leaders, teachers and support staff;
- appropriate resource allocations to ensure sustainable development;
- availability, access and technical support;
- pupils with high ICT capability;
- schools as the lead community's learning and information hub.

There are two main agencies supporting the government's ICT strategy: the British Educational Communication and Technology Agency (Becta) and the National Grid for Learning (NGfL).

For a school to qualify for NGfL funding to buy ICT equipment it needs to have a development plan for ICT that addresses current issues. The NGfL is concentrating on improving levels of ICT infrastructure and connectivity and providing access to worthwhile education resources. An e-confident school must strive to provide excellent ICT facilities and resources to expand the ICT curriculum beyond current provision. The facilities should also be interconnected with the home and community.

Becta is the government's lead agency on the use of ICT in education and has useful guidance about content and drafting of ICT development plans and policies. Its main focus is the development of ICT pedagogy and whole-school improvement. A school should be seen as an ICT-rich institution, at the heart of its community, which can offer learning beyond the classroom.

SBM Toolkit – ICT:1

Becta has annual ICT in Practice Awards to identify excellent models of practice and to help disseminate excellent practice more widely. This is useful in that SBMs can have extended access to these schools through the schools network. You may also wish to devise a brief questionnaire which you can use to interview the winners and find out the all-important detail behind the initiative.

From this, you can then establish your own benchmarks for elements of the provision.

Every school should now be focussing on making excellent use of ICT resources to raise standards in learning and teaching and to support the changes which followed the introduction of the national agreement and workforce reform. Every member of staff must be confident in applying ICT to their role in school. SBMs have a significant role to play in supporting their schools with this agenda. Schools need to have a strategic vision for ICT and must understand how they are progressing on the journey towards becoming an e-confident school. SBMs can contribute to several aspects, *not least* via

- hardware and software provision including the infrastructure;
- health and safety relating to installation and usage;
- provision of technical support;
- provision of high quality training;
- ICT supporting learning and teaching;
- internet provision and safe use;
- licensing;
- security, data backup and restoration.

NAACE (originally the National Association of Advisors for Computers in Education, but now encompassing a broader membership including teachers, lecturers, consultants, inspectors and other ICT leaders in addition to advisors), in association with Becta, has developed a quality assurance scheme for ICT known as the NAACE mark to provide a framework for schools to develop ICT capability against national standards. This recognises the extent to which a school has successfully developed and implemented a strategic approach to ICT.

One fully recognised part of the role of SBM is to research and report to the leadership team on purchasing appropriate resources to make sure that products and services meet identified needs. One of the factors supporting effective use of ICT to reduce teachers' workload is the provision of high quality hardware and software, both of which should be available for use when and where they are needed. There are two initiatives that will support an SBM. The first is provided by the independent ICT Procurement Advisory Service (IPAS: available at: http://ipas.ngfl.gov.uk) which takes schools through a logical sequence of six steps in a procurement process, to help mitigate against risk and to ensure that those services and products received meet the needs of that school. The second is the Accredited ICT Service Suppliers (AISS) which complements the IPAS process and provides schools with an additional ten-step process for the selection of suppliers.

Mobility counts

Many schools developed ICT suites as the best option for ICT delivery but have since appreciated the restrictions this can impose and the need to have ICT capability within each classroom. The purchase of wireless technology can greatly increase flexibility and enable pupils to interconnect from various learning spaces, including home. Therefore, schools need a mixture of desktops, laptops and handheld devices to deliver e-learning. Becta's *What the Research Says* series (www.becta.org.uk) has suggested that portable ICT devices

- increase enthusiasm, motivation, confidence and a sense of ownership;
- allow greater classroom and curriculum integration of ICT;
- increase greater independence and self-initiated learning in pupils.

Every classroom will need to be furnished with new technologies such as electronic whiteboards and digital projection and furniture that is more adaptable. Such technology will encourage teachers to develop active learning with more engaging materials and to bring new resources into their teaching, thus making a significant contribution to embedding ICT in the classroom and raising standards through improved learning and teaching.

One key benefit of whiteboards is the high level of interaction which engages pupils and increases their motivation and the presentational capabilities they offer, so that videos and websites can be seamlessly included. The curriculum is being expanded and enriched and matched to the personalised learning needs and styles of individual pupils. A National Whiteboard Network has been established to offer support and guidance for schools to make the best use of interactive whiteboards. Staff need to become confident in their use and a suitable training programme is essential.

Again, a key element of the role of the SBM is to establish a requirements analysis to determine the most appropriate whiteboard. Being a substantial investment, value for money is an important consideration. Recommendations need to be based on extensive research and analysis into functionality, reliability and usability of the whiteboards and any technical issues relating to projectors.

SBM Toolkit – ICT:2

Conduct room surveys to ensure that the whiteboards will be located in the best position, at the appropriate height for pupil use, and to determine if additional furniture or furnishings such as blinds are needed: do this on both sunny and dull days and project the difference into different seasons.

In addition, all the health and safety implications of the installation such as cabling, lighting, temperature and humidity must be considered as well as post-installation security. Schools must also give consideration to peripherals such as software, technical support and insurance. Becta has developed standards and performance specifications and undertaken a full supplier evaluation process for interactive whiteboard solutions. It is advisable for schools to refer to this advice in order to make sound decisions. For further information see the Becta website (www.becta.org.uk/leas/whiteboards/).

Other technologies

To support schools in making the right choice and to ensure that they are getting value for money, SBMs should compare whiteboards with other low cost options and emerging technologies such as tablet PCs.

Learners also need access to a range of audio-visual tools to enable them to record and publish their own creations. Video conferencing offers further possibilities to enrich learning, from the use of a webcam on a stand-alone PC to purpose-built video conferencing studios with specialist equipment. *The key factor is the use of the technology, not the technology itself.*

The SBM, in consultation with relevant staff, will need to prepare a functional specification for video conferencing equipment and services, taking into account connectivity and bandwidth, location, equipment, support and training needs and the budget available. Devon's LEA has published a guide to video conferencing in the classroom with both primary and secondary case studies.

Many schools are already using this technology and Becta has published a paper (www.becta.org.uk) about the impact on teaching and learning. The research identified that using such technology:

● allows interactive access to experts;
● enables collaboration with peers by teachers and learners;
● enriches the experience of distance education by reducing feelings of isolation and encouraging interaction;
● raises student motivation.

CASE STUDY

Hallam Fields Junior School Ilkeston Derbyshire

School Business manager   Sharon Siddons

The school has made significant advances in both infrastructure and connectivity as a result of NGfL funding meeting the required pupil/PC ratio, providing laptops for teachers and investing in interactive whiteboards. The priority for the school was to become an e-confident school and to gain an understanding that e-learning is not about putting more and more ICT equipment into school, but realising the potential of the ICT already there and maximising its value to enhance teaching and learning. (DSBM)

Sharon determined that a strategic response was needed to optimise the potential of the infrastructure. Her intention was to:

- review and evaluate current practice in the use of ICT by teachers;
- identify training needs suited to individual teacher's capabilities;
- identify staff who could disseminate good practice;
- provide a cost analysis to ensure effective use of the Standards Fund Grant 31a;
- facilitate the team and ensure a positive impact from the changes.

She used a PESTLE (Political, Economic, Sociological, Technological, Environmental) analysis to determine the benefits the school would gain by becoming involved in the Hands on Support project. All teaching staff accessed the HOS matrix which produced an individual profile and enabled them to produce an individual action plan. Having gathered this information, the school was able to determine its spending priorities by identifying what proportions to spend on hardware provision and professional development. Consequently staff will be able to embed ICT across all aspects of the curriculum, enriching the learning experience for pupils and bringing lessons to life.

Safe technology

The internet has provided schools with exciting opportunities to improve learning and teaching which are helping to motivate pupils and make lessons more interesting. But there are also risks associated with its use, especially for young people, and SBMs must be aware of and address these risks to ensure safe use of the internet.

The Department for Education and Skills and Becta have long been providing advice and guidance on all aspects of internet safety through the Superhighway Safety website (www.safety.ngfl.gov.uk). Pupils must understand the appropriate and effective use of technology. There are several measures schools can take. An audit of internet safety practices in schools (www.safety.ngfl.gov.uk) identified a number of issues:

1 Exposure to inappropriate material that is sexual, hateful or violent in nature is a key concern for schools. Such material could encourage involvement in activities that are illegal or dangerous. Schools must have suitable filtering software, a firewall and/or a walled garden to prevent pupils from finding these sites.

Filtering systems prevent or block access to unsuitable material using a range of measures. Firewalls prevent unauthorised access to private networks and their contents from either malicious use or accidental damage. (Unfortunately these measures can also block many sites which staff need, including Becta and some of the NCSL's site!)

2 Pupils are in danger of being exposed to advertising. Research suggests that most pupils cannot determine the difference between advertising and reality.

3 Whilst the use of individual e-mail addresses for pupils can help improve communication skills, it is clearly another area of concern. Many SBMs would concede that apart from the work involved to manage the system there are many dangers, especially from attachments and viruses. For example, pupils can get involved in online bullying or arrange meetings that could put them in danger.

  One solution is for the school to subscribe to Gridclub (www.gridclub. com), an official website for primary school pupils: this can also be subscribed to from home. Gridclub allows pupils to have individual e-mail addresses, use search engines and contribute to forums. The site has an online mediator who will report any inappropriate behaviour.

  In addition, schools must have policies to support safe use of the internet. Becta's Superhighway Safety website gives advice about useful procedures and policies for safe use of the internet. Each school must have an acceptable use policy where students or their parents sign an agreement setting out the acceptable ways in which their internet services can be used.

  Such a policy in itself is insufficient: there needs to be regular monitoring of student use of the internet with suitable sanctions for misuse, such as removal of privileges, to encourage self-discipline. It is also a good idea to have posters prominently displayed outlining the rules of responsible internet use.

4 Because many pupils have access to the internet at home or in the community, they need to be educated about internet safety just as schools teach stranger danger. The Internet Proficiency scheme has been developed by Becta, the DfES and the Qualifications and Curriculum Authority (QCA) to develop a set of safe and responsible behaviours for pupils to adopt when using the internet.

  This is designed to provide pupils with the knowledge and skills to use the internet sensibly, evaluate the materials they find, and know how to react if they find unacceptable material. In addition to the scheme material there is a website cyber cafe (www.gridclub.com/cybercafe) to promote further discussion.

5 Many schools now have a website to promote their activities. Safety must again be considered. The identity of pupils must be protected and parental permission must be obtained before using any photographs.

One area of considerable growth is that of software resources and the SBM must ensure that any software in school has an appropriate licence for its use. They must also be aware of the terms and conditions of the licensing agreement and monitor them in practice. The SBM will need to have systems in place to track software licences, ensure that the terms and conditions are adhered to and also to consider value for money, as considerable amounts are spent on licensing.

In order to improve access to ICT and multimedia resources, the DfES has provided funding to individual schools via their LEAs in the form of e-learning credits: as SBM you will probably hold the budget account for these. E-learning credits enable schools to buy curriculum online digital learning resources to support the teaching of the curriculum. The website gives access to thousands of multimedia resources that have been given independent evaluations, star ratings and teacher reviews. Websites such as Evaluate (www.safety.ngfl.gov.uk) and Schoolzone (www.schoolzone.ngfl.gov.uk) were appointed by the DfES to run a contents evaluation service for Curriculum Online and are a valuable source to help schools make informed decisions before choosing software.

Managed services

Schools have the option to choose a managed service to access ICT equipment and services. After rigorous testing, NGfL Managed Services has approved a number of suppliers. Under a managed service, which could cover internet access or the supply of hardware or software, the supplier undertakes to support a school's ICT facilities to a contractually agreed service level. This has the advantage of leaving the school to concentrate on learning and teaching. There are several levels of managed service available to schools, but normally the supplier:

● provides technical support for the ICT infrastructure whilst ownership of the facilities rests with the school;
● supplies all ICT facilities and under an additional contract agrees to manage them;
● makes ICT facilities available to the school through a lease purchase;
● is responsible for all ICT requirements, including sourcing, installation and maintenance of all equipment.

Here the role of the SBM is to present the school leadership team with carefully researched options (including a cost benefit analysis) for their consideration.

A critical factor in the success of the use of ICT in schools is the need for effective technical support. Currently the quality and provision of such support are variable. Managed services can be part of the solution but the appointment of ICT technicians is the most favoured solution. General maintenance does not need a trained teacher, but teachers need to be confident that troubleshooting will be addressed quickly to enable continuous use of the equipment.

Demand for ICT technicians is increasing as schools develop their infrastructures. The job requirements have also increased from simply troubleshooting to the use of a technician to support ICT teaching and training. Becta provide a competences framework to help schools to judge the quality of their provision and to determine professional development needs. The SBM should play a significant role in both the line management of technical staff and in ensuring that their school has an effective strategy for dealing with technical support.

MANAGEMENT INFORMATION SYSTEMS

The SBM is often the person with management responsibility for their school's network and needs to be certain that the MIS chosen is efficient, effective, able to facilitate management processes and to also provide integrated curriculum and management information systems to enable schools to effectively and easily monitor the progress of individual pupils and provide assessment for learning. Since an MIS is used to store data there is clearly a security issue to be considered. Different users will need different levels of security.

SBM Toolkit – ICT:3

Start by assessing your needs and decide which of the following areas are essential and which you may wish to add on at a later date:

- assessment;
- asset management;
- attendance;
- home–school communication;
- communication between staff;
- finance;
- human resources;
- planning for learning and teaching;
- pupil data;
- report writing;
- self-evaluation;
- SEN management;
- timetable construction;
- miscellaneous.

Use a simple project planning tool (GANNTT Chart, Microsoft Project Planner) to ensure this 'later date' doesn't stretch into infinity.

Becta provides a planning grid for schools to use and offers guidance on the interoperability agreement managed by them. The DfES has encouraged software suppliers to sign up to the agreement and use the same definitions, called the Common Basic Data Set (CBDS), as the recommended standard for data importing and exporting. This means that data can be transferred between different MIS software and to other bodies, essential as children's services become more integrated.

The benefits of an MIS fall into three categories:

1   raising standards in the classroom;
2   leadership;
3   communications.

Raising standards

The MIS can provide access to accurate information about pupils and through analysis of this data can improve teaching and learning by:

- transferring pupil records more efficiently;
- setting and monitoring targets;
- informing teacher planning;
- targeting support for individual pupils and giving easy access to Individual Education Plans (IEPs);
- reporting to pupils and their parents/carers what pupils are achieving and what they need to do as their next steps;
- streamlining record keeping and reporting.

A school's MIS is also used to submit assessment data to the Data Collection Agency via the School to School (s2s) service which also creates the common transfer file and sends it to a pupil's new school. The transfer file is mandatory and the MIS needs to be kept up to date with pupil assessments.

The Pupil Achievement Tracker (PAT) has been designed as a diagnostic and analytical tool. It imports its attributes from the IMS (Information Management Strategy) and follows IMS principles that data are entered once and used several times. The DfES provides files for PAT at www.dfes.gov.uk/ptforms. Graphical data can be produced on the progress made by pupils and also on trend graphs and value added data. Teachers, informed by the progress made by similar pupils nationally, can use the PAT to set challenging targets as well as undertake a diagnostic analysis of test papers to compare performance in each of the national curriculum's test questions. The senior leadership team can view their school's recent performance against other similar schools, analyse achievement of different groups and look at the achievement and progress of pupils. The PAT will also support them in setting school targets.

In January 2004, David Miliband, the then Secretary of State for Education, launched a New Relationship with Schools (NRwS). He outlined the vision for personalised learning to improve opportunities for every learner. NRwS aims to reduce the burden of data collection on schools and LEAs but improve access to, and use of, available data to improve learning and teaching. As part of the NRwS remit, it plans to merge PANDA (Pupil And National Data Analysis) and PAT to streamline the provision of data analysis to schools. The resulting interactive website will provide schools, LEAs and inspectors with a common set of analyses.

CASE STUDY

Boughton Leigh Junior School Rugby

Warwickshire

School Business Manager   Jean Sinclair

Following a very successful Ofsted Inspection the school wanted to build on its strengths and address any areas of development. One area was the use of pupil data and turning assessment of learning into assessment for learning (CSBM). Jean conducted a project to:

- develop a shared understanding of the benefits of data analysis;
- work up strategies for using the data available to raise standards;
- help the school target resources, for example booster classes;
- assist learners to understand how they can improve their performance;
- celebrate success.

Jean appreciated that although the school had a wealth of data it was only using this for summative assessment. Examination of the autumn package and value added charts had indicated that some pupils were underperforming. She realised that better use was required of the information held by the school.

She led a small focus group in conducting an audit of the current situation using tools such as PESTLE and SWOT (Strengths, Weaknesses, Opportunities, Threats) analysis and they concluded that the current use of data was not as effective as it ought to be. It was decided that with a networked curriculum and administration system in place, teaching assistants could input and access data. The following actions were recommended:

- purchase of an extra assessment and data analysis tool;
- development by a focus group of user-defined reports to suit the school's individual requirements;

CASE STUDY

- use of web-based tools for more assessment. As these are automatically marked by the system, teacher workload is reduced but relevant target setting and monitoring information is produced
- establishment of a clear baseline;
- ensuring that staff are fully conversant with the use of assessment, data analysis, benchmarking and target setting and addressing any professional development needs;
- development of personalised learning programmes for individual pupils;
- use of data to inform the school's improvement plan and to raise standards.

By using this data, staff have become far more focussed on teaching and learning. By utilising the reports, teachers, parents and pupils will have a shared understanding about individual progress.

Leadership and management

Some schools are significantly behind other organisations when using an MIS to support leadership and management. Reports from an MIS system will provide the school leadership team with accurate, accessible and objective information to inform future decision making. One example is the use of a financial benchmarking website to help schools challenge how they spend their budget and decide if there is scope for improvement.

As well as being e-confident, schools should also improve their e-delivery. Staff should be using e-mail and the school intranet as the main forms of internal communication. Parents and governors will increasingly expect electronic access to information about a school and its pupils, particularly assessment and attendance data, and ICT can have a positive impact on home–school relations.

Communication Information Management Strategy

This was first introduced in April 2000 to save time, reduce workload and support schools in their efforts to raise standards. Information needs to be easily accessible so that schools can make decisions about learning and management using reliable and relevant information and improve the quality of the information they offer to parents.

The IMS is based on the following principles:

- minimising demands on schools;
- collecting only essential information;
- gathering information once and using it many times;

- storing and transferring information electronically;
- automating information collection – one-button solutions;
- improving the value of information returned to schools;
- achieving compatibility between systems from different suppliers;
- upgrading and maintaining ICT infrastructure;
- setting high standards for training and technical support.

An effective strategy is designed to make simpler and faster the provision of information for others such as the DfES and is an area covered during Ofsted inspections. In 2005 the IMS and annual school census sites will be amalgamated and renamed the School Census and PLASC (Pupil Level Annual School Census). The annual school census is the largest data collection for the DfES and is a statutory requirement since the Education Act of 1996. The PLASC return is essential to support PANDA and Autumn Package publications. The MIS issues pupils with Unique Pupil Numbers (UPNs) as part of this development. These UPNs are allocated to pupils when they first start school according to a nationally specified formula and will remain with them throughout their school careers.

In order to reduce the burden on schools a new school census will replace PLASC for secondary schools from 2006 and for primary schools from 2007. The main features of the school census will be:

- three collections per year in January, May and September with different items to be collected in each of the three terms;
- historical as well as snapshot data collected;
- additional data to include exclusions, attendance, extended services and home address information.

Such data should already be readily available in schools with an efficient and effective IMS. Collecting this information on a regular basis will replace several existing surveys including:

- termly exclusions;
- the gifted and talented;
- absence surveys both annual and termly;
- the contextual and absence survey;
- sections 1 and 2 of the September pupil count;
- identification of the Youth Cohort survey.

Data about the school workforce are still collected through a variety of surveys but will possibly be included as a module within the new census, with a national roll-out planned for 2008.

The MIS in school contains vast quantities of data and the SBM has the responsibility for its security and protection, and for ensuring that the systems used comply with current legal requirements. These procedures should be reviewed with consideration of possible risks. Under the 1998 Data Protection Act, which replaced the 1984 Act, all schools processing personal data must comply with the following eight enforceable principles of good practice. The government's website (at www.dpassist.co.uk) will provide more detailed information. Data must be:

● fairly and lawfully processed;
● processed for limited purposes;
● adequate, relevant and not excessive;
● accurate;
● not kept longer than necessary;
● processed in accordance with the data subject's rights;
● secure;
● not transferred to other countries without adequate protection.

The Data Protection Act covers the collection, storing, editing, retrieving, archiving and destruction of data. Schools, as data users, must annually notify the Information Commissioner of the purpose for which it is holding data. An application for notification can be made either by telephoning the Notification Department (on 01625 545740) or by visiting the website (on www.information-commissioner.gov.uk).

All personal data need to be kept securely and only made available to authorised personnel. Under the first principle of fair processing, schools must inform subjects about the purposes for which their personal data will be processed. This information should be provided at the same time as the data are collected. Pupils over twelve are considered able to understand the process and make their own decisions.

Schools must also ensure that hard disks are appropriately cleared when disposing of management hardware. Deleting files is often not considered adequate protection since some of the data could be retrieved. It is therefore advisable to destroy the disks. The Act does not define or elaborate on its fifth principle of how long data should be kept but it is recommended that schools keep finance data for six years and pupil and staff data for seven years after people have left.

SBM Toolkit – ICT:4

East Sussex has produced an information access and security policy template for their schools and this is available from the Becta website if other schools want to use it. It also produces an ICT audit programme.

Under the Freedom of Information Act 2000 and the Environmental Information regulations people are entitled to gain access to recorded information held by, or on behalf of, public authorities. This right came into force on 1 January 2005 and state schools are considered a public authority. They must respond to requests within 20 working days.

To avoid data being lost, schools need to make regular daily back-ups of data on the MIS and store this in a secure fireproof container off site in accordance with a schools disaster recovery policy.

Clearly, as a result of such vast amounts of data and regular updates and upgrades, together with varied use of the IMS, the SBM will need to ensure that staff have the appropriate training and are well equipped to do the tasks required of them. The Teachernet site (at www.teachernet.gov.uk) has a framework for information management and ICT competences which sets out the range of competences needed in a school to ensure that staff are effective in their jobs. It can be useful for the SBM, as the line manager of the support staff team, to use the framework to assess individual levels of competence and to identify training and development needs. The framework covers three areas:

● personal productivity tools;
● information management;
● technical support.

In addition there is a toolkit to identify who does what in terms of administrative tasks. This toolkit can be used to inform managers that segregation of duties is in place and to manage the allocation of administrative tasks and deploy staff effectively.

CONCLUSION

This chapter has considered the key role the SBM can play in supporting their school to raise standards in learning and teaching through the development of its ICT infrastructure, training and increased use of technology, with the procedures and policies provided to ensure safe, efficient and effective access to data. The case studies illustrate how the role of the SBM is important in helping and supporting their school to move forward towards e-confidence. In providing their school leadership team with information, options and cost benefit analysis for any aspect of their work, the SBM can enable the team to make sensible informed decisions which support the strategic direction and development on the journey to becoming an e-confident school.

SUGGESTIONS FOR FURTHER READING

DfES (2003) *Fulfilling the Potential: Transforming teaching and learning through ICT in school* (DfES 0265). London: HMSO.

DfES (2005) *Harnessing Technology: Transforming Learning and Children's Services,* (DfES 1296). London: HMSO.

Lucey, T. (2005) *Management Information Systems* (9th edn). London: Thompson Learning.

OFSTED (2004) *ICT in schools: The impact of government initiatives five years on.* Norwich: HMSO.

USEFUL RESOURCES

Becta (www.becta.org.uk).

Data Protection (www.informationcommissioner.gov.uk).

DfES (www.dfes.gov.uk).

Gridclub (www.gridclub.com).

IPAS (http://ipas.ngfl.gov.uk).

Ofsted (www.ofsted.gov.uk).

Teachernet (www.teachernet.gov.uk).

NCSL www.ncsl.org.uk/useofdata

3

Facilities Management

Dave Evans

INTRODUCTION

In this chapter you will find a review of the increasing delegation of facilities responsibility to schools and the resulting implications for the School Business Manager (SBM). The various aspects of school premises and equipment that fall within the category of 'facilities' are covered and the emerging issues for strategic planning and managing the change agenda will also be explored.

You will also find a discussion about the extent of facilities management as it currently is, where it may go in the future, and the SBM's role in managing this range of facilities in schools. A clear overview of possibilities for schools to plan their future procedures for effective facilities management is also provided.

Prior to the introduction of Local Management of Schools (LMS) (Education Reform Act) 1988, the provision and management of school premises lay with the local education authority (LEA). Therefore the school's strategies for development prior to this innovation were inevitably linked to the LEA's overall plan for their city or county. The gradual change from centralised provision managed by the respective LEA to school-based provision has given schools the opportunity to plan and manage their premises and facilities to meet their own local and community needs.

Initially the role devolved to the headteacher. With the incremental change in the laws on governance since 1986 the expectation has developed for shared leadership of LMS between governors and the senior management team. In the last five years the emergence of the school business manager as an integral part of the Workforce Reform initiative has changed expectations within school leadership teams. The requirement for an expert in facilities management has influenced the training of new SBMs.

EXTENT OF FACILITIES MANAGEMENT

'Facilities' include all the physical assets of the school: buildings, grounds and all the materials in or on them. Managing them requires the school business manager to maximise the effective use of all these in meeting the educational needs of the community. These should be addressed through:

- strategic planning and development processes;
- the safe maintenance and operation of buildings and grounds;
- consultation, advice and collaboration with governors, local authorities (LAs) and other external agencies;
- continuity of supplies and services, as well as the maintenance of equipment;
- transport, catering and community involvement.

Regardless of size, many schools are now embarking upon their own management of areas such as cleaning, catering, maintenance and transport. Many are beginning enterprise ventures that will not only address their facility but also create income for the school. A survey of recent case studies from the CSBM programme run by the NCSL (available at: www.ncsl.org.uk) indicated a steep increase in schools embarking upon managing their own facilities. These included cleaning, catering, electrical maintenance, buildings maintenance, furniture refurbishment, building plans, transport arrangements, grounds maintenance and business of facilities letting, in addition to more ambitious ventures that will enhance income as well as address community needs.

The following extracts are from CSBM and DSBM case studies and project extracts (available at: www.ncsl.org.uk).

Large Primary School

> I have investigated the risks and benefits of managing our own catering service by visiting other schools within the area that have already changed over, and have compiled a draft business plan for consideration by the governors.

Middle School

> The main purpose of the upgrade of the phone system is to enable targeting of calls, thereby improving the efficiency and effectiveness of administrative staff and relieving pressure at key times by enabling certain calls to be dealt with in an automated way.

Medium High School

> The building of a new entrance hall with reception offices will improve the school's security as well as meeting the needs of a growing administrative team.

STRATEGIC PERSPECTIVE AND EFFECTIVE FACILITIES PLANNING

Successful schools will have a clear vision as to future direction. This applies to all aspects of school and includes curriculum development, staffing arrangements and facilities planning.

> Schools need to think in terms of long-term planning through 'futures thinking' and 'scenario building' to show strategic intent in a clear vision statement. In drawing this up it is important that stakeholder groups are fully involved ... *What you do today can build into influencing what you get from the future.* Candidate for CSBM cohort 2 and DSBM cohort 1: SBM, primary school.

In order to ensure a school's vision for future direction is met, it is necessary to ensure an appropriate strategic plan is in place. This needs to address the requirements for a school to sustain its planned development through effective management of all its facilities.

> The SIP (School Improvement plan) is formulated by a number of groups, covering areas such as community, personnel, and teaching and learning, and is very much a working document. I am a member of the personnel/CPD group. The SIP impacts on my role in a number of ways, primarily though through the financial/budget implications identified in the plan, any building implications relating to teaching and learning, the allocation of resources, staff training etc. It is completely appropriate therefore, that I am involved in these processes.

(CSBM candidate, finance and premises manager, secondary school)

SBM Toolkit – FM:1

To accomplish effective facilities planning it is necessary to review current facilities against pupil and staff numbers. Once this is done, you should project forward to the expected numbers based on actual pupils: from these figures you should be able to work out the future facilities needs for the school.

This is an essential exercise for all SBMs in order to give a rationale for facilities overall planning which may include the need for additional building or a change of usage (and so on). In addition it will give the necessary information to inform estates management, premises usage and asset acquisition or disposal (see Asset Management on p. 48). The strategic plan is therefore the blueprint for all facilities decision making.

Once this exercise is completed the information gained should inform school leaders about development needs for the short-, medium- and long-term planning of facilities that can be included in the school's development plan for premises and site development, in order to meet overall development needs.

Implementation of the strategic plan requires the SBM to make certain informed choices. These will depend upon many variables including the expertise available, the school's size and development requirements. Some of these choices are explored below.

In-house or outsourced

The first choice a SBM may need to make is whether to use internal expertise, if it is available, or to outsource professionals such as architects, engineers, risk managers, contractors, or other service providers in order to meet the need. This will depend upon the knowledge and skills of the school staff. With regard to maintenance many schools do not outsource, but for minor projects most do and therefore need to have procedures developed to ensure all outsourcing meets legal and ethical requirements, as well as a school's needs.

Where schools have the necessary internal expertise and may wish to use it, then procedures have to be in place that check for suitability:

- Are they appropriate for this particular task?
- Do they meet the legal building regulations, specifications and insurance requirements?
- Do they meet value for money criteria?

Any checks should always include outsourced comparisons to ensure the first and last questions are answered with quotes as evidence for governors.

PFI – Planning pitfalls and opportunities

Private Finance Initiatives (PFI) are popular in certain political circles and therefore can not be easily dismissed, but need to be reviewed on the same basis as any other source of finance that has contractual constraints attached. These initiatives offer opportunities for finance that will not necessarily be available from local government sources. However, they do have conditions attached that can tie the school concerned into serious long-term commitments. The SBM should review the options and list the benefits and commitments clearly, and then present implications for different long-term scenarios for the school before governors and/or LAs make any decisions.

There will be a tendency for some heads and governors to focus on the benefits and not on the commitments. It is important that pitfalls and opportunities are looked at equally so that the implications for the future are clear and explicit.

> I have heard some excellent stories and some real horror stories about PPP/PFI ... whilst you have a fantastic school now, what happens if your financial backers

experience financial problems in the future and cannot maintain the level of support you are currently receiving? Who now has control of your facilities and what is the link between the contractor and the SBM regarding premises and grounds? (Facilities Hot Seat, Talk2Learn 1-9-05)

Talk2Learn is a secure online community learning environment, developed by the National College for School Leadership (NCSL) specifically for school leaders. Those who have been enrolled into CSBM and DSBM have open access to these. Others need permission from NCSL.

Awarding Contracts

The SBM will need to become conversant with drawing up specifications for various contractual works and must develop protocols to ensure correct procedures are always followed. It will be their role to enforce these. Therefore some knowledge and understanding of building regulations for schools and the legal requirements for safe working conditions will need to be acquired. This may be onerous, but if it can be achieved then the SBM can assume the responsibility for advertising contracts for their school's minor projects or maintenance jobs. This will include awarding and managing these using DfES and LA guidelines on tendering and safe working conditions for schools.

Extended school requirements

One new initiative fully supported by the government is that of extended schools. Schools will need to respond to the DfES challenge that by 2010, all primary and secondary schools will provide extended services to their pupils. The government's belief in the importance of links with the community reinforces the fact that *all* education relates to the wider community and the world of work and professional practice. Of course, from an SBM perspective, increased use of school premises can lead to improved security for the school site and reductions in vandalism and graffiti in the surrounding area. 'It is about making best use of existing space outside of school hours', Ruth Kelly – Extended Schools Hot Seat, Talk2Learn October 2005.

In order to ensure advanced planning, each school will need to address this initiative as achievable and each SBM will need to explore the facilities implications and draw up an appropriate plan for resource allocation. They will also need to investigate income and expenditure to meet the costs of these additional requirements for schools. Will the benefits outweigh the costs? Any new initiative adopted for extended schools should form part of the strategic plan.

The Extended Schools initiative requires all schools to draw up plans to address their community needs if appropriate, and to share facilities where these public assets would enhance community well-being. Therefore SBMs will need to investigate current community usage of school facilities and consult on further usage that may be appropriate to their school and/or the community. There may well be reciprocal arrangements for community facilities being used by schools. A usage audit of both school and community facilities should be a part of the strategic plan.

Health and safety

In carrying out the strategic plan it is often necessary to include health and safety issues as additional people on site always involves security procedures and safety regulations being invoked. It is important that these procedures and regulations are written down, disseminated to all staff and reviewed after each project (refer to Chapter 1).

MAINTENANCE, REVIEW AND FACILITIES IMPROVEMENT

> School Business Managers have to look at whether their buildings are fit for purpose … (*'Age Concern, School Buildings,' Talk2Learn, September 2005*)

Staffing issues – planning and programming

Staffing procurement and procedures will be covered in Chapter 4. However, the point of addressing staffing here is as a planning tool to inform on facilities needs.

Bearing in mind the section on strategic planning (see pp. 42–45), it is important to work on *actual numbers* of pupils – ideally three years ahead of arrival. However with parental choice this will always be an inexact science. Each school will have its own data base spreadsheet that will use LA numbers but will not rely entirely on them. Once these numbers are as accurate as they can be, they will inform the school leadership team of future staffing needs as regards teachers and support staff. This is known as manpower planning. In addition it will inform on facilities' needs in terms of classrooms, specialist rooms, furniture, equipment, and maintenance of same. It will also inform on staffing for support of these facilities such as cleaning, although SBMs should always be aware of new technologies and materials.

All these operations will need to be carefully programmed so that building work is planned well in advance of need. Before building or alterations are complete furniture and fittings will need to be acquired and allocated. Staffing will also be programmed in advance of building completion. In schools where there are no building projects, it will still be necessary to review staffing in relation to facilities maintenance to ensure these are meeting a school's changing needs.

```
┌─────────────────────────────────────────────────────────────────┐
│                                                                   │
│                     SBM Toolkit – FM:2                            │
│                                                                   │
│   School furniture is improving almost exponentially. For example, many South │
│   African schools have their cleaning requirements met through enhanced fur-  │
│   niture and floor coverings which do not easily deteriorate and have low main- │
│   tenance requirements.                                           │
│                                                                   │
└─────────────────────────────────────────────────────────────────┘
```

Premises register and scheduling

To fulfil the SBM's role in promoting effective and efficient use of facilities within school buildings and grounds, it is necessary to ensure servicing and maintenance according to specified requirements laid down by the suppliers or providers. For each aspect of the school's facilities within buildings and grounds there will need to be a fully surveyed schedule of work to ensure they all perform at maximum efficiency. In order to devise an appropriate schedule for such servicing and maintenance it is necessary to create and maintain a register of premises.

A premises register should list all assets that make up the buildings and their fixtures, fittings and contents, and should include; age of buildings; construction type; plans and areas; equipment and plant; operational manuals and warranties; servicing and inspection records, energy and water consumption records, together with additional information on assets held. This differs from the asset register (see below) in that it includes all data required to ensure maintenance of facilities are fully scheduled according to the makers' or providers' specifications.

In order to create this register it will be necessary for each SBM to survey all buildings to record the condition and requirements for each area and facility. Once this has been compiled, it will need to be updated annually as condition and usage change. Condition surveys will provide a systematic means of showing objectively the state of the premises, and from this information it should be possible to ensure a planned programme of maintenance is implemented. Sources here will include professional inspections, surveys and reports from architects, engineers, fitters, building inspectors and any other key person required to carry out these operations as part of their servicing contracts. Where applicable, the LA has a duty of care to the pupils and must ensure the buildings are fit for purpose. Their involvement can be important, although it is possible even this role will be passed to schools in the near future.

The register will enable SBMs to create a timetable of maintenance scheduling. This should show the timings for servicing and inspections of all plant and equipment, some required monthly, quarterly, six monthly or annually and so on, indicated in table form in the schedule within the premises register.

Links to Other Plans

The Audit Commission believes it is good practice for the school development plan to include summarised information from other, more detailed, strategic plans to show how the allocation of resources and the budget for the year support the priorities identified in these.

These would include, for example, the:

- asset management plan;
- property development plan;
- staff development plan;
- IT/ICT development plan. (CSBM/DSBM candidate, July 2005)

Costing, prioritising and planning for sustainability

Once the school's condition is detailed in the premises register, work for repairs and maintenance should be costed, prioritised and planned. This information, fed back to the leadership team, will enable strategic decisions to be made with regards to repair, replacement or improvement.

The sustainability of school facilities requires the SBM to put in place a rolling programme of school refurbishment, covering items such as redecoration, furniture and equipment replacement, floor and fittings refurbishment or replacement. Costings will depend upon the contractors, although in-school staff can often complete these tasks more cost effectively than outside contractors. Each SBM will need to estimate a cost for such a programme based on a percentage of the replacement cost for furniture and fittings.

The involvement of others in these processes is important. Stakeholders will be involved through appropriate meetings such as whole governing body, committee and parent teacher meetings. Each school will have communication procedures. It is important for the SBM to use these to ensure full involvement of interested parties in the information dissemination and, where appropriate, the decision-making process. The LA will have the right to be involved through its duty of care role, as well as its responsibility that the school buildings are fit for purpose. There should also be a wider community involvement through less formal communication means, such as newsletters and newspaper articles.

The management of energy and water are the responsibility of the school, whether carried out by the LA's specialist department or by the school themselves. There is a need to look at energy and water through a whole-school approach which will be picked up in Chapter 7 ('Managing Environmental Issues'), however it is necessary to cover certain requirements here that impinge upon facilities management.

There are important statutory requirements that SBMs need to ensure are addressed in providing water, heating and lighting for pupils and staff. These will require schools to ensure the minimum requirements are met and all safety regulations enforced. There is also a commitment for schools to reduce water and energy consumption in line with international government agreements. In addition to these financial and technical aspects, there are educational aspects that need to be addressed by the school through appropriate schemes (see Chapter 7).

Asset management – control, acquisition and disposal

Management of a school's assets requires the creation and maintenance of an asset register that will list all assets to ensure effective utilisation and planned-for replacement. This provides a security record to ensure who is responsible and where the asset is held. It is important to ensure all stores and equipment are secured and access to them controlled and documented. The SBM will need to undertake checks on the safe custody of assets on a regular and scheduled basis. The register will be an important source of evidence for auditors and governors.

Although it may be necessary for each department to keep their own register, it should be done under the direction of the SBM or another responsible person who will ensure a whole-school approach to all record keeping and acquisition checking, monitoring and recording. This may be particularly true of smaller items such as calculators. The governors will need to agree the procedure for this control and suggest guidance for disposal procedures.

The acquisition and disposal of assets will require recording and checking through the agreed procedure before being written into the asset register. This should follow a proper financial procedure, ensuring segregation of duties as indicated in Chapter 6 on financial management.

Estate management

The management of school sites requires that each school should have a site plan that shows the location of:

- all buildings, grounds and the extent of the boundaries together with adjacent buildings and grounds;
- all services such as underground pipes, cables and drains;
- each area that requires different servicing or maintenance requirements marked out clearly, defining the area boundary with an indication to link them to the appropriate servicing contract.

The plan should include a service specification as follows:

- servicing contractors with relevant named contact in each case;
- each area's specific requirements;
- frequency of operation;
- performance specification (such as grass length and so on).

In addition it is important to have procedures for acquisition and/or disposal of estate assets which would require the involvement of various other parties, including the LA, the DfES, the school governors, and in some circumstances the Audit Commission.

Health and Safety Regulations

In carrying out all the duties described in this chapter, the SBM will need to ensure adherence to all the relevant health and safety regulations listed as follows:

● Health and Safety at Work Act 1974;
● Management of Health and Safety at Work Regulations 1999;
● Control of Substances Hazardous of Health (COSHH) 1999;
● The Manual Handling Operation Regulations 1992;

and these others according to circumstance:

● The Noise at Work Regulations 1989;
● The Control of Asbestos at Work Regulations 1987;
● The Construction (Design and Management) Regulations 1994;
● Personal Protective Equipment Regulations 1992.

School has a legal duty of care to whoever is carrying out the work. It is important that each school identifies one person to ensure all health and safety regulations are known, enforced and adhered to by everyone working within or adjacent to the school's grounds. This is required regardless of using in-house or external contractors.

All regular and occasional contractors will need to be informed in writing of the school's requirements as regards the specific health and safety requirements that they need to adhere to for the safe completion of their contract. When major work is carried out or regular contractors agree to share the responsibility for health and safety transference of any such responsibility should be recorded clearly in writing and agreed with the health and safety officer and representative (see Chapter 1 on 'Managing Risk').

Analysis of future needs is a key feature of sustainability. When the school reviews facilities and looks at the acquisition of new buildings, equipment or fittings, the SBM should research the maintenance and servicing implications of any such change and indicate this to the leadership team and governors prior to any decision being made.

> I can see now that we need to take a more holistic and long-term approach. As the only member of the senior management team who is not a classroom practitioner, I

already ask a lot of 'what ifs' and 'whys' at meetings but now I feel I need to actively encourage a look at future scenarios. (DSBM Candidate Reflections: Talk2Learn, Cohort 1 July 2005)

TRANSPORT

Transport will often fall within the SBM's remit. There are clear distinctions between statutory transport for pupils to and from school, and additional transport which is solely the responsibility of the school alone.

Pupil transportation requirements

The following guidance is based on UK and EC education institutions, but is generally regarded as good practice internationally.

At present it is the LA's responsibility to provide free transport to and from the designated school where pupils live beyond walking distance. This is defined as either those aged under 8 who live up to 2 miles from the school, or those pupils aged above 8 who live up to 3 miles from the school (as per the 1996 Education Act). This does not apply to the school that would be the parent's choice. Within these distances the school can provide transport but there are strict regulations that the vehicle must operate under (defined as a 'Section 19 permit'). The relevant White Paper in 2005 (DfES, 2005) suggested changes to these regulations for certain pupils.

The use of transport for school activities will fall within the school's responsibility. Any additional use of transport as well as school hired or owned vehicles will also fall within the school's responsibility (see Chapter 1 'Managing Risk').

Many schools operate their own mini-buses and some other vehicles connected with ground maintenance and the like. Once purchased, the school accepts responsibility for the condition of the vehicle on the road. To regulate this responsibility it is important that procedures are followed in recording all servicing, inspections and defects as they arise. Defects may require immediate action with the vehicle not allowed into use until these are satisfactorily repaired. The school may contract out maintenance to a garage; this does *not* absolve the school from their overall responsibility as the vehicle's owner from the task of recording all checks and drivers' records before and after each journey.

In addition to mechanical condition the vehicle must be equipped with a first aid box of a defined design and can only be driven by people designated as suitable by the school, taking all legal considerations into account. Where the mini-bus has more than 12 passengers it is necessary for all drivers to hold a Public Service Vehicle licence (PSV), unless they are designated 'non-commercial' which means no contributions are made. In addition the vehicle will need to be tested by a designated council or at an HGV testing station. Under this permit scheme the bus cannot carry members of the public but only those to whom the permit is issued – the school. Drivers must adhere to 'EC drivers' hours regulations'.

It will be the school's responsibility to ensure all drivers entitled to drive hold full current driving licences with category B and D1 entitlement, are over 21 years old and are not disqualified by way of convictions.

Meeting educational and environmental needs

There are excellent educational reasons for schools being influential in discouraging parents from using certain types of private transport for their child (also referenced in Chapter 7 'Managing Environmental Issues'). Indeed the DfES is encouraging schools, LAs and parents to think about safe and sustainable school travel that makes use of walking, cycling and public transport. It is important for SBMs to assess the balance between cost effectiveness and moral and ethical actions in facilities management. This is probably best shown in the way a school encourages or discourages the use of polluting transport, whether instigated by parents or the school itself. At best a school must be seen as a benign influence in such matters.

Therefore many SBMs are now instigating environmentally sympathetic policies for transport for pupils, even if the school grounds are only being used for picking up or dropping off children. Indeed many are now actively encouraging healthy and environmentally friendly programmes, such as 'walking trains' or secure bicycle storage and so on.

> The school I am being sponsored by launched its first walking bus in June 2003 and it is still running to date. The walking bus is organised by the school, but volunteer parents are the 'driver' and 'conductor'. Children are collected from a number of specified 'bus stops' throughout the village in the mornings and are dropped off at these points in the afternoon. (CSBM Candidate: National Module Discussions, Talk2Learn, July 2005)

Staff vehicles on site

There are several issues that the SBM may need to address in ensuring all staff that use their cars for the travel of pupils and park on school grounds are advised correctly. Therefore they will need to ensure there are written school guidelines about:

- the risk of parking on school grounds and the liability the school will accept;
- which staff can use their cars for transporting pupils, the insurance requirements, and 'child protection' safeguards;

- the school's requirements for using their car for other school business such as transporting school equipment and so on;
- the need to indemnify the authority against third party claims if they use their cars for authority business (business use cover is normally sufficient here).

CATERING

In the UK, the publicity for school lunches instigated by Jamie Oliver's programme over the summer of 2005 has had a marked effect upon the future development of school catering.

> I have been visiting a different school each day for the past four years and I have noted the wide variation in the quality of school meals. I always ask if I can eat in the dining hall when I am assessing in a school, because it tells me so much about the culture of the institution. I have noted a clear correlation between the quality of the meals and the quality of the education provided by schools. Maybe this is because the meals are an indicator of the care that the school takes of the pupils' welfare. Certainly the bursar contributes a great deal to the creation of a civilised atmosphere in school if they run a high quality meals service. (CSBM discussion on school meals facilities, 2004, Talk2Learn)

After many years of retreat on school catering this has now become the latest 'hot' issue. Jamie Oliver's initiative on school dinners has had a significant effect. Therefore, the SBM will need to address the service levels in their school, whether in-house or contracted out. Do they meet the legal, organisational, nutritional and free school meals requirements?

The provision of a school meals service lies with a school's governing body (The School Standards and Framework Act 1998). The SBM's role will be to oversee that the provision is meeting both the pupils' and the school's needs. These include:

- the legal aspect, in terms of free school meals – the LA will indicate to the school those eligible;
- fulfilling other government initiatives such as The National School Fruit Scheme, Every Child Matters and Extended Schools, through addressing pupil well-being in all school policies;
- the organisational level, in terms of ensuring those with entitlement are provided with the opportunity for a meal;
- health and safety arrangements are fully adhered to and known to all concerned;
- nutritional standards being met;
- working with LAs to ensure correct procedures and outside agencies where a school outsources the meals provision;

● additional issues that the SBM might be involved with, if their school runs a breakfast club or tuck shop and so on.

Nutritional requirements and well-being issues for school meals

New nutritional standards are laid down by the DfES in three documents for each type of school. The SBM will need to ensure these regulations and guidelines are being met in relation to all catering carried out for, or on behalf of, their school.

School caterers must meet nutritional standards laid down by the government in an effort to curtail the rising cases of obesity among school pupils. Good health is important for everyone. The government wants to secure, maintain and improve children's and young people's health. (*School Lunches, Healthy Living, Teachernet*)

I am an office manager in a Cumbrian junior school with 188 on roll. I am looking at the feasibility of in-house catering for my case study and last week I visited a local infant and nursery school who took their catering in-house in Sept 2004 with great success. Numbers taking a school meal have risen to 97 per cent (from 68 per cent with 320 on roll), sandwiches and tray bake cakes are sold to parents picking up their children and they project a profit of £5k for 05/06 for this alone.

The headteacher invites parents into school one day a week and provides a 'meals-on-wheels' service to the elder members of the community. He is also planning to introduce Sunday lunches for the school community. His recommendations for in-house catering were: find a good butcher and a good cook and you can't lose. He was extremely enthusiastic about in-house catering and promised us that if we took the plunge we wouldn't look back! We are seriously considering going with in-house catering. (NCSL in Dialogue October 2005)

SBM Toolkit – FA:3

Use of outside agencies

Many schools have developed breakfast clubs or after school clubs that require additional catering. In trying to extend the school there are a host of pitfalls into which an SBM could fall. In schools in the UK, there are 23 Acts or regulations applicable to catering or catering premises. The DfES recommends schools to work in partnership with other local providers and organisations such as the local environmental health service, and the LA or other local suppliers.

> Therefore you, as SBM, may wish to see yourself as a *coordinator* of various providers in developing the extended school. This fits well with the concept of 'federations' of schools and peripatetic SBMs. There is even a case for rotating the responsibility among SBMs, but do remember the issues of competence and training. A certificate-level SBM can undertake this role, but (untrained) others may not comply with regulations.

CHANGE MANAGEMENT AND FUTURE REQUIREMENTS

In meeting all the changes taking place in schools today, the SBM needs to be conversant with the various change management tools which are now available to review, reflect, analyse, evaluate and plan for future school needs. These can now be accessed through the Training and Development Agency – Schools, or the local authority remodelling adviser.

The CSBM and DSBM provide candidates with additional tools for addressing quality of management and developing team approaches. The use of such tools will give SBMs a repertoire of problem-solving abilities that should enable them to meet the present dynamic in schools as they effect the management of facilities and business.

SBMs will need to ensure they have the opportunity to influence and implement improvement. Where schools have change teams they should be involved, as they are able to give a different perspective and drive through more effective use of school facilities both for the pupils and the local community.

The implementation of the school curriculum requires that appropriate facilities are available in the classrooms or specialist rooms where they are needed. The increasing use of interactive white boards or overhead projectors in addition to laptops is an example of the developing needs of modern teaching to ensure effective learning. The SBM's role is to ensure the correct equipment is sought using the agreed procedures.

Looking at the change in facilities requirements now compared with five or ten years ago indicates the accelerating and changing requirements of schools. There is a need for the SBM to be able to meet these new needs as they arise and to be able to recognise false needs. They will need to develop processes for ensuring the demands of teachers are required and sustainable for their school of the future. This process will need to involve the leadership team and other stakeholders, and be able to inform itself of influential trends and changes that are pertinent to the school's developing situation. This demands a long-term perspective which the SBM will need to provide.

It is the SBM's role to be able to translate policy into practical action. The leadership team will agree the policy; the SBM will need to plan the action that staff will need to follow in order to meet this policy. SBMs must have procedures ready for all aspects of audit, review and evaluation of current facilities before embarking upon new minor works, maintenance contracts or equipment and furniture procurement. In this way the SBM will be able to respond to need by creating an action plan for each instance that will meet the new demands that any venture and its implementation will place on the school.

> Bursars can also offer headteachers other kinds of support – such as advice on remodelling the school workforce and developing the role of support staff. And precisely because most bursars have a different perspective from colleagues who have trained as teachers, they can be a useful sounding board to test new approaches, and indeed put forward solutions themselves. (*CSBM Candidate, (Cohort 4) Talk2Learn, April 2005*)

Maintaining momentum

In addressing change management, one of the most difficult things to achieve is to maintain the momentum that changes bring to school improvement. Success breeds success and in the same way improvement in one area affects the desire for improvement in others. Once schools set about the process of continual facilities review, with action plans where change is needed, the SBM's role will be to ensure the change agenda is sustained.

The new agenda for school facilities management does require the widest possible community involvement. The schools facilities should be seen as community amenities held in trust by the school for the whole community. Policies should include the community, and action plans should ensure interested stakeholders are fully informed and where appropriate involved. It is common practice to actively seek parental involvement in all school facilities ventures; it needs to be equally so with the wider community for future usage and this may affect the perspective of need in the future.

CONCLUSION

Effective management

If all buildings and equipment within school are fit for purpose, with full usage and no waste, then the facilities management in the school is deemed effective. If that is not so, then procedures and/or personnel need to be reviewed and improved.

Realising the possibilities

The quote below indicates a positive outlook to future thinking. New development opportunities for bursars and school business managers are only just beginning. Therefore the outlook for the future of school facilities management is bright. If all SBMs can focus on the possibilities their school facilities can offer, and strive to meet those in the near future, schools will be much more able to meet their community needs and so improve their educational environment.

> Since starting the CSBM in 2002 my role in the school has changed dramatically. My job title has changed from finance officer to school business manager. My work has changed from bookkeeping to leading a growing administrative team and becoming part of the school leadership team. I feel the areas we have covered in this DSBM module have already given me the confidence in team meetings to contribute more fully. I have now learnt to think of the wider picture and to try and consider options that can continue into the future instead of focussing on easy answers to current operational problems. (*DSBM Candidate, Talk2Learn, (Cohort 1)*)

This chapter has emphasised certain key elements. These can be summarised as follows:

1 To ensure a school's vision is met in terms of facilities management to meet school needs it is necessary to have a strategic plan. This strategic plan will include:

   - A review of current facilities audited against future needs. This will include a future numbers survey.
   - Clear procedures for deciding on in-house or outsourced services, PFI options and implications, review protocols for awarding contracts, all of these being identified for short-, medium- and long-term future projects.
   - A school's response to extended schools, community involvement and health and safety issues.

The strategic plan should relate to, or be integral with, the school's improvement plan, and be available to all staff, governors and other appropriate stakeholders.

2 Maintenance is a pro-active task, constantly changing procedures as a result of review of practice. The effective SBM will ensure:

   - Adequate provision of facilities through an effective pupil projection procedure that will ensure appropriate staffing.
   - The management of a comprehensive premises register that records the facilities' condition which informs scheduling of maintenance operations.
   - Redecoration and facilities refurbishment or replacement on a costed, rolling programme.
   - The management of assets through a regulated asset register that indicates responsibilities as well as location and condition of assets.
   - Effective estate management through a scheduling of contractual work that is monitored and reviewed.
   - Adherence to all health and safety regulations as laid down in the various relevant Acts of parliament.

● Regular updates on maintenance programmes as each school improvement plan is implemented.

Maintenance is crucial to ensuring an effective learning environment is fit for purpose for all pupils.

3   Transport requirements to and from school for pupils beyond walking distance are the responsibility of the LAs but schools must ensure these are monitored for pupil safety. In addition an SBM will need to ensure their school:

● Regulates the use of vehicles, on site, regardless of origin.
● Legislates for the use of staff vehicles, as well as informing staff of the requirements for their vehicle use for pupil travel.
● Has an environmental policy for vehicle use by parents and others using the school site and entrance that relates to the school's environmental curriculum.

There should be a unity of practice in curriculum philosophy and organisational arrangements in meeting the schools transport needs.

4   Catering is the responsibility of the school's governing body. Many now have opted to provide meals in-house others to outsource to private contractors. Either requires the SBM to oversee and review the provision to ensure the school is getting the best deal for its pupils in terms of:

● Free school meals arrangements.
● Nutritional standards being met.
● Meals and additional catering arrangements within the school site and/or kitchen meeting all health and safety rules and these are known and enforced.
● Good use made of LAs and other agencies, whether providing meals, supplying ingredients or giving advice.

There should be unity of practice in curriculum philosophy and organisational arrangements in meeting a school's catering needs.

5   Change management is an area of expertise that the effective SBM must become confident with. They need to be influential in solving problems that will help the school meet the needs of tomorrow with the funding and facilities of today.

6   Putting policy into practice is a prime role for the SBM. There will need to be clear procedures for audit, review and evaluation to ensure expectations on facilities' usage is entirely met not only within the school but for the whole community.

7   The current political imperatives together with the new development opportunities for SBMs mean the management of facilities in school is dynamic

and gives excellent opportunities for 'blue sky' thinking to greatly improve current practice for the benefit of all pupils/students.

SUGGESTIONS FOR FURTHER READING

Alexander, K. (Ed.) (1996) *Facilities Management*. London: Spon Press.

BNF, (no date) *Establishing a Whole Food Policy.* British Nutritional Foundation and Design and Technology Association for DfES: available at http://www.teachernet. gov.uk/_doc/4865/BNF_Food_in_Schools_BT.pdf.

DfES (1999) *A Safer Journey to School: A Guide to School Travel Plans for Parents* (Transport 2000). London: HMSO.

DfES, (1999) *The Education (School Premises) Regulations 1999, Statutory Instrument No. 2*. London: HMSO.

DfES (1997) *School Grounds: A Guide to Good Practice, DfES Building Bulletin 85*. London: HMSO.

DfES (2005) Extended schools: Access to opportunities and services for all, a prospectus (ref 1408-2005DOC-EN): available at http://www.teachernet.gov.uk/management/atoz/e/extendedschools/.

DfES Architects and Building Branch (2001) *Inclusive School Design*, London: HMSO.

DfT (2004) *Walking and Cycling: An Action Plan*. London: DfT.

HSE Books (1992) *Workplace (Health, Safety and Welfare) Regulations 1992: Guidance for the Education Sector*. London: Health and Safety Executive.

Kowalski, T. J. (2002) *Planning and Managing School Facilities* (2nd edn). Westport, CT: Bergin & Garvey.

O'Sullivan, F., Thody, A. and Wood, E. (2000) *From Bursar to School Business Manager*. London: Financial Times/Prentice Hall.

Park, A. (1998) *Facilities Management: An explanation* (2nd edn.). Basingstoke: Palgrave Macmillan.

TDA (formally TTA) (2005) *Building the School Team*. London: TTA Publications.

Wood, J. and Littlewood, M. (1996) *A Guide to Management and Maintenance of School Grounds*. Crediton: Southgate Publishers.

USEFUL RESOURCES

DfES, *Standards for School Premises*, DfES Guidance: available at premises. schools@dfes.gsi.gov.uk.

DfES, *Consultation on School Lunches:* available at http://www.dfes.gov.uk/consultations/.

DfES, *Nutritional standards for (each phase of) School:* available at

http://www.dfes.gov.uk/schoollunches/juniors.shtml

http://www.dfes.gov.uk/schoollunches/juniors.shtml

http://www.dfes.gov.uk/schoollunches/secondary.shtml

http://www.myschoollunch.co.uk/

Managing Human Resources

Anne Bryson

INTRODUCTION

Human Resource (HR) is without doubt the most valuable resource any organisation can possess, undeniably the key to its success or failure. In his book *A Handbook of Human Resource Management Practice* (2004: 1) Michael Armstrong defines human resource management as 'a strategic and coherent approach to the management of the organisation's most valued assets'. In the case of a school, which has the development of people as its purpose, fair and effective management of human resources is critical as the value it places in its staff will impact on the young people in its care.

This chapter will explore some of the practicalities of Human Resource Management. You will find guidance on fair and objective procedures for recruitment, selection and induction of staff as well as grievance and discipline. The legal minefield related to staff appointments and the termination of personnel contracts is explored and the issue of how appropriate rewards packages can help motivate staff and ensure that you get the best from your human resource is investigated.

POLICIES AND PROCEDURES IN PRACTICE

Schools are encouraged to establish and regularly review a range of policies outlining the values of the organisation and how it intends to fulfil its responsibilities. In relation to HR one would expect to find, at the very least, policies for recruitment and retention, staff grievance and discipline, staff pay and performance management and of course many policies will apply equally to staff and students. This last point is well served by codes of practice produced by the Equal Opportunities Commission, the Commission for Racial Equality and the Disability Rights Commission which encourage all organisations in the UK to introduce policies to eliminate discrimination on the grounds of gender, race and disability.

In order to evaluate the effectiveness of these policies, it is recommended that data are collected and analysed on the composition of the workforce, applicants for vacant posts and career progression. This procedure is one of many which need to spell out in detail the steps managers should take to ensure that HR policies are consistently applied. The development of such procedures should take place in consultation with all relevant stakeholders and both legal and ethical requirements should be taken into account. The existence of documented procedures which are transparent and well publicised will ensure that everyone knows exactly what steps to take, or what will happen in the event of a particular HR issue arising.

RECRUITMENT AND SELECTION

Good practice involves eight clear stages, each of which is addressed below.

1 *Review of vacant post*

An effective recruitment procedure would ensure that when an existing member of staff left, the needs of the school would be reviewed in the same way as if it were advertising a new position. One way of tackling this is to use the questions in Toolkit – HRM:1 below.

SBM Toolkit – HRM:1

The following questions might be asked:

- Do we actually need this post?
- What do we want the individual to do?
- How should the job description be defined?
- What skills and qualities are required?
- How does this post fit in with the longer-term aims and priorities for development?
- At what level should it be remunerated?
- What are the budget implications?
- Who should the post holder report to?
- Are there any implications for the overall staffing structure?

Once these questions have been answered and the decision to appoint has been made, it is necessary to draw up a job description and person specification so that the post can be advertised. Timing also needs to be considered:

- When do you require this person to start?
- How much notice might their existing employer require?
- How much time will you need between advertising, short listing, inviting individuals for interview, making an appointment, and following up references?
- What other steps (such as induction procedures) might need to be put in place before the new employee can begin work?

2 *Job Description*

The job description should provide basic information about the post including:

- job title;
- purpose of the role;
- main duties and responsibilities;
- reporting relationships;
- any special features of the job;
- the scope of the role;
- statements on, for example, equal opportunities polices.

Job descriptions should not be so detailed as to stifle flexibility and team-working but at the same time need to be clear enough for the post-holder to understand the contribution that he or she is expected to make to the whole school team.

3 *Person specification*

The person specification identifies the human characteristics and attributes which are required to undertake the role effectively, covering such headings as skills, knowledge, experience and attitudes and often divided into either 'essential' or 'desirable' qualities. There are a number of well-known and widely-used models for compiling person specifications, such as Alec Rodgers' Seven Point Plan (1952) and Munro Fraser's Fivefold Grading System (1954) www-users.york.ac.uk/naew6/Peop–Qual.htm. In both cases, despite the passage of time, the models provide a consistent framework for short listing and selection interviews.

At every step of the recruitment process it is essential to ensure that equal opportunities legislation is complied with, thus both of the models shown above need to be interpreted in a legal and ethical manner and considered within a twenty first century context. It could be wrong, for instance, to

Rodgers' Seven Point Plan	Fraser's Fivefold Grading System
1 Physical make-up – health, appearance, bearing, speech.	1 Impact on others – physical make-up, appearance, speech, manner.
2 Attainments – education, qualifications, experience, achievements.	2 Acquired qualifications – education, vocational training, work experience.
3 Intelligence – intellectual capacity, learning capacity, ability to analyse, etc.	3 Innate abilities – natural quickness of comprehension, aptitude for learning.
4 Special aptitudes – ability to use words, figures, etc.	4 Motivation – the kind of goals set by the individual, his or her determination in following them up and success in achieving.
5 Interests – practical, social, artistic.	
6 Disposition – influence over others, dependability, maturity, humour.	5 Adjustment – emotional stability, ability to cope with stress, ability to get on with people.
7 Circumstances – domestic, family.	

discriminate against someone under Point 1 in both models because they had a particular accent or under Point 7 of Rodgers' Seven Point Plan, because they had a young family. Other models exist, and can be acceded on the Chartered Institute of Personal Development's website (available at: www.cipd.co.uk).

4 *Advertising*

Advertising is an expensive business, therefore it is important to consider not only the content of the advert, but the timing and where the advert should be placed, for example the local or national press, professional publications, websites, job centres and so on, all of which should be appropriate to the position being advertised. Remember also that you might have internal interest for the vacancy, and these applicants should be treated in the same professional way and be subject to the same procedures as external candidates.

Thought needs to be given to the information provided for applicants and whether you require them to submit a CV with a standard letter to be signed, a CV along with a letter of application addressing specific points, or a standard application form. Whilst a CV can save time you can be more specific about the information you need by asking them to complete an application form, which along with the person specification can be used as the framework for short listing and interviewing. In schools in the UK, there are also particular requirements relating to candidates having criminal records.

5   Selection interviewing

The selection process traditionally consists of a formal interview and depending on the position, a requirement to provide evidence of competence in certain aspects of the role, for instance in tray exercises, presentations, problem-solving scenarios, and/or exercises in the use of standard computer software in which the post-holder will require expertise. A range of more formal selection tests are available should the position justify this, but they need to be applied, interpreted and evaluated by suitably qualified professionals. The British Psychological Society hold a certificate and register of competence, which can give some security here (available at: www.bps.org.uk).

Thought should be given to where the interviews can take place, the set up of the room and the make up of the interview panel. Every effort should be made to put candidates at their ease so that they perform naturally. Barriers, such as tables between the panel and interviewee, should be avoided as should chairs of differing heights. Questioning needs to be 'open': 'Tell me about ...', 'Give me an example of ...', 'How would you deal with ...?' As much information as possible must be collected to inform the decision-making process and a proforma is useful to record answers, helping to ensure consistency and fairness.

After the selection process has been completed and a decision has been reached, a provisional offer of employment can be made. It's worthwhile, if possible, making the initial offer by telephone and where the decision is very close, identifying a reserve in case the preferred candidate does not accept the post. It should be made clear in any communication that the offer is subject to satisfactory references being received and any other conditions being met, such as pre-appointment checks relating to health or criminal records. It should also be stressed at this point that any documentation relating to the selection process, (including applications and notes related to short listing or the interviews themselves) should be retained for six months in case the decision is challenged under equal opportunities legislation.

6   Letter of appointment

The letter of appointment is an important document, as along with the candidate's letter of acceptance it forms the basis for the contract of employment. The following information should be included in the letter of appointment:

Job title
Date of commencement
Salary
Terms of employment, that is

- whether the appointment is full-time or part-time and if part-time the numbers of hours per week
- in the case of support staff, whether for the full year or 'term time only' and if so the number of weeks worked and paid
- whether the post is permanent, temporary or fixed term and if appropriate the end date

Whether any probationary period applies
Any special conditions or benefits
Notice periods for termination of contract
Procedures for accepting the post.

Letters of rejection should be brief but sensitive, focussing on an applicant's strengths and offering the opportunity for feedback should the applicant wish to take it.

7   *Staff induction*

The staff induction programme is one of the most important stages in the recruitment process. You have invested a great deal of time and effort in getting the right person for the job and this process not only eases the new recruit into the strange environment, it also helps establish a favourable impression and enables them to perform effectively more quickly. Research shows that employees are more likely to leave during their first six months in post than at any other time and induction helps avoid the cost and inconvenience of this.

The induction programme is likely to cover a period of time and includes a number of stages as indicated in Toolkit–HRM:2 below.

SBM Toolkit – HRM:2

Use these three stages as the basis of a proforma for both you *and* the new recruit to record the experience. This is useful if there is an issue at any later stage about, for example, conflicting advice.

- First day: Make sure the first person the new employee will meet knows that they are coming and what to do with them. It is likely that they will have been asked to bring certain documents with them (their P45, for example) and also there may be documentation which needs to be issued to them such as a staff handbook and/or induction checklist.

  Whoever has been briefed to look after the new recruit should run through the main points, such as health and safety, toilets, refreshments, layout

---

> of the building and so on. Although the most important appropriate person to undertake much of the induction process is the line manager, it's also good practice to allocate a 'buddy' from within the team to act as guide and to whom the new member of staff can direct questions.
>
> • First Week: The employee should be introduced to different elements of their work throughout the first week. It can also be useful to arrange for them to meet some of the people that they will come into contact with on a regular basis.
> • First Month: Further work shadowing and on the job training will take place over this period, as well as introductions to other key people. It may also be appropriate for the new starter to sit in on meetings to get a wider view of the aims and objectives of the school.

8 *Probationary period*

It is not uncommon for schools in the maintained sector in England and Wales to appoint new support staff subject to an initial period of probation, usually of six months. If this is the case it should be made clear in their letter of appointment. Regular meetings should be held between the line manager and employee during this time so that progress can be reviewed, with support or training being offered to remedy any shortcomings. At the end of the period the employee should be informed in writing of the fact that the probationary period has been successfully completed.

Where an employee has failed to meet the necessary standard, but has shown progress, the probationary period can be extended should this be felt to be beneficial. Any extension should include clear targets and a new end date and should be confirmed in writing. Where a line manager considers a probationer to be unsuitable in spite of the additional support and training offered, a full report should be made to governors setting out the reasons for recommending termination of employment.

GRIEVANCE AND DISCIPLINE

Hopefully you now have a suitably qualified, well-inducted employee on their way to being a model employee. Well, actually, if you get it 51 per cent right, then that could be the best to hope for, as even the best employee may find themselves subject to grievance and disciplinary procedures. Every organisation has the need for certain rules and acceptable standards of behaviour, many of which will be unwritten and adhered to as a matter of common sense. It is however necessary to have a formalised approach to dealing with some issues so that everyone knows exactly where they stand and what steps will be taken in the event of a particular problem arising. The main areas which require to be covered in this way are

- discipline;
- grievance;
- absence;
- capability;
- redundancy.

In each case the various procedures will spell out the policy on handling the issue in question and the approaches to dealing with it including the different stages of the process.

The Employment Rights Act 1996 sets out the details that should be contained within a statement of employment and given to employees within two months of commencing employment. Included within this statement should be details of any disciplinary procedures which apply. This can be found at: http://www.opsi.gov.uk/acts/acts1996/1996018.htm.

A code of practice and detailed guidance on setting up disciplinary and grievance procedures, can be downloaded from the ACAS website at: http://www.acas.org.uk/.

Disciplinary procedures are aimed at encouraging employees to maintain the required standard of behaviour and to provide an employer with a fair means of dealing with those who do not. Grievance procedures, on the other hand, provide a forum for employees to raise serious complaints, whether they are about individuals or practices within the school which cannot be dealt with through the normal line management process. New rules concerning grievance and disciplinary procedures in England, Wales and Scotland came into being in October 2004, details of which can be found on the ACAS website at: http://www.acas.org.uk/faqs/discipline.html#3.

Capability is a complex issue involving the skill, aptitude, health or any other physical or mental quality an employee requires to be able to perform their work to an adequate level. When an employee fails to demonstrate the necessary competence in spite of additional support, guidance and training being offered, it is sometimes necessary to instigate capability procedures. This is a legal minefield and any SBM would be well advised to obtain professional advice before going down this road.

ABSENCE

Absenteeism is a drain on school resources and long-term absence is a particular problem in many schools. Whilst the absent employee continues to receive a salary, the cost of replacing the individual also has to be met and the disruption to the smooth running of the school can be considerable.

Whilst there are a variety of reasons for absence, many of which can't be avoided, steps need to be taken to manage and minimise unnecessary absence and the disruption it causes. Proper procedures for reporting and analysing staff absence will equip the school business manager with information to help address these issues. Guidance on dealing with staff absence and turnover can be found at the ACAS website at: http://www.acas.org.uk/publications/B04.html.

TERMINATION OF EMPLOYMENT

Redundancy

Under the UK's employment law as defined in the Employment Rights Act 1996, there are number of possible causes for an employee to be made redundant:

- the employer has ceased, or intends to cease, to carry on the business for the purposes of which the employee was employed; or
- the employer has ceased, or intends to cease, to carry on the business in the place where the employee was so employed; or
- the requirements of the business for employees to carry out work of a particular kind have ceased or diminished or are expected to cease or diminish; or
- the requirements of the business for the employees to carry out work of a particular kind, in the place where they were so employed, have ceased or diminished or are expected to cease or diminish.

In other words, where the school closes down completely, or closes in a particular location, or where the number of employees required has reduced or is expected to reduce, an employee can be dismissed as redundant. In certain circumstances redundant employees are entitled to compensation payments and unless the school has a fair and consistent redundancy policy in place, which has been agreed by the trade unions, the school may leave themselves open to claims of unfair dismissal.

The ACAS website (available at http://www.acas.org.uk/publications/b08.html#2) provides extensive guidance on handling redundancy, including the contents of a redundancy policy and good practice in consultation. This, however, is a particularly complex area and advice from an HR specialist should be sought.

Terminating a contract of employment

The ACAS website (see above) states

A contract of employment may be ended by mutual agreement or by the employer or employee giving the required notice of termination. If the employer fails to give the required notice the employee can make a claim to the courts for damages for wrongful dismissal. Alternatively, if the employment has been terminated, a claim can be made to an employment tribunal. Where the employee leaves without giving the required notice, the employer may also have, in certain circumstances, a right to claim damages in the courts or at an employment tribunal. Either party can terminate the contract without notice if the conduct of the other justifies it … Resignation without notice (and a possible claim of constructive dismissal) is only justified where the employer makes a 'fundamental' or 'repudiatory' breach of the contract. Whether or not the breach is considered fundamental will depend on the particular circumstances but may include such actions as a reduction in pay, withdrawal of benefits or change of duties. In the event of a dispute, the question of justification can finally be determined only by the courts.

As you can see this is an incredibly complex area requiring detailed knowledge of the law and well-documented procedures. Where the employer terminates that contract, this constitutes a dismissal. For a dismissal to be fair, the employer must have acted reasonably taking into account all of the circumstances. ACAS suggests that any employer contemplating dismissal should satisfy themselves that:

- there is sufficient reason for dismissal on the grounds of capability, conduct, redundancy, or some other substantial reason for dismissal is necessary to comply with the law;
- reasonable alternatives to dismissal were considered;
- the dismissal is consistent with previous action by the employer and any disciplinary procedure;
- the dismissal is fair, taking all relevant factors known at the time into account – for further information see the Department of Trade and Industry's leaflet PL712 (*Unfairly Dismissed*);
- they have, as a minimum, followed the statutory disciplinary and dismissal procedure. This involves the employer informing the employee in writing about the alleged offence; a meeting to discuss the issue; and, where necessary, an appeal. http://www.acas.org.uk/publications/h03.html#6

Further guidance on fair and unfair dismissal can be found on the ACAS website at http:www.acas.org.uk/publications/ho3.html#6 and the Department of Trade and Industry's website at http://www.dti.gov.uk/er/regs.htm.

TERMS AND CONDITIONS OF EMPLOYMENT

In addition to the letter of appointment and subsequent acceptance letter, a contract of employment will include a written statement of terms and/or an employee handbook and/or other rules referred to in either the written statement or the appointment letter. A contract is an agreement between two parties, which is why a written acceptance of the appointment is required. In accordance with the Employment Protection (Consolidation) Act 1978, as amended by Schedule 2, Employment Act 1982, written detail of terms and conditions must be given to all employees within 13 weeks of them commencing work, with the exception of employees working less than 16 hours per week (although it is good practice in this case also).

Employees must be notified of changes in terms and conditions within one month of changes taking place.

EMPLOYEE RELATIONS

The term 'employee relations' is often used in the context of industrial relations which usually implies the relationship between management and the trade unions. In fact employee relations covers a much wider spectrum than this; it is a partnership approach between employers, employees, representative trade unions and a variety of other bodies. Good employee relations are positive and participative; they will include formal processes, procedures and channels of communication but they will also include informal day-to-day relationships between employees, team leaders and line managers which are intuitive and based on initiative and common sense.

Employee Relations is also about policy development and review, continuous improvement of conditions and ensuring that relevant changes in employment law are implemented.

Collective Bargaining is a key feature of employee relations and is defined by ACAS as …

> a system of rules, jointly agreed by employers and employee representatives, for negotiating matters such as pay and conditions of employment and resolving any differences that can arise from them. Collective bargaining can only exist in organisations where employees have some form of representation, usually in the form of a trade union.

Further detailed guidance can be found on the DTI's Employment Relations Directorate website, available at www.dti.gov.uk/er and the ACAS website to be found at www.acas.org.uk.

REWARDS AND BENEFITS

Maintained schools in England and Wales are required to have policies in place to ensure the fair and consistent applications of pay and performance management strategies. In the main, employees are paid in accordance with nationally agreed pay and conditions which relate to their profession; this will include entitlement to additional allowances and benefits such as pension schemes and sick pay.

There is much to be said for establishing a rewards policy as opposed to just a pay policy, thus focussing on the total rewards package available to staff and reflecting the value a school places on the people it employs. The objectives of employee benefits to an organisation are described by Armstrong (2004: 272) as:

- providing an attractive and competitive total remuneration package which both attracts and retains high quality employees;
- providing for the personal needs of employees;
- increasing the commitment of employees to the organisation;
- providing for some people a tax efficient method of remuneration.

Armstrong goes on to say that 'motivates employees' is not included in the objectives because normal benefits seldom make a direct and immediate impact on performance, although they can improve commitment to the organisation in the longer term.

Employee benefits fall into two main categories:

Tangible benefits are of quantifiable value to the employee. Some of these are mandatory such as entitlement to a pensions scheme, annual leave, sick pay, maternity and paternity pay; others are discretionary such as loan or hire of equipment, mobile phone, health insurance, discretionary leave, training and career development opportunities, free on-site parking and free school meals for adults undertaking lunch-time duties.

Intangible benefits contribute to working life and say more about how an employer values staff. A recent CSBM candidate identified the following intangible benefits offered in her school:

- well-equipped staff room kitchen;
- water cooler;
- lunch provided on inset days;
- doughnuts provided during difficult weeks or as a 'thank you' to staff;
- bouquet of flowers for long-term illness or birth of a child;
- staff social events;
- fresh flowers in the office once a week.

She went on to reflect 'in discussions with staff is it apparent that in general the intangible benefits are those most appreciated by staff and contribute to a sense of value and well-being within the school community'.

It should be remembered that with one or two exceptions such as pension schemes, car parking spaces and meals, most benefits will be taxable as benefits in kind. When considering a benefits policy in your school, consideration should be given to the tax efficiency of the benefit, or in other words the tax payable on the benefit should be less than if the equivalent cash sum is paid instead.

LEGAL REQUIREMENTS

You will already have gathered that the law in relation to Human Resource Management is extremely complex and getting it wrong could have disastrous consequences. In this chapter we have only been able to scrape the surface of the legal and ethical minefield surrounding staff appointments, grievance and discipline, termination of contracts, remuneration and benefits. No-one expects the SBM to be a specialist in every aspect of the role, but they need to know their limitations and have the confidence to seek advice where necessary, and this is one area where specialist professional expertise would be valuable.

There are a number of excellent web-based resources detailed throughout this chapter and in the Useful Resources which give guidance on UK's the employment law. In particular the ACAS website provides guidance on a range of potentially difficult areas. The DTI Employee Relations Directorate also provides interpretation and guidance on various aspects of employment legislation.

The main acts of parliament with which the SBM needs to be familiar are

The Employment Rights Act 1996, which includes:

- employment particulars;
- protection of wages;
- guaranteed payments;
- time off work;
- suspension from work;
- maternity rights;
- termination of employment;
- right not to be unfairly dismissed;
- redundancy payments;

and the Employment Relations Act 1999 (amended 1 October 2004) which covers fairness at work, including:

- trade union recognition and de-recognition;
- industrial action ballots;
- unfair dismissal of strikers;
- maternity leave;
- paternity leave;
- time off for dependents;
- employment tribunal awards;
- the right to be accompanied in grievance and disciplinary hearings;
- part-time work.

EQUAL OPPORTUNITIES LEGISLATION

Discrimination and harassment in employment and vocational training on the grounds of gender, race, disability, religious belief and sexual orientation are outlawed under UK law; the fine detail can be found within the following legislation:

- Equal Pay Act 1970;
- Sex Discrimination Act 1975;
- Race Relations Act 1976;
- Disability Discrimination Act 1995;
- Race Relations (Amendment) Act 2000;
- Employment Equality (Religion or Belief) Regulations 2003;
- Employment Equality (Sexual Orientation) Regulations 2003.

Only in exceptional circumstances are schools and colleges exempt from applying these regulations. Any further information on equal opportunities regulations as they apply to schools and colleges can be found on the NASUWT Website at: http://www.teachersunion.org.uk/Templates/Internal.asp?NodelD=70235.

DEVELOPING STAFF – PUTTING VISION AND VALUES INTO PRACTICE

In addition to the expectation that the SBM will understand the legal and technical obligations of human resource management and will manage the appointment process and payroll system, line management of support staff usually falls within their role. Implicit in this is a consistent and coherent staff development strategy which enables:

- the identification of both school and individual development needs through a variety of means, for example, questionnaires, self-review using prepared checklists, discussion with line manager, changing priorities of the school development plan, changing local and national priorities;
- a consideration of how these needs could be met, for example, external courses, in-house training, shadowing a colleague, job rotation, coaching, mentoring, guided reading, web research;
- the development of an appropriate programme to address needs including timescales and allocation of funding;
- the monitoring and evaluation of a programme to ensure that training and development had achieved its purpose and performance has improved as a result.

For some time now schools have been required to have performance management in place for members of the teaching profession and the Education

(School Teaching Appraisal) (England) Regulations 2001 provides the latest regulations on this. Although there is still some way to go, it is increasingly recognised that a clear performance management strategy within a school provides an important way of developing the potential of all staff.

When performance management is seen as a whole-school policy, the likelihood is that all staff will have a better understanding of:

- the vision, ethos and culture of the school;
- school policies and procedures and how they impact on individual roles;
- how personal and professional development needs are identified through a coherent and consistent process;
- how professional development is linked to the aims and priorities of the school through the school development plan;
- how professional development is monitored and evaluated;
- how annual appraisals or performance management reviews check progress against pre-set targets and identify further development needs for the coming year.

Do not underestimate the importance of providing appropriate support and development for support staff. Failure to do so will result in low morale, with staff feeling unvalued which will without doubt have a negative affect on their performance.

A recent CSBM candidate chose as her case study to undertake a review of the administrative support within her school where she had been appointed to the newly-created post of school business manager the year before. Morale amongst the support staff in general was low, systems and procedures were slapdash, there was no ownership of work and the admin team in particular came in for constant, often well deserved, criticism. Whilst there was a well-developed appraisal process for teaching staff, no such system existed for support staff, nor were there any obvious or logical means of identifying training or development needs.

The SBM's plan included interviewing a selection of stakeholders who benefited from admin support, as well as interviewing each member of the administrative team. When discussing the proposed admin staff questionnaire with her headteacher, she was somewhat surprised at his reaction to one of the questions, which was, 'What support do you feel you need to enable you to fulfil your role in school?'. The headteacher's response was 'What do you mean by support? They are there to support us'. In this instance, the school vision talked about valuing the whole-school community and developing them so they could achieve their full potential. Sad then, that this apparently didn't extend to a vital section of the school's human resource – the administrative staff.

Twelve months on, and the administrative staff structure has been revised, job descriptions have been rewritten, communications have improved and a performance management system has been introduced for support staff, with targets linked to the school development plan. It has been a long and complex process which has been painful for some and even now not everyone is convinced about the need or desire for such a system. Although still in the early stages the school is starting to benefit from a better informed, more motivated and more demanding team of people who feel more involved in, and understand better, their contribution to the life of the school.

In cases like these it often falls to the SBM to ensure that the development of support staff is seen as a priority, that funding is allocated and that appropriate structures and systems are in place.

OTHER ISSUES WHICH IMPACT ON EFFECTIVE HUMAN RESOURCE MANAGEMENT

In England and Wales, the Workforce Reform Agenda, initially introduced to improve recruitment and retention of teaching staff, has been the single most significant catalyst for the increasing status of the SBM. A few years ago it was inconceivable that a non-teaching staff member could hold this level of responsibility which is under the control of today's SBM. HR is no exception to this as it was common practice in large schools for one of the deputy headteachers to have responsibility for resources (encompassing HR, Finance and Premises) whilst the rest took care of curriculum issues.

Although, the tide is changing and forward-thinking headteachers now recognise the skills that an appropriately qualified professional can bring to a complex area such as human resource management, it is still the fact that resistance will continue to be met in this area for some time to come. Although outside the brief of this chapter, change management skills will be an essential requirement of the successful school business manager in negotiating this transition effectively.

CONCLUSION

In this chapter is has only been possible to scrape the surface of some of the human resource management issues with which the SBM will be faced and refer you to sources of further information. Human Resource Management is without doubt one of the most exciting, challenging, yet rewarding elements of this role and you would be well advised to access the recommended resources and explore this topic further. When you have completed this chapter, you might like to consider the following:

SBM Toolkit – HRM:3

- How often the HR policies in your school are reviewed and how well they meet the needs of the changing educational environment.
- How well HR procedures interpret the policies and provide a fair and consistent framework for dealing with issues.
- How the benefits available to staff in your school make them feel valued and increase their commitment to the organisation and whether any other tax efficient benefits could be considered.
- How well your staff development systems support the whole school workforce and how you could influence their improvement.

SUGGESTIONS FOR FURTHER READING

Armstrong, M. (2004) *A Handbook of Human Resource Management Practice*. London: Kogan Page.

Robbins, M. and Baxter, M. (2004) *Policies: A Guide for School Governors and Headteachers* (2nd edn.). Ely: Adamson.

USEFUL RESOURCES

The DfES Standards site includes a section on the importance of staff development in relation to school improvement: this is available at http://www.standards.dfes.gov.uk/otherresources/publications/investors/two/twoc/.

The IIP website includes a selection of case studies which can be searched on the basis of sector: this is available at http://www.investorsinpeople.co.uk/IIP/Web/Homepage1.htm.

The Training and Development Agency have set out plans for the training and development of all school support staff in their document 'Building the School Team'. Further information can be found at: http://www.teachernet.gov.uk/wholeschool/supportstaff/.

Further information on the professional development requirements for members of the teaching profession, for example Education (School Teaching Appraisal) (England) Regulations 2001, and the Teachers' Standards Framework (2001) can be found on Teachernet at: http://www.teachernet.gov.uk/management/payandperformance/performancemanagement/.

Guidance on good practice and equal opportunities legislation in Scotland, England and Wales can be found on the following websites:

Equal Opportunities Commission
http://www.eoc.org.uk/.
The Department of Trade and Industry's Employment Relations Directorate
http://www.dti.gov.uk/er/index.htm.
The Commission for Racial Equality
http://www.cre.gov.uk/.
The Disability Rights Commission
http://www.drc-gb.org/businessandservices/employment.asp.

New guidance was issued in July 2005 in light of the Bichard Enquiry entitled *Safeguarding Children: Safer Recruitment and Selection in Education Settings*. Details of this and the checks recommended prior to the appointment of school-based staff can be found on the Teachernet website at: http://www.teachernet.gov.uk/wholeschool/familyandcommunity/childprotection/goodpractice/saferrecruitment/.

Guidance on grievance and discipline policies, handling redundancies, fair and unfair dismissal, employee relations, collective bargaining and employee rights: http://www.opsi.gov.uk/acts/acts1996/1996018.htm

Guidance on grievance and discipline policies, handling redundancies, fair and unfair dismissal, employee relations, collective bargaining and employee rights can be found at the following:

Department of Trade and Industry website:
http://www.dti.gov.uk/er/.
ACAS website:
http://www.acas.org.uk/.
Tailored Interactive Guidance on Employment Rights (TIGER): www.tiger.gov.uk.

Office Systems Management

Jean Blair

INTRODUCTION

In this chapter you will find background information and illustrations relating to current techniques, processes and tools associated with Office Systems Management (OSM). Through personal case studies, it will be seen how this pivotal area of school management is being transformed and will continue to develop. The role that Office Systems Management can play in contributing to the strategic management of schools in the future is discussed and promoted. The key issue of communication skills is briefly explored leading into the concluding question – where next for the school business manager of the future?

THE BACKGROUND TO OFFICE SYSTEMS MANAGEMENT

If we were to take a comparatively short journey back in time as far as the early 1980s and walk into a school office what would we expect to see that would mark the office set-up as being different from today? In a secondary school the office staff would probably comprise the school secretary – usually female and, maybe, qualified in shorthand and typing, whose main role was to look after the headteacher – and possibly a clerical assistant, who would manually process the requisition orders for new text books and stationery. In a primary school, there would probably be one part-time secretary, combining both roles.

In both cases, we would probably see electric or even manual typewriters, the Gestetner and Banda machines for reprographic work, one phone and maybe a very small manual switchboard, a cupboard for the stationery and possibly the odd filing cabinet or two for storing the paperwork. Communications with the LEA (local education authority) were received in a weekly delivery by hand when the school meals van from the local office stopped by after completing its earlier deliveries. Management of finance would comprise looking after the school fund and the petty cash.

This is how Audrey Stephens, currently a school administrator at a Cheshire primary school, remembers her role back in the 1980s in a primary school in Leicestershire.

A step back in time ...

My role as part-time school secretary began in 1987. I was employed at the local village Church of England primary school for 18¾ hours per week. I recall working for 5 hours on three days and 3¾ hours on a Friday to make up the time. There were approximately 210 pupils on roll and it was a three term intake then. They had just introduced admitting children at the age of 4+.

I came from a banking background and found that the work meant I could call upon skills and attributes I had gained during my seventeen years in the banking industry.

A lot of my time was spent calculating dinner money and bringing forward credits not taken during the week and balancing these very carefully indeed each Friday. A complicated weekly return was produced to forward to County Hall.

My desk was situated in the staff room and I was expected to make coffee; three of the teachers had it made with all milk, one half milk and water and one took hers black and it had to be ready by their break time – or else! I had to try to balance the books, type confidential letters, count, record and bank money with constant interruptions. No change there then! In between, there was always 'Time to Move' and the other radio programmes I had to remember to tape; two on a Tuesday and one at 10.10 on a Thursday, etc. This was a nightmare as more often than not

- they forgot to give me the tape;
- it wasn't re-wound to the correct place;
- or the phone went, the delivery man came and darn it! I'd forgotten to tape it again!

Oh, how I hated having to own up to that one and how glad I was when the time came when it finished!

I worked for Leicestershire LEA and I believe in hindsight they were quite innovative. We piloted LMS (Local Management of Schools) and I was coding grid slips for the capitation budget in those days. We had to put in requisitions for toilet paper to County Hall and all the exercise books were kept in a locked cupboard. I can still feel the smoothness of

CASE STUDY

the cover of a new one when I had been asked to get it – one child at a time! I'm still not sure if it was locked to prevent the pupils or the teachers from helping themselves without asking first!

Technology was very basic. The school had only one telephone; I used a manual typewriter at first, then one day, deep joy, I had an *electric* one! Wow! Do you remember changing those 'daisy wheels'? The reprographic department consisted of one very old Gestetner machine. Producing and distributing a school letter to parents was a major event. Oh, I can remember all the pink blobs on the 'skin' we had to type on. No computer word processor to allow you to cover mistakes made in a hurry in those days.

There was one old and very battered metal filing cabinet which doubled up as the filing system and the safe.

One day one of my more unusual duties was to perform a Christian burial for a mouse that had been found in the boys' toilet. The teacher had wondered why so many of the junior boys were asking 'Please can I be excused miss?' She asked me to investigate; they were all using it as target practice! I was dispatched with a spoon to dig in the frozen ground as it was winter time. Well, I guess it came somewhere in the job description!

I do recall I was always busy: I took work home in the evenings on some occasions and also went in unpaid during the summer holidays to catch up. Some things never change then?

At the end of her recollections, Audrey wryly notes the unchanging nature of some elements of OSM, and this leads to the key point of OSM: it is about enhancing the efficiency and effectiveness of an organisation. This in turn rests on effective communication since good communication is the lifeblood of successful organisations. If you stop to think for a minute, communication takes up almost 100 per cent of the working day, and it involves only five methods: written word, spoken word, symbolic gestures, multi-media and visual images. In Audrey's time (as she recalls it!) the key methods used were written and spoken words in limited media modes. How has this changed?

THE CHANGING FACE OF OSM

Contrast the picture painted above with a modern day school office and look at the role of a school business manager delivering effective OSM in the twenty-first century.

They, and their team, will be involved in management of pupil data, have responsibility for finance, have oversight of building projects, management of significant numbers of staff and play a part in recruitment and marketing. And as for equipment there will not be a typewriter or shorthand pad in sight, but computers everywhere. In many of our secondary schools there will be several teams set up to deliver these services, with staff specialising in finance or administration or data inputting. They are likely to have the latest in reprographic equipment at their disposal, a modern switchboard with automated answering of calls and communication by e-mail, including that sent to parents.

SBM Toolkit – OSM:1

Before considering how to improve office systems, it is sensible to think about the objective(s) of that change. One method of doing this is to think of the change in terms of four categories:

1   Improvement of support services, for example faster document preparation;
2   Improved communications, for example better data processing facilities;
3   Cost benefits, for example replacement of paper documents;
4   Operational improvements, for example more and wider use of facilities.

The management of all of this, and many more areas besides, are everyday tasks for the SBMs of today and have to be accomplished against a background of increased accountability and monitoring of performance.

THE SBM TODAY

Linda Byrne, the bursar at a primary school in Sefton, Merseyside, describes her current role and responsibilities and puts a new perspective on how she has faced up to the current challenges facing school business managers.

CASE STUDY

I became a 'voluntary mum' helping out in the school office in 1993. I had been working for an international company for over twenty years at the time, however because of child-care commitments I had decided to work part time. During the second half of the week, whilst my son was in school, I offered my services on a voluntary basis to the school office for two days each week.

In 1994 the school secretary retired and rather reluctantly I applied for the position. I say 'reluctantly' because the salary was considerably lower and I did not think school life was for me.

I began my career in the school office as the school secretary for 29 hours each week, term time only. As time progressed I became the bursar, 35 hours each week, full time, and we employed a school clerk for 12 hours each week to assist me. I am now also a member of the senior management team.

As many of my colleagues will understand, my workload was increasing, yet because of a restricted budget there was no opportunity to employ extra help in the office. In addition, we now have more immediate demands for information and indeed, for *more* information through the impact of computers. One day a group of parents chatting in the playground 'caught my eye'. I began to wonder how they had passed their time each day up to 3 pm. I knew that several of them had word-processing skills and that many of them wished to work in a school environment.

I asked the headteacher if one of the 'mums' could work in the school office for just two hours on a Wednesday afternoon. I would provide them one hour training in basic school office procedures; in return the trainee would answer the phone and take messages for the next hour.

The 'mums' loved it! Most of them had young children and had been away from the work place for a considerable time. Eventually, the 'mums' were working every day on a voluntary basis, and I now often have a waiting list of people wishing to train in the school office. They had so much to offer our admin team and they proved it. The 'mums' all have CRB (Criminal Records Bureau) clearance and in the several years we have been involved in the training, not one single complaint has ever been made! Their skills were encouraged by the admin team and the headteacher. On many occasions it has been difficult to encourage them to leave our school and seek paid employment.

We are extremely proud that seven of our 'volunteer mums' have gone on to work as bursars, assistant bursars, school clerks and even in the health service! They received their training at our school, and we received their support in the school office. We use an in-house training programme and now offer the parents NVQ (National Vocational Qualification) level 2 in Administration. I have undertaken training myself and am about to complete my assessor award for NVQ2.

At our school we have a strong sense of pride about our pupils, our parents and the community. Each one of us has a talent, but sometimes we need help to find it. I will always encourage opportunities for any individual to improve their self-confidence. It is an amazing privilege to see an individual grow in self-confidence. If you have confidence in yourself you feel motivated and develop a strong sense of self-worth.

I know that without doubt I have the best job in the world!

As this example and the previous illustrate, the face of school administration has changed beyond all recognition in the past twenty five years and will continue to do so at an ever increasing rate.

To cope with and successfully deliver all of this calls for staff who can display a wide range of skills and expertise, well-trained individuals who can offer strong leadership and management skills and cope with the myriad array of challenges that will face them on a day-to-day basis; people who are flexible and adaptable, who can think strategically and contribute positively to the value and vision for their school for the future, who have at the core of their being a desire to provide the best for the young people in their care, young people whose futures rest upon them.

However, it is of no value if all these valuable attributes are not married to good communication skills – in other words, if they exist in isolation. This is especially important if you consider the wider range of communication techniques necessary in our second example above! The emphasis is clearly still on the written word, but to take full advantage of technology, other media (especially the spoken word) are obviously more apparent. Consider, for example, the symbolic gesture of Linda's *first* successful 'volunteer mum', and the importance of the visual image of a helper from the community in the office.

Perhaps most importantly, is the development of communications *between machines* and between remote offices, which were until recently regarded as separate entities. The immediacy of these processes demands enhanced competence in all five communication methods. A poorly-scripted/typed e-mail can cause more damage than a more considered letter, as can a poor answer-phone message. The automated, high tech office of the future demands considerable expertise – especially in communications!

Audrey Stephens here reflects on the impact of studying the OSM aspect of the CSBM (Certificate of School Business Management):

CASE STUDY

Effective School Communication

Although I was always aware of the effectiveness (or not) of communication within the school, it also became apparent that we should put more consideration into the image the school was giving during its communication with the stakeholders.

One area I identified for improvement was the ad hoc way in which certain members of the teaching staff were sending information to the parents. Although there was a policy stating that all letters to parents should be checked first with the headteacher, this was clearly not being adhered to. One letter regarding a netball match was hurriedly copied from a previous one with the result that the date was incorrect (last year instead of this), the incorrect website address had been put on by mistake and there were also spelling and grammar faults.

I was only made aware of this letter when a parent telephoned the school to check the details and my response was 'what netball match?' On further investigation I discovered to my horror that she was also asking for parental help with transport, but taking no risk assessments and not distributing the LEA letter asking parents to complete disclaimers or details of their car insurance cover, both of which are requirements.

As a result I asked for a slot in the next staff meeting where we clearly identified the problems: the risk that both the school and the head-teacher were being put in under the current situation and devising a strategy where all communications were proof-read by me.

The implications of a situation like this are obvious to a school business manager but not necessarily to a member of the teaching staff, who through perhaps trying to be helpful at best was giving a very poor image of the school and at worst could have put the school in a situation where we could have been sued for negligence.

There are more details of impact in Chapter 11.

BACKGROUND TO THE DEVELOPMENTS AND CHANGES OF THE PAST TWO DECADES

In UK schools the origins of all of these developments came with the 1986 Education Act which gave new responsibilities and delegated additional powers to governing bodies. This role was further developed with the introduction of the 1988 Education Act. Additional powers included responsibility for recruitment and dismissal of staff and financial management of the school budget, with the latter, as a power which has increased significantly in subsequent years as the control of finance has moved away from local authorities.

The composition of governing bodies was extended by this act to include representatives from the world of industry and business, together with greater representation of parents. Many of these governors brought with them a whole wealth of experience and new sets of ideas and practice from the world of business, causing headteachers and their management teams together with many of the existing governors to look at things in a new light. 'No bad thing', many would say.

Some people started to reflect and look outside the box for the first time. Headteachers were asked about business plans, not just for the next year, but for the next five years and the impact and links with the school budget. A whole new world began to open up, that would impact on OSM. It soon became very evident that no single leader could successfully manage all the changes that would follow; the door was beginning to open – extremely slowly it must be admitted in some cases – for SBMs and the new systems that needed to be set in place.

SBM Toolkit – OSM:2

Accountability

The SBM's role is a reality, but with increased power has come increased accountability. One of the outcomes of further delegation of funds to schools has been a growing accountability regarding how this additional public money is being spent. This places additional responsibilities on the school business manager, working in conjunction with other members of the senior leadership team, to ensure the principles of best value are applied and that value for money is achieved in all transactions.

These areas are addressed in more detail in Chapter 6. However, you should clarify this as soon as possible, and then look to ensure yourself (by training, by the role's terms of reference, and so on) that the accountability can be accepted with confidence.

IMPROVED PERFORMANCE

Another outcome of increased power is the constant pressure to improve performance at all levels. This applies not only to standards achieved by pupils, standards of learning and teaching and those of leadership and management, but to the performance of all members of staff. What role can the school business manager play in this process? Possibly the most difficult hurdle to overcome in some schools will be gaining acceptance that they, or indeed any member of the support staff, can make any contribution whatsoever to managing strategic improvement and can contribute to effective change in any form within their individual school.

Linda Byrne explains that as a result of her completing the OSM module she introduced a weekly meeting of the administration team:

> Before completion of the administration module I simply distributed tasks to the administration staff. The staff did not have an opportunity to discuss the workload or to make suggestions about improvements in systems and procedures.
>
> The introduction of the weekly team meeting has proved to be an opportunity for individuals to be creative, innovative and to discuss tasks and targets. At the meeting

each member of staff talks about their priorities and targets both in the short term and the long term. We discuss issues that have affected the team during the previous week.

We work more effectively as a team and the self-esteem of each individual has grown. We have discussed and implemented new systems and procedures for the benefit of the whole school.

In this final account we hear how Diane Lane, a school business manager at a primary school in Leicestershire, changed her role from that of school administrator to school business manager and became of member of the senior leadership team when the deputy headteacher of the school retired.

CASE STUDY

I never imagined two years ago just how much my job would change. At that point, I had been in post for nine years having previously worked as a PA in a large engineering company. As the sole administrator/ bursar with 300 pupils on roll, there was never a dull moment in the office. I was 'Jack of all trades' but never had responsibilities out of the office. However, I have always liked challenges and the opportunity to move from the 'comfort zone' into the unknown came my way. I heard about the Certificate of School Business Management which whetted my appetite for professional development. I was already aware that more and more was being expected of bursars, so with the full backing of my headteacher and governors I embarked on a course that has opened up a new career path for me.

The CSBM gave me the confidence to suggest and make changes which would benefit the whole school. I became part of the school management team where I was able to exercise my newly acquired leadership skills and became a valued and respected member. The completion of my course also coincided with the National Agenda for Workforce Remodelling and I was involved in the strategic planning of staff changes and development opportunities. Teachers were to get PPA (Preparation, Planning and Assessment) time, ancillary assistants were studying NVQs to become teaching assistants and teaching assistants were applying to become higher level teaching assistants – there were definitely going to be changes.

As the deputy headteacher was approaching retirement, I discussed the possibility of having a new leadership role if she was not replaced. The CSBM had made me aware that a school business manager could fulfil most of this role and would have the added advantage of financial and administrative knowledge.

By appointing two assistant headteachers with responsibility for curriculum at Key Stage 1 and Key Stage 2, a new management structure has evolved. The new leadership Team now has the combined expertise of the headteacher, two assistant headteachers and a school business manager.

I am responsible for all aspects of site and property maintenance with line management responsibility for the premises officer. This is an area I am finding particularly challenging as I learn more about health and safety issues. I am also responsible for six midday supervisors and have appointed a part-time admin officer to assist in running the office. This has enabled me to manage the efficient running of the school which in turn allows the headteacher to concentrate on wider issues such as improving standards and sustaining success following our last excellent Ofsted inspection.

These changes, together with my recent appointment as clerk to the governors, have exceeded all my expectations and who knows what challenges the future will bring!

> The inclusion of the school business manager on the management team has resulted in aspects which have not always been previously considered such as Health & Safety, finance and personnel issues being fully considered before decisions have been reached (Headteacher).

One factor in the acceptance of the changing role has to be the demonstration by individuals that they can make a difference. This is most visible in the way that they carry out their responsibilities in the school. As more SBMs undertake additional responsibilities, gaining expertise in areas previously considered outside their remit such as facilities and risk management, acceptance and recognition of their skills will hopefully come about. Improvements in office systems management is an obvious area of activity where SBMs can demonstrate that they *are* making a difference. In my case, this involved a 'system' for dealing with Human Resources.

As schools take on extended roles more support staff are being required. Management of these ever-increasing and extended teams of support staff is more and more becoming the province of the school business manager; a role that encompasses not just the day-to-day management of their work, but responsibility for their recruitment, induction into their often newly-created posts and their ongoing professional development. In all of this, the needs of the school business managers with regard to support and training must not be overlooked.

LEGAL REQUIREMENTS

A major concern for all educational institutions has to be how they can ensure that they keep up to date with ever changing legal requirements and how their office systems can support the school in this area. The SBM can play a vital role in this process. A first step is to ensure that all relevant documents and policies are available and accessible within the school and can be referenced by staff and governors alike. If they familiarise themselves with the content of the documents that impact on the work of the school, school business managers are then in a position to draw the attention of other members of the senior leadership team and the governors to these documents and can both contribute and advise on relevant school policies that must be written and implemented to ensure that all legislation is complied with. The school business manager, however, should never consider themself a legal expert. We live in an increasingly litigious society and it is always vital to estimate and understand the limits of our own knowledge and expertise and at what point it becomes an appropriate time to consult others.

However, this in itself leads to a basic first step: SBMs should ensure that all staff are familiar with (or at least have access to) documents detailing policy.

Other issues that need to be addressed

Reference was made earlier to the skills and expertise required of a successful school business manager. Effective communication skills must be considered as a pre-requisite for the role. Without doubt, this can be further enhanced when the ability to simultaneously manage and work within teams is achieved.

I have a passionate belief in teams and in the effective impact that these can have. All members of teams have an important role to play in contributing to the success of their particular team, which in turn contributes to the overall effectiveness of an organisation. For the successful school business manager knowledge, skills and expertise in systems alone will not be enough. They must be a good team player themselves, understand what makes an effective team and most importantly possess the knowledge and understanding of what it takes to be an effective team leader.

In my opinion successful organisations are underpinned by successful teamwork and communications and undermined when these characteristics aren't evident or put into practice.

THE SBM OF THE FUTURE

If schools as we currently understand them still exist, who will manage them? Will a familiar picture be the SBM responsible for all aspects of office systems management and the headteacher responsible for teaching and learning? The concepts of federated and extended schools are certainly adding weight to the argument, as OSM will become even more important in such devolved structures. Systems guarantee quality, and managing them will become more complex.

The following is a suggested checklist for anyone considering change(s) to OSM in their organisation:

1 Register of equipment.
2 Survey of staff workload (broken down by type of work – filing, telephone queries and so on).
3 Mail census – volumes, times, disposition (destroyed, filed and so on).
4 Survey of demand for facilities not currently available – estimate expansion costs, and so on.
5 Staff survey of operational issues.

When *all five* have been considered, then the change will at least have been considered at length and a robust rationale produced!

CONCLUSION

Through personal case studies we have seen the effect of change in OSM on the role of the SBM. The importance of communication has been stressed and possible future directions considered.

SUGGESTIONS FOR FURTHER READING

Belbin, R.M. (2004) *Management Teams: Why they Succeed or Fail* (2nd edn.). London: Butterworth-Heinemann.
Covey, S. ([1995] 1999) *Seven Habits of Highly Effective People*. New York: Simon & Schuster.
Davies, B. and Ellison, L. (2005) *School Leadership for the 21st Century: Developing a Strategic Approach.* (2nd edn). London: RoutledgeFalmer.
Katzenbach, J. and Smith, D. (2003) *The Wisdom of Teams: Creating the High Performance Organisation*. New York: Harper Business.
Mullins, L. (2004) *Management and Organisational Behaviour* (7th edn.). London: FT/Prentice Hall.

USEFUL RESOURCES

Administrative Support website (DfES)
http://www.teachernet.gov.uk/wholeschool/remodelling/cuttingburdens/good prac/gpindex/gpadmin/
http://www.teachernet.gov.uk/management/atoz/
Benchmarking
http://www.teachernet.gov.uk/mamagement/atoz/
Communication
http://www.cba.neu.edu/

Cutting Burdens
http://www.teachernet.gov.uk/cuttingburdens/wholeschool/remodelling/bursars
Freedom of Information/Data Protection Act
http://www.informationcommissioner.gov.uk
Investors in People
http://www.iipuk.co.uk/IIP/Web/Default.htm
Management Information Systems
http://www.teachernet.gov.uk/management.atoz/
Performance Management
http://www.cognology.com.au/default.htm
http://www.teachernet.gov.uk/cuttingburdens/wholeschool/remodelling/
Training Needs Analysis
http://www.trainingneedsanalysis.co.uk/tna_article1.htm
http://www.teachernet.gov.uk/wholeschool/remodelling/bursars/Bursarkeyrole/
http://www.teachernet.gov.uk/wholeschool/remodelling/bursars/

6

Financial Management

Jenny Moore

INTRODUCTION

In this chapter you will find:

- an overview of current thinking about effective financial management;
- a consideration of the key elements involved in efficient and effective financial management;
- a critique of accepted tools and techniques;
- discussion about the role of the 'new' SBM (school business manager) in financial management.

Ever since the emergence of the self-governing school in the maintained sector in the early 1990s, the role of the financial manager has taken on a steadily increasing profile. It has gradually come to be accepted that state schools need well-trained and professional financial managers, just as private schools have always had financial managers (traditionally called 'bursars').

This need should not really surprise us, for it is somewhat self-evident that any organisation that generates and expends significant amounts of money and employs significant numbers of people will require sound and proper financial management. Schools may attract annual funds ranging from £250,000 in a tiny rural school, to £10,000,000, in a large secondary. The average school is equivalent to a medium-sized business in terms of its turnover and number of employees, but add on the fact that it is public money, raised by taxation, and effective use and good management become imperatives.

What we have seen in the past fifteen years has been a transition. This transition was fairly rapid in those schools that took up the grant-maintained experiment; these schools quickly emulated the private sector and many governing bodies appointed accountants or similarly well-qualified administrators to manage their finance and other support services. In other schools the transition is still in its earliest stages; there are LAs (local authorities) where the financial and other experts are still all at the centre and where full devolvement of the control and any decision-making processes has yet to be fully realised and felt. And there is a third group of schools, somewhere in the middle and probably in the majority, where the devolvement of budgets has taken place, where the LA has relinquished its day-to-day control, but where the need for professional financial management at school level has not yet been fully recognised.

In many such schools there has, of course, been some progress towards sound financial management with a growing number already employing a bursar or finance officer. However, all too often this has been merely as a response to the tasks that now need to be performed at school level, not a recognition of the added value that a professional financial manager can bring to a school and its senior management team.

A FELLOW PROFESSIONAL?

It has been a feature of recent school culture, over the past fifty years or so, to regard teachers as the professionals; all other staff have been ancillary to them. But in the age of self-governing schools, one has to ask the question – professional at what? The reality is that when it comes to finance, teachers have actually been the amateurs, fitting in a bit of budget preparation here and a touch of finance monitoring in order to get by – or not, as the case may be! But the well-run school, just like any other well-run organisation, whether it be in the private or the public sector, demands proper financial management set up and implemented by a trained professional, and that professional must have influence in the organisation.

How can professional expertise be exploited to the benefit of a school if it does not have a voice that is heard? It is not enough for the financial expert to be shut away in the office expertly performing financial tasks. However well these are performed – with all the figures added up perfectly and all the reports accurate and all the accounts balanced and correct to the penny – this demonstrates only good accounting practice, but it is not sufficient to ensure a school is financially well managed.

Strategic financial management is the key and to give strategic input the finance manager needs to come out of the office, engage with all the school's activities and fully understand how the school works in its entirety. A holistic approach is required! The SBM needs to be a party to the decision-making process, from inception through to evaluation of the options, to development, implementation and review.

In my commercial experience I was taught that a perfect senior management team consists of:

- a managing director who knows the business inside out, has the drive and instinct to lead his or her team to success and makes the tough decisions;
- a creative person or two, full of ideas and with the enthusiasm to fully exploit the talents of the workforce; and
- a finance director who acts as the disciplinarian.

The disciplinarian! It sounds rather dour, doesn't it? But the truth of this is obvious; organisations that don't have clear systems, access to sound information, well-structured procedures, consistent policies, efficient administrative processes, objective evaluation of ideas, meaningful review and analysis cannot make good decisions or sound judgements. All these things require a disciplined and systematic approach. Organisations that do not have someone with their finger firmly on the budget button, someone who can expertly advise, measure and evaluate possibilities, assess when to, and when not to, take financial risks, cannot succeed in the long term.

Does this disciplinarian in the guise of finance manager sound familiar? Does this sound a little like the role of an SMB? Because teachers are so close to the problems they are trying to solve, because they are often so enthusiastic about their ideas, they sometimes forget to be objective. Sometimes their ideas are brilliant and their rationale sound, but they lack the experience or knowledge to know how to implement efficiently. The presence of a disciplinarian can add the questioning voice, acting as devil's advocate, the person who puts on the brakes, suggests different means to the same end or ensures that plans are fully thought through and costed – *before* they are implemented! And because SBMs invariably have experience outside the education sector, they can often bring that external dimension and experience to the decision-making process. A wise headteacher will recognise how much the support and strategic input of such a person can assist them in day-to-day decisions, policy implementation and in their search for success.

SBM job descriptions vary enormously from school to school but, almost without exception, and for many of the reasons outlined above, the financial element of the role is centre stage. This is because it is widely recognised that financial management is the tool by which all other processes and developments are enabled. *Everything* that happens in a school is in some way related to financial management, and financial considerations are to some degree or another a factor in every management decision that is made. No area of school life should escape the analytical attention of the SBM.

Financial management is therefore not a thing apart but a thread that must run through every single aspect of an organisation. This realisation does not always sit easily with teachers; their motivation, they will tell you, has nothing to do with money, it is all about pupils, education, learning and caring. The astute finance manager does not see this as a contradiction, but adopts the same motivation; they just approach it in a different and more objective way, constantly looking for every opportunity and utilising all their business and financial skills to ensure the best possible outcomes. School financial management *is* also all about pupils, education, learning and caring.

SBM Toolkit – FIM:1

Ask for five minutes at the next staff meeting, and make the following points to all staff.

- Managing finances in a not-for-profit organisation is different from the business sector. The cultural dimension does need to be taken into account.
- Because schools have a guaranteed income stream and are effectively spending other people's (taxpayers') money the danger is that they can too easily become complacent or wasteful in their spending. But if, where a private sector counterpart would look for profit an SBM looks instead for added value, those differences are minimised.
- The objectives and measurement of success may be different but the means are the same.
- Complacency is the enemy of good financial management and good business practices deter complacency.

This is your values statement and clearly sets out where you are coming from.

But what differentiates good from poor financial management and what are the rewards of the first and the consequences of the latter? There is a growing body of data, evidence and experience that recognises and disseminates good practice. The pressure is now firmly upon schools to take advantage of the knowledge and expertise that have been developed and to implement policies and practices that are shown to improve financial management and performance.

Government policy has clearly hardened in this area; no longer will poor financial management in schools, and condescending indulgence by paternalistic LAs, be tolerated. No longer is well-intentioned amateurism acceptable. Minimum standards are being set and schools are expected to adopt them. The old excuses – hard-pressed headteachers with too many other things to worry about, slow provision of information or lack of support by LAs, insufficient money – have all been made null and void by workforce reform, by significant injections of additional cash and by the good practice guides, resources and toolkits that now abound in the sector.

The DfES's value-for-money unit has done much work in this area; the introduction in 2002 of consistent financial reporting allows school-by-school comparison across all areas of spending. Schools are now not only encouraged, but expected, to undertake self-evaluation against all areas of financial management. By 2008 all schools will be required to have achieved the DfES's financial management standard. This evaluates performance against all areas of financial management from budget and development planning to procurement practice, from financial controls to governing body participation.

It is not enough for schools to make their budgets balance and to show they have adhered to the financial regulations; they must be innovative in their use of resources and in income generation, make the most economical and effective use of the funds available and demonstrate that they have provided good value for money and the best possible education for all the pupils in their care. Schools will be judged for consistency, good practice and results.

But what are the key skills for the finance manager? What expertise is required? As ever, knowledge is power and SBMs must arm themselves with good information. Start with the context; learn about the financial, legal and political framework which the school operates within. An SBM must become the school's financial expert and that expertise must extend to every aspect of financial management.

FINANCIAL DELEGATION

All LAs must publish a 'Scheme of Delegation and a Formula for Financing Schools' which sets out the LA's financial policy and specifies how funds will be distributed to each school. This is essential reading for the finance manager. All SBMs should obtain a copy. Analyse the formula and then question the rationale. The objective is to find out which 'pots' of money are retained at the centre and which services have not been delegated or fully delegated. If there are anomalies or apparent inconsistencies in the scheme, if the LA retains and controls funds for services that would be better delegated, then the SBM needs to challenge this. One basic challenge principle is to compare your school's scheme and formulae with others in a different LA area. The same principle applies to LSC (Learning Skills Council) funding for sixth forms and a multitude of other funding schemes and initiatives; these areas are complex and require a professional's attention and scrutiny.

The SBM must be equipped to verify that a school's allocations are correct in every detail and that it receives every penny to which it is entitled. If a school is to be truly self-governing it must have a view of the whole picture, not just parts of it. Too often schools fail to make the best possible decisions, because they concern themselves with only part of the equation. They accept as a given and unchallengeable fact that 'the LA takes care of that, so we need not worry about it' and assume it means that all is well. But good decisions need all available information and to passively accept the LA's guidance or to slavishly follow its instructions or rules without question does not always produce the best or most cost-effective outcomes. The more responsibility the school has to take for its own decisions, the more careful analysis and consideration it will give to all its activities and expenditure. This philosophy is now firmly embedded in government policy.

Under current arrangements, each local authority determines for itself the size of its schools budget, although the Secretary of State does have power to require a LA to increase its budget to a prescribed level. The LA will determine which sums to set aside as funds from this budget for centrally provided services and the funds that remain are termed the Individual Schools Budget (ISB). The ISB must be distributed amongst the LA's schools, on a financial year basis, in accordance with the School Standards and Framework Act 1998. Delegation to each school of its 'budget share' is then made via a Section 52 statement (S52 of the act) and this statement lists all the component parts of the allocation made to that school. In future schools will be allocated three-year budgets, the rationale being that this will assist them in longer-term planning. From 2006/2007 a new Dedicated Schools Grant will be allocated by the DfES to each LA. This grant will be ring-fenced for expenditure on schools and related educational services.

It is a requirement of the act that a minimum of 75 per cent of the ISB must be distributed to all primary and secondary schools on the basis of pupil numbers. This pupil-led funding is intended to ensure that, in broad terms, the more pupils a school educates the more funding it will receive. The actual sum of money for each pupil is allocated in accordance with the age or, more precisely, the national curriculum's key stage of the pupil. Thus Key Stage 5 pupils, on GCSE courses, attract significantly more funding than Key Stage 2 pupils in junior schools.

Each authority's scheme sets out the mechanisms for capturing pupil numbers, using PLASC (the annual pupil census) data to determine the number of pupils to be funded. The remainder of the ISB is distributed to schools using formulae to take account of other factors that may be variable between schools; for example, level of social deprivation (usually measured by the number of pupils entitled to free school meals), number of pupils having special educational needs, local authority business rates and other variable premises and catering costs, area salary weightings, and so on. It is also common for LAs to allocate sums in the formula which are then passed back to them by the school in return for that particular LA service.

LAs retain statutory responsibilities for the education of individual pupils with a statement of SEN; it is usual, therefore, for schools to receive additional funds to ensure this statutory provision is met for these pupils, and this funding is over and above a school's S52 budget share.

Special schools have slightly different arrangements, the main one being that they are allocated funds according to the number of places catered for, rather the number of pupils actually on roll.

IMPLICATIONS OF DELEGATION

It is, of course, largely due to pupil-led funding that a competitive market has grown between schools; a school that fails to recruit an adequate number of pupils suffers financially. Thus in recent years, schools have seen increasingly large sums spent on marketing and advertising, with various glossy brochures and DVDs.

The LA's Scheme of Delegation will also set out in detail the obligations upon schools in the use of their budget share, including, for example, how surplus and deficit funds will be treated at the end of each financial year, the regulations relating to school bank accounts, and so on.

The level of autonomy that schools have in managing their budgets varies from LA to LA and with the status of the school (that is whether it is a foundation, voluntary aided or community school). The trend is most decisively towards self management and self-governance. Most LAs now offer schools the option of cash management at school level, with 'cheque-book' schools receiving all of their budget share, usually on a monthly basis. Such schools may therefore open their own bank accounts, invest their cash as they choose (although risk investments may not be made) and manage their cash flow to obtain maximum interest. Other schools operate at an interim level of self-management in that the LA retains the bulk of the cash for payment of salaries, just passing the balance over to the school bank account for the purchase of non-payroll goods and services. There are also many LAs and schools, predominantly in the primary sector, where the LA still holds the cash and the school, although it makes the spending decisions, carries out all transactions via the LA's central systems.

With regard to payroll, in foundation status schools (where the governing body rather than the LA is the employer), schools make their own payroll arrangements. They are free to decide their own provider and although many still contract to the LA for payroll provision, a number have opted for private sector bureaux or for administering their own payroll in-house. Payroll and associated pension matters are important areas for SBMs; as more responsibility is delegated to school level, it becomes increasingly important that schools are well-informed and have sufficient expertise in these areas. It is another example of specialist knowledge shifting to schools, having traditionally been the preserve of the LA.

BUDGET PLANNING AND MONITORING

The governing body is responsible for determining how a school's budget share will be spent. In practice, most governing bodies will delegate authority to the headteacher for the majority of day-to-day spending decisions within the framework of the governing body's approved budget plan. Each governing body must determine and document the extent of delegation to the head and will normally set specified expenditure limits and parameters in respect of the head's authority to appoint staff, procure services, and so on.

Annual budget setting is one of the most important tasks a governing body will undertake. Unfortunately, all too often it will be seen as a task in isolation; in this scenario, a school will wait until mid-March to find out how much money the LA has allocated, and will then update all the costs, add a bit for inflation and hey presto, the school has a budget plan. It's called 'incremental budgeting'. If there are sufficient funds the plan can be approved; if money is tight, something must be trimmed. This is frequently the pattern, but if this is a process that is simply repeated year after year, this will not be conducive to sound financial management.

Zero-based budgeting is a tool which requires a total review of all activities; no assumptions are made about budget needs, all monies from a range of possibilities and the wish-list are analysed and costed. The approach is that if we do (a), it will cost £x; if we do (b), it will cost £y, and so on. All conventions and potential developments are prioritised discussed and argued over. A school that adopts this method of budget setting and developmental planning is a school that avoids complacency and will spend its money in those areas where the objectives are clear and where the most progress will be made. If a school only ever produces a budget incrementally, it tends to constantly be trying to find additional money to cover additional costs. People will tell you that additional costs are inevitable if things are to improve! But this is obviously not feasible or sustainable in the long term and at some point budgets will run out; the school will be in deficit. By the use of zero-based budgeting, not necessarily every year but maybe every two to three years, a school can re-prioritise and lose as well as gain costs. Only by doing things better rather than just doing more things, can the old make way for the new and real development take place.

On average, 80–85 per cent of a school's budget will be spent on staffing; it is obvious therefore that this area must be given considerable attention to ensure value for money. However, it is not uncommon for schools to maintain without question the same staffing structures year on year. Extra appointments may be made where it is affordable, but the structure will remain unchanged and unchallenged. It's not difficult to recognise that a school's staff are potentially its most valuable asset, but how valuable? How does one measure value-for-money from employees?

Performance management is a topic for another chapter but in terms of budget planning, staffing establishments and staffing costs are an essential part of the process and need to be measured for best value against the same criteria as other services. Schools have seen the cost of ICT rocket in recent years; if staffing remains at the 85 per cent level, how can these additional ICT costs be sustained? Schools may well receive special grants to update here but if these

ICT infrastructures are to be properly maintained and updated, which parts of the budget get squeezed? Fewer books? Less well-maintained premises?

These questions demand radical analysis based on a regular monitoring of data, which in turn, demands a systematic approach. The monitoring system itself can be devised and its rigour guaranteed by registration for quality systems such as the ISO 9000 or EFQM (European Foundation for Quality Management) models.

SBM Toolkit – FIM:2

With the provision of sophisticated ICT tools and the advent of a very diverse workforce, difficult decisions need to be taken. Old predictable patterns of provision – one classroom, one teacher, 30 pupils, five hours of lessons a day – are becoming less predictable. Ask yourself the following questions:

- Will children's education be better served where a teacher can deliver lessons to groups of 20 pupils, or where a teacher plus a higher-level teaching assistant and state of the art ICT provision cater for 35 pupils?
- Are pupils' interests better served by teachers paid an additional teaching and learning allowance to perform academic or pastoral mentoring duties, or by a dedicated mentor for part of the week?
- Will a secondary school operate most effectively with two deputies or with a single deputy plus an ICT manager?
- How can resources be provided for additional lessons to be delivered after school to ensure personalised learning goals can be achieved?

These are just some of issues that will require discussion as part of the development planning process and the solutions will often be complex. The issues also need to be considered *with* the professionals in the area of teaching and learning – that is, the teachers. Of course this is a clear example of team working, using the expertise of *all* within the school.

EXPENDITURE AND INCOME

Preparing a school development plan requires whole-school discussion, substantial senior management time and considerable input from the financial manager. If the headteacher and/or senior teachers prepare the development plan and then just pass it to the SBM as a finished product simply to be costed, a vital step has been missed out and hugely important opportunities are likely to have been missed. Worse still, if it is then presented to, and approved by, governors before all the cost implications are considered. So much more can be gained if a financial manager has been on board to review, analyse and advise and with their expertise utilised throughout the process. SBMs can make excellent development plan co-ordinators – forecasting pupil numbers; analysing their effect on future budget allocations; reviewing existing provision; challenging assumptions; evaluating and costing alternatives; obtaining quotations; comparing results – all these are areas where an SBM can ensure a professional approach. Thus, by the time a school receives its Section 52 budget share statement, its strategic plan and draft development plans should already be in place with all parties having a firm grasp of priorities.

We have seen that the emphasis in schools has traditionally been on spending rather than income generation. The UK's maintained schools, being relatively well-funded, find their attentions drawn more towards recruitment of pupils and control of expenditure. It can be, however, that parental contributions form a large chunk of a school's income and debtor policy and control can be a big factor in a school's financial well-being.

With specialist status, private finance initiatives, a plethora of standards funds and other government initiatives to encourage schools to seek sponsorship and alternative sources of funding, they cannot afford to sit back and wait for money to be handed over unconditionally. A large number of these opportunities require pro-active and time-consuming participation and acquiring additional money is a good deal more difficult than merely spending it. Again, in this area, schools will find it difficult to function effectively without a professional financial expert. An SBM can be required to take on anything from a straightforward LA capital maintenance bid, to business sponsorship, to a full-scale bid to the lottery fund.

Potentially, schools can access many different external pots of money, but it can be difficult to assess the likelihood of success. Unless a full-time fund-raiser is employed, and few schools can afford or justify that option, no school will be able to access every pound that is potentially available. Careful judgement must therefore be made, taking into account the amount of time input and the cost of investment versus the potential benefit. Consultants can be effective in this area, but again cost-benefit analysis must be made before commitment and, as the 2005 Impact and Evaluation Report (avaliable at: www.ncsl.org.uk) illustrates, SBMs *do* have great success in this area.

Governments constantly promise transparent funding formulae and simplified funding streams but the reality seems often to deliver ever more complexity. Some funding routes, for example standards funds, have been simplified to some degree, but other initiatives and complexities seem to arrive with predictable regularity. For example, performance management for teachers brings with it the need for schools to ensure that the LA makes the correct allocation for threshold and post-threshold funding. With each point on the upper pay spine attracting a different percentage of LA contribution, schools need to take active steps to ensure that they receive all of their entitlement. Claims also need to be made for such things as post-threshold supply teachers; the additional cost of employing advanced skills teachers; and the leadership scale progression attracting additional financial support. All these areas require an SBM to remain vigilant and protect their school's interests.

BALANCE AND DEFICITS

Schools are often, in the national context, criticised for the collective sum of their balances. Newspaper headlines shout about the millions sitting unused in schools' or LAs' bank accounts. Legislation has, until recently, determined that once correctly allocated, a school's budget share belongs to that school and unspent funds at the year end remain in the ownership of the school. However, with some schools having accumulated balances that are deemed excessive, pressure has led the government to allow LAs the right to recover some of this unspent money. Schools in this position must now justify any large balances held; funds are allocated to schools on an annual basis for the delivery of education to the pupils on roll at that time and it is argued, therefore, and with some justification that if these funds are not spent these pupils have not received their just entitlement.

Of course for many schools, the luxury of a large balance is not something they have to concern themselves with. It is usually considered when budget setting that a contingency fund of 1 per cent is sufficient to meet unforeseen eventualities, with any additional balances brought forward usually having been saved and earmarked for specific development projects. The important thing is that a school is not taken unawares by either a deficit or a surplus. The inference from such criticism of excessive balances is that these schools have found themselves with these large surpluses without actually planning for them and therefore this indicates a lack of good financial foresight and monitoring.

This is not always the case: sometimes schools find themselves with very difficult dilemmas and unavoidable additional costs. When faced with the choice of additional expenditure or a detriment to educational delivery, schools will often opt for the additional expenditure despite a lack of funds. However, these problems should be *short term* and sound planning and monitoring should ensure that the resultant budget difficulties are not unexpected. If a school has quantified its current and future costs and made contingency arrangements, the risks are minimised.

Schools will often, when expecting falling rolls or seeing fluctuating rolls, seek to set aside funds to protect their staffing levels until the position stabilises. Rising rolls are often just as difficult to manage; a primary school with unusually large September and January intakes needs to accommodate and educate the additional pupils before receipt of the related funds, so forward planning is essential.

If schools find themselves in a deficit situation, they will be required to prepare a recovery plan to ensure the deficit can be managed and overcome. It is important to know and understand why a school has reached a deficit situation. It is not enough simply to say there are insufficient funds. Some in-depth analysis is required. Budget management in a complex world means difficult choices must be made and a deficit generally means that a school has not made those difficult choices – it has just carried on spending in too many areas.

Cash flow considerations also become crucial in a deficit situation; far more precise attention needs to be given to the timing of expenditure to ensure that sufficient funds are available to meet fixed commitments and outgoings, such as salaries. Examination fees, for example, are a large commitment for secondary schools early on in the financial year; if a school is in a deficit situation it may need to request an additional advance from its LA in order to meet this necessity. At the time of writing the UK's schools are not allowed to borrow money from external sources, but this is being mooted by the current government.

MANAGING THE MONEY

LAs have a statutory role in the management of school budgets, primarily to monitor expenditure and support any schools in financial difficulty. LAs will require schools to submit returns at regular intervals and at the year end. Most schools manage their budgets on a cost-centre basis, often delegating specific funds to budget holders within the school, for example departmental heads or premises managers.

Internal delegation can be a means to better financial management; in a large school especially, an SBM cannot be expected to scrutinise every single item of expenditure to measure best value or ensure value-for-money. Investment in a little training to impart basic financial management skills to budget holders can be a very worthwhile use of an SBM's time and effort. Not only will this raise awareness of good financial practice and ensure that common pitfalls are avoided, but from an individual perspective, especially for a teacher with designs on headship, it can be a valuable inset.

LAs and the DfES now monitor school budgets in accordance with a national coding structure so that all schools, regardless of whatever internal budget management techniques they use, are required to report their actual income and expenditure under designated headings. Consistent Financial Reporting (CFR) is now a requirement for all English maintained schools and the data provided give government and other interested parties accurate information regarding schools' income and expenditure. It also allows individual schools to benchmark their own expenditure against that of other similar schools. If a school sees, for example, that its energy costs are hugely at variance to other similar-sized schools, it can investigate further and may find that those other schools have obtained far more economic contracts. In this regard benchmarking can be a useful tool, but it remains only one tool that requires a level of knowledge and expertise to utilise effectively.

Benchmarking will not tell a school why its costs exceed those of other schools; it can only highlight areas for further scrutiny and the conclusions drawn will be a matter of judgement. Staffing costs are a particularly difficult area to assess; if administrative staff costs are high, for example, does this indicate overstaffing and poor value for money or does it indicate that the school has been more successful than others in transferring all levels of administration from teachers to support staff, with consequent educational benefits? If large sums of money are spent on books, in comparison to other schools, is this indicative of a school where classroom resources are a clear priority, or one where the book supplier is too expensive? If catering costs are on the low side, is this because the pupils are receiving poor quality, unhealthy food or has the school pursued policies that have achieved exceptional value? Only investigation and discussion between schools will give answers to these questions and a diligent SBM can pursue best practice in these areas to the clear benefit of their school.

PROCUREMENT AND PURCHASING

All UK public bodies are required by legislation to seek best value in all their contracts for goods or services and although schools are not bound legally, they are strongly encouraged to follow best practice and develop their own best-value policies.

As a minimum, schools should set out agreed limits for quotations and tenders and ensure that all staff with any purchasing responsibilities are aware of the policy. For example, a school may determine that all purchases for goods or services exceeding a value of £3,000 require three written quotations to be obtained and recorded and/or that anything over £15,000 requires formal tender procedures to be adopted. These types of safeguards will ensure basic economy. They will not necessarily, however, deliver value for money; to meet this test, efficiency and effectiveness also need to be considered.

SBMs will always find areas in their schools where value-for-money and best value can be sought; the difficulty will always be time. It can almost become a full-time job. Realistically, therefore, an SBM will only be able to investigate fully certain areas in any one year.

SBM Toolkit – FIM:3

Guidance, and the ideal scenario, suggest that all contracts should be reconsidered every three years or so, but often if a school is happy with and has confidence in its supplier the SBM's detailed scrutiny and attention can be better focussed elsewhere. As ever the danger is complacency and one must guard against cosiness with suppliers which can deter objective analysis. It can be good practice when deciding to stick with existing arrangements to document the reasons, or even minute them at the finance committee so that objectivity has been demonstrated and recorded.

Often one of the most difficult, best-value considerations occurs when a school is deciding whether to contract to an external supplier or to set up in-house provision. In this area, as well as in straightforward contracting, using the '4 Cs' test – compare, consult, challenge, compete – will assist the decision-making process. The danger with in-house provision can be a failure to assess *all* costs, although this must be measured against unquantified staff time that may be taken up managing and liaising with external providers, especially where service is poor.

Catering, cleaning, payroll service, grounds maintenance, minor repairs and maintenance; all these are traditionally the areas where schools have real choices. In some of these smaller schools tend to have more limited choices; it is unlikely to be practical, for example, for a small school to employ its own grounds staff and purchase necessary machinery to deliver its own grounds services. However, schools can confederate or make consortium arrangements and these can be very successful, although it does require one particular school to take on the administration and management responsibilities of such an arrangement.

In-house provision does give a school far more day-to-day control and success stories, where schools have transformed provision and service, are common. In economic terms the cost differences at the outset can be small, but in terms of effectiveness and quality in-house provision can show demonstrable improvement. But again, complacency is an ever-present danger and costs can creep up or even spiral if they are not tightly controlled.

Supply cover for absent teachers is another area where difficult decisions will need to be taken. Many schools choose to insure against longer-term absences, with policies available at varying levels of cover, for example after the third day or after ten days. Premiums, however, are high and many larger schools particularly choose to cover their own risk and hope that absence in any one year remains within affordable limits.

ACCOUNTING AND AUDITING

It is arguable whether SBMs should be accountants. Certainly an accounting qualification will be useful; a basic level qualification will arm an SBM with the basic tools to do those parts of the job that require specialist skills and knowledge. There is no doubt these will be useful; some would say essential. A higher-level qualification, or a full professional qualification, will arm an SBM with a more sophisticated set of techniques and it is clear that in some aspects of the role these too will be very useful. To perform the SBM role without a basic understanding of double-entry and other accounting conventions such as accruals, prepayments, control account reconciliations and the like, is difficult and would-be SBMs are well advised to up-skill themselves in these areas as a minimum. Likewise, capability in use of spreadsheets is essential. If the SBM is a professional and is to be regarded for their expertise and specialist knowledge, then the assumption will be that the financial tools of the trade are all present and in working order.

In some areas the use of financial accounting software is determined by the LA and schools have no choice in the matter. In most schools, however, the decision will be theirs and although there are a number of packages available there is a small number of clear market leaders whose systems are used by the majority of schools. This has advantages in that SBMs and finance officers are able to readily gain support and training in their use and can discuss and compare practices with colleagues. It also means that skills and knowledge are transferable between schools and continuity of staffing can be maintained. Most software packages now provide the facility to manage all the accounting stages; ordering, invoicing, cheque payments, journals, bank reconciliation, debtor control and so on, through to trial balance.

The format of school accounts tends to be on a straightforward income and expenditure basis, in a financial year that runs from 1 April–31 March. In the past, some schools have been required to prepare accounts on a fixed asset accounting basis, but as UK schools currently may not borrow in the private sector markets (although they can, and do, speculate with income in these markets), this is not generally a requirement. Capital expenditure will be recorded in the year it is spent and depreciation is therefore not an issue either.

All major software providers have made their products compatible with DfES reporting requirements and CFR (Code of Federal Regulations) coding structures, in order that schools may easily provide the necessary reports and returns. These returns invariably require electronic transfer, so compatibility and integration with the internet and/or e-mail formats are essential.

PROBITY AND ETHICAL PRACTICE

Although a computerised accounting system, if correctly used, will provide sound information and a clear audit trail, it will not in itself ensure robust systems and good practice. All schools must have clear procedures and systems to ensure separation of duties and proper authorisation. Care needs to be taken with access levels in the accounting system and all procedures to be followed should be documented and circulated to everyone concerned to ensure clarity of expectation.

It is clear that the vast majority of school staff are honest, ethical and act with integrity with the interests of their school at heart. But it would be naïve to assume that theft and dishonesty cannot occur. Each year we see in the press examples of misappropriation, misuse or embezzlement of funds and audit departments throughout the country will attest to seeing cases of theft, in all its forms, with depressing regularity. The cases that hit the headlines tend to be headteachers or other senior staff, where the opportunity for theft or excessive expenses claims is enabled by their position of power. The lower profile cases tend to be finance assistants who perform their theft or borrowing by diverting income, as when preparing it for banking or by duplicating petty cash claims.

There are a number of things a vigilant school can do to minimise the risk, such as putting in place random checks or rotating tasks (where staff numbers allow). One must also be constantly aware of the signs of fraud; an employee who seems to live beyond their means, someone who is negative about checking procedures or guarded in their willingness to share paperwork or particular tasks and so on – all these can be warning signs, although of course in themselves they are not conclusive.

Headteachers and indeed SBMs need to ensure that they protect their own interests by ensuring that the processes they oversee, and the authority that they exercise especially in relation to their own salary and benefits, are very well documented. Staff will tend to comply, without question, with whatever their headteacher instructs them to do. If a head is casual about authorisation or documentation, if they become accustomed to just issuing instructions – 'Pay Mr Smith £50 for the extra work he did at the weekend, don't put it through payroll' or 'Give me £100 cash to buy a present for Ann's retirement' – and expect compliance without due process, then they are acting foolishly and putting their integrity at risk. Financial rules and procedures must be applied equally to every person in the organisation and a wise head will go out of their way not only to follow the rules scrupulously, but will also make sure that their compliance is visible and transparent, seeking the SBM's advice regarding proper procedure whenever there may be any ambiguity. In some instances it can be prudent to make governors aware if a particular decision may be seen as contentious.

The more people that are involved in various processes, the more opportunity there will be for checks and balances to be made, but of course this can be difficult on a day-to-day basis in a small school office. It is also pointless to involve an individual by merely getting them to sign a piece of paper if they do not understand what it is they are verifying. Any member of staff involved in financial procedures, in any way, should receive minimum training so that they know, for example, that when they put their signature on an invoice or cheque, they are really saying 'Yes, I verify this as a valid school expense, properly due for payment and I authorise it.'

Payroll is an area where particular vigilance is required and every instruction to pay, or vary the pay, of an employee should be clearly authorised in writing. Payroll fraud can potentially involve large sums of money; it is therefore crucial that checks are thorough and that all staff responsible for payroll input should always be different from those dealing with outputs and the recording of related accounting records.

Of course not all problems arise through misappropriation; most poor practice arises from ignorance or laziness. Teachers who cost the school unnecessary expense by failing to fully and accurately cost a school trip, or leave cheques in drawers for months on end; staff who fail to inform the finance officer that cover costs can be claimed from an exam board; these are all areas where schools can lose money. Any checks or systems that SBMs can put in place will be time well spent; again, it is often a case of training or raising awareness.

SBM Toolkit – FIM:4

Think about appointing a responsible officer (RO) to provide independent checks on a school's financial systems and procedures. Where schools have done this the RO is usually, but not necessarily, a governor and acts as an internal auditor; checking transactions, verifying figures, questioning systems, following audit trails and generally testing the school's processes.

This practice can be invaluable, especially where a school has insufficient staff with the relevant expertise to perform valid checks. An RO will ideally be an accountant, or have some financial expertise; their checks and reports can give reassurance to the governing body that independent scrutiny is being applied.

If not an accountant, somebody who works in a small- or medium-sized enterprise (SME) office will usually have the skills!

Requirements upon schools in respect of audit are variable. Many rely solely on their local authority's audit of their processes and accounts, which may be annual but often is much less frequent. Where an annual audit does not take place, it is imperative that other systems checks are in place and carried out regularly. Some governing bodies prefer the assurance of an annual audit and will pay for the cost from school resources, hiring independent sector auditors and accountants to perform the work.

CONCLUSION

The biggest factor in the success of an SBM in their role as financial manager, after knowledge and expertise, is likely to be their relationship with the head-teacher. If that relationship is to be successful and fruitful, it must be one of utmost and mutual trust. A head needs to believe that the financial advisor is not only knowledgeable in their field of responsibility, but fully understands the needs of the school, its pupils and staff.

If this understanding is to develop, old barriers between teaching and support staff must be abolished. The SBM and other support staff must invest time and effort to really understand the difficulties faced by teachers and what they need to perform to optimum capacity. The tendency of teachers to try to hold on to tasks and responsibilities – this frustration is often quoted by support team members – is usually due to a fear that others, who do not fully understand the stresses and problems they face, will take control away and their working lives will thus become even harder. This fear and insecurity must be replaced by trust; trust that others do truly understand what is needed and can actually make it happen.

Teachers in turn must recognise that a modern school needs more than teaching skills to function effectively and that some of those skills are every bit as hard-won as their own. A school may employ the best teachers in the world but without good management and effective use of resources, that school cannot guarantee success. Teachers must understand and accept that financial scrutiny and the drive for good business practice can really enhance their school's performance and are not merely bureaucratic burdens upon them. They must come to see and trust that good systems and processes potentially benefit everyone in a school and ensure that resources are available where they are most needed. They must also recognise the duty that schools have to the public to spend their taxes wisely.

The SBM too needs to feel that the advice, support and financial expertise offered are heard and valued. Headteachers, with all their responsibilities and conflicting demands, need as much support as they can possibly get. The more professional that support, the more can be achieved. One would not expect the managing director of any organisation to take financial decisions without the input of a financial director and in this regard there is no reason, other than one of history, why schools should be any different.

SUGGESTIONS FOR FURTHER READING

Blandford, S. (1997) *Resource Management in Schools: Effective and Practical Strategies for the Self-managing School.* London: Pitman.
Davies, B. (1994) 'Managing Resources' in T. Bush, and J. West-Burnham, (eds), 1996 *The Principles of Educational Management.* Harlow: Longman.
DfES (2001) *Promoting Benchmarking and Accountability in Schools.* London: HMSO.
Ofsted (1997) *Managing Financial Resources Effectively in Schools.* London: Stationery Office Books.
Ofsted (2000) *Keeping Your Balance: Standards for Financial Management in Schools.* London: Stationery Office Books.

USEFUL RESOURCES

The following helpful websites can be found at the addresses listed below:
http://www.dfes.gov.uk/valueformoney/
http://www.ofsted.gov.uk/publications/index.cfm?fuseaction=pubs.displayfile
&id=603&type=pdf

http://www.teachernet.gov.uk/management/atoz/b/bestvalue/
http://www.standards.dfes.gov.uk/locate/management/schoolsfinance/rfm/bv/
http://www.schools.audit-commission.gov.uk/
http://www.teachernet.gov.uk/management/schoolfunding/schoolfinance/
http://www.standards.dfes.gov.uk/locate/management/tar/fbfs/
https://sfb.teachernet.gov.uk/login.aspx
http://www.ncsl.org.uk/fmis
http://www.ipfbenchmarking.net/consultancy_dfes_update/

7

Making Sustainable Environmental Management Work in Schools

Tony Shallcross, Mary Jackson and John Rodway

ACTIVITY

Before you read this chapter make lists of who is involved in environmental management in schools and who should be involved.

INTRODUCTION

The embryonic profession of the school business manager (SBM) is another indicator of the increasing pressure on schools to model their practices on those of private sector enterprise. Devolved management of schools was a major step in this direction in the 1990s. However, this developing business ethos created a major anomaly in the management of schools. The introduction of the National Curriculum (NC) in the late 1980s reduced teachers' and headteachers' roles and responsibilities as curriculum managers. Prior to this time, schools had largely controlled teaching methods and content and examination boards dictated courses for 14–19 year old national examination candidates for which examination board syllabuses dictated course content. Paradoxically, as schools and teachers relinquished power over curriculum management, an area of significant professional expertise, their responsibilities for financial management, an area in which most teachers and headteachers had little or no training, increased. The growing administrative workload created for schools and particularly headteachers, as initiated by the Education Reform Act (ERA) (1988), was one of the reasons for the eventual development of the Certificate in School Business Management (CSBM).

However, there is an issue here of much deeper educational significance. The move towards a stronger business ethos may be an overdue development in the evolution of schools as effective managers of financial and other resources. However, to many educationalists this evolution represents a fundamental ideological change because it diverts attention away from schools' prime function as centres of learning and teaching. To some teachers the role of the SBM symbolises the commercialisation, application of market principles, the profit motive and competition to schools. While schools are clearly small- or, in some cases medium-sized business enterprises, as Michael Fullan (1999) observed most teachers consider them to be fundamentally social organisations, driven by the moral purpose of educating pupils rather than financial motives.

On the other hand there are lessons to be learned from each sector. Historically, maintained schools in England may have been in the opposite position of encouraging their development as educational organisations while neglecting their role as economic enterprises. Many businesses fail because they focus on changing the economic aspects of production while neglecting their function as social enterprises whose success lies in promoting human as well as economic development (Argyris and Schon, 1996). These rather divergent histories of private enterprises and maintained schools suggest that by taking advantage of links between schools' enterprise, educational and social functions SBMs can make a significant contribution to the development of schools as more innovative and sustainable centres of organisational learning, and not just to their development as more business-focussed organisations. This focus on education in schools has led to their evolution as organisations in which learning occurs, but not necessarily to their development as learning organisations. The term 'SBM' rather than 'bursar' is one indication that the remit of the SBM should extend beyond financial management and seek to locate business decisions closer to the locus of teaching and learning in schools (Summerson and Shallcross, 2005).

This analysis could place the SBM in a quandary. On the one hand, to try to avoid conflict SBMs could confine themselves to the management of the financial, business-focussed aspects of their schools and steer clear of initiatives that encroach on the formal curriculum – the traditional territory of teaching staff, unless invited into this territory by teachers. But such isolationism and fragmented management are not the characteristics of dynamic learning

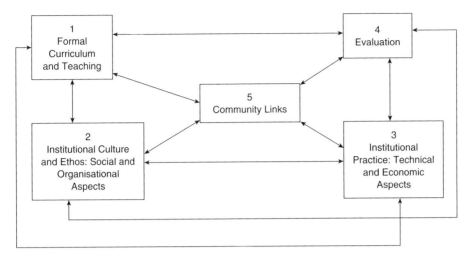

Figure 7.1   The Five Attributes of a Whole-School Approach

organisations, successful distributed leadership or good business management in schools.

Conversely SBMs can get involved in, or even stimulate, initiatives that promote distributed leadership by forging links between their own work and the formal curriculum. Such attempts at integration are likely to be more successful if SBMs recognise that the core business of schools is learning and teaching. In addition if SBMs can show that linking the formal curriculum with aspects of institutional practice, such as energy use or school grounds development, is of mutual benefit to the economic, educational and social functions of schools this further enhances the SBM's prospects of success. The answer lies in whole school approaches which provide a rationale for such an integrated approach to school education and a model for integrating the formal curriculum, institutional practice, school culture, community links and evaluation (see Figure 7.1).

WHOLE-SCHOOL APPROACHES AND SBMs

The two strands of whole-school approaches that appear most directly relevant to the SBM are community links and institutional practice (see Figure 7.1). Some argue that education cannot address environmental issues or sustainable development if it does not extend beyond the school gates into local communities (Elliot, 1999; Uzzell, 1999). But links with local community-based actions such as involvement in a 'safer routes to school' scheme are more effective when they are linked, in children's minds, with knowledge about wider regional and planetary transport issues. Local actions directed at concrete issues in communities and/or in schools have real impact on children and young people, especially if these children and young people are involved in deciding to implement action to address these issues (Jensen, 2002).

SBM Toolkit – SEM:1

Modifying institutional practices is an example of local action within a school. Energy conservation, developing school grounds or supporting elderly people within the local community are more tangible and immediate than learning about the deforestation of the Amazon Basin. A focus on energy conservation can benefit a school's budget especially when pupils become monitors and regulators of energy use in school.

Energy saving has environmental, educational and personal impact as well as financial consequences. It reduces schools' greenhouse gas emissions, develops children's understanding of energy and energy conservation and when it results from pupils' active participation, it motivates learning by promoting children's and young people's self-worth, self-confidence and their personal, social and environmental competence.

However, care has to be exercised when working with local issues as some may be highly controversial. Discussing fishing quotas in a fishing community (Schnack, 1998) or the reduction of greenhouse gas emissions from the burning of fossil fuels in a coal-mining settlement can be difficult for schools because these issues may create friction and conflict with parents, local citizens and/or politicians. The emotional immediacy of such issues can obscure wider, considered judgements.

However, by separating environmental knowledge in the formal curriculum from sustainable practices schools and local communities socialise hypocrisy (Shallcross, 2003). When schools fail to practise what they teach, children accept that being concerned about the environmental crisis while doing little or nothing about it is normal adult action (Titman, 1994). Whole-school approaches can break this cycle by modelling sustainable actions in schools' social and institutional practices, after these actions have been discussed and decided through a collaborative culture (UNESCO, 2004) that involves pupils and school support staff as well as teachers and other stakeholders. This is perhaps why one SBM felt that all those involved in senior management should be aware of whole-school approaches.[1]

---

[1] All the direct quotations from SBMs in this section are taken from the evaluation of a pilot for the NCSL/CSBM environmental management module (Shallcross and Moorcroft, 2004).

All senior management/leadership should have to read this!

This continuity of social relationships in whole-school approaches not only reduces defection, it increases the mutual trust that leads to cooperation (Ridley, 1996). By belonging to a functioning social community adults and pupils can become agents of change (Uzzell et al., 1994). In relation to sustainable development, collaborative cultures entail progressively stronger links between schools and their local communities because the seeds of sustainability lie in extending collaboration (Ridley, 1996). If pupils participate in deciding to conserve energy in their school, it becomes easier to persuade those adults and children who might waste energy by not switching lights off to do so because not switching lights off would become culturally unacceptable (Clayton and Radcliffe, 1996). There is evidence that through whole-school approaches schools can influence actions in local communities (Uzzell et al., 1994; Shallcross et al., 2006).

If a whole-school ethos is to promote local action and community links by empowering pupils and staff, then a collaborative, participative, democratic culture of communication and decision making based on mutual adult–child respect is crucial. Collaborative cultures (Nias et al., 1989) are built on the belief that values and actions are caught rather than taught through a school ethos that promotes openness, respect and a sense of mutual security. For SBMs the development of such collaborative cultures applies not only to their own sphere of management within schools, but to schools as a whole. Some SBMs recognised this need after a workshop on the CSBM environmental management module. Here are a few general (anonymous) comments:

The important bit is the pupil, the community and everything else.

It's good in the fact that it's showing what the children can do. What can be done in classes, what can be done with links outside.

I think the whole-school approach in this module has been really important, because it is a module which encompasses everyone and everything within the school and the local community …

Collaboration means that the roles of support staff and teaching staff become more associated with teams that develop practices such as those which are:

- organised and efficient;
- proactive rather than reactive;
- linked to theory;
- focussed on discussing decision making;
- based on written records (Fullan and Hargreaves, 1992).

COMPETENCE FOR WHOLE-SCHOOL APPROACHES

If collaborative cultures are to develop school staff, including SBMs and support staff, need to be proficient in interpersonal skills and knowledgeable about group processes such as communication and conflict resolution. Developing these skills becomes an important training agenda for SBMs if their staff are to play a full part in developing collaborative, whole-school cultures. What SBMs also need to remember is that school culture looks different depending on ownership of the viewpoint being examined (Smyth and Hattam, 2002). Neither culture nor ethos is the property of a single group in a school, be they teachers, support staff, pupils or governors. Some of these differences in perspective may arise because of gaps between policy and practice in schools. Pupils in schools are likely to draw conclusions about school culture based on what actually happens in school, whereas senior management may be more influenced by policy statements when forming such judgements. We have already seen that the less coherent policy and practice are in a school, the more likely pupil cynicism becomes (Titman, 1994).

But collaboration does not mean hollow consensus as collaborative school cultures are continuously constructed by struggles within and between groups in schools (Smyth and Hattam, 2002). Formal discussion of difference is a characteristic of collaborative cultures because these cultures create safe professional spaces in which dissenting opinions can be expressed and considered, often leading to deeper organisational consensus and understanding (Nias et al., 1989). However, it is links with parents and communities, which involve SBMs, which may be the most important feature of collaborative cultures. Such links form the productive alliances that help to disseminate a school's message and create ethical meaning within that school and beyond its gates (Fullan, 1999). This, then, is democratic collaboration because it is about the common good and not just self-interest.

Democratic schools are concerned with collaboration and cooperation rather than competition. Pupils believe that democratic classrooms display tolerance, mutual respect, a valuing of individuals, active participation, listening and fairness (Council of Europe, 2000). The procedures and principles of a democratic institution include equality, freedom, tolerance, consideration and respect for other people and their interests. These values are not only expressed in the committees, school councils and meetings which are often *the only overt symbols* of democracy, but also and perhaps more significantly, in the social networks, interactions and daily institutional practices that constitute the non-formal curriculum of a school and frequently involve support staff.

USING ENVIRONMENTAL INITIATIVES TO DEVELOP THE SBM's ROLE

We now want to see how whole-school approaches can be encouraged and sustained through the development of school grounds and energy and water management in schools, areas of that fall under the managerial remit of SBMs. Focussing on one area such as water use helps to avoid the danger of feeling swamped by the range of potential initiatives that could form part of a whole-school approach. The skill for the SBM and their school's senior management is not only in selecting which feature of the school is addressed as the first small step towards whole-school development, but more importantly how this step is selected. Focussing on small steps that promote win–win situations is also one way of reducing anxiety:

> I feel a bit overwhelmed with it. More emphasis on the smaller things at first.

The development and use of school grounds is nothing new. Playing fields have been a feature of schools' estates for many years, but there have been other significant uses of school grounds in outdoor education. At the beginning of the twentieth century, Margaret and Rachel McMillan highlighted the importance of the outdoors to young children in the UK while in the 1950s forest schools were established in Scandinavia. Outdoor education became an integral part of Danish early years education in the 1980s and has more recently been incorporated into many nurseries and schools in the UK, where use of the outdoors is also seen as a vital part of young children's experience of nursery and school (Titman, 1994).

During the 1930s children with tuberculosis were taught in open-air schools in the UK as this was thought to be the best treatment at the time. Since then the use of school grounds has had its ups and downs and by the end of the 1980s, research showed that many schools in the UK had poorly developed and used school grounds (Adams, 1990). Towards the end of the twentieth century a great many of these acres were sold off in the UK for development until legislation was strengthened to give school grounds and particularly playing fields greater protection.

One result of 1980s research was the establishment in 1990 of Learning through Landscapes, the UK's national school grounds charity (Adams, 1990). Throughout the world similar organisations have been set up; some national, some local, some with an environmental focus and others with a broader remit, covering all aspects of school grounds use, design and management. All these organisations support schools who wish to make the most of their grounds for the benefit of schools, pupils and often their local communities.

Further research around the world (EDC and the Boston Schoolyard Funders Collaborative, 2000; Johnson, 2000; Dyment, 2005) has shown that school grounds are an essential feature of a school's estate – they can support learning (Chawla and Duffin, 2005), encourage different aspects of play, promote positive behaviour and have a positive impact on the attitude of pupils to school as a whole (LtL, 2003). In some less economically developed countries, such as South Africa, school grounds can become a very important source of food for schools and communities, in some cases producing the nutrition needed to support HIV/AIDS sufferers in local communities (WEESA, 2004). Grounds have much more potential than to be used only for sport.

Much of a pupil's time at school is spent in the grounds – at the beginning and end of the day, for play and socialising at break and lunch times, for after-school activities such as gardening and wildlife clubs and for some lessons during the school day. As extended schools develop in England the use of school grounds will become even more important. For very young children the outdoors use is essential. In primary schools much of the curriculum can be taught outside and some aspects are best taught outdoors, while in secondary schools more and more teachers are realising that hands-on learning in the outdoors can provide an added motivational dimension to lessons (Malone and Tranter, 2003; Chillman, 2004).

SBM Toolkit – SEM: 2

Think about raising the profile of the school grounds as a cash-benefit exercise. A school's grounds are the first feature of a school that members of the local community encounter, including parents who are selecting a school for their children. School grounds can also be the location for school events such as fetes and can be hired by other groups – such as uniformed organisations and sports clubs. Schools can be a central focus for the community and the grounds, in turn, can reflect the community they serve. The way in which the grounds are managed is also important. Schools grounds that are not well-maintained are prone to vandalism.

Because of all these factors, school grounds are an important asset and one that should be developed and managed with care. The role of the SBM whilst varied can also have a significant impact on the success of the improvement and function of the school site, in turn enhancing the asset.

THE ROLE OF THE SBM IN SCHOOL GROUNDS DEVELOPMENT

Each SBM will have their own responsibilities relating to school grounds and will have to address differing issues. One example of an SBM's involvement in a school grounds project is given in the short case study below.

An Exmouth secondary school

The SBM managed the school grounds project. The first phase of the project involved erecting marquees in a courtyard area to provide much-needed shade and to create an area for pupils and staff to socialise in at different times of the day. However, the next phase of the project was put on hold as most of the teachers who had been involved in the initial phase of the project left the school.

Despite this loss of teaching staff the project did not stop completely. In another part of the grounds a determined Year 9 pupil was busy creating an allotment out of a disused area of land. This he managed in less than a year, transforming not only the space but also boosting his own self-esteem and confidence.

This project showed how even a few resources and commitment from the local community can make a big difference. A local DIY store was persuaded to donate tools and split bags of compost and another firm donated carpet which was used to suppress weeds. The local Royal Marines constructed a polytunnel. The pupil who set the project up now organises fellow pupils and with the help of learning support staff the project has now become self-sustaining, as sales of produce grown by pupils finance future purchases.

Although the SBM managed the project at this Exmouth school the loss of teaching staff meant that it was unable to be completed. This highlights the importance of having distributed leadership that represents different sectors of the school community in the team that manages and participates in projects. If there had been a wider group of people involved in this project from the outset it might have been able to continue in its original form. This breadth of involvement is particularly important when the turnover of teaching staff is high in a school. Other members of the school community that can get involved are support staff, pupils, parents, governors and members of the local community. The more varied the members in a team the wider the cross-section of views, experiences and skills that can be brought to projects.

One pupil's enthusiasm and resolve made this Exmouth school allotment project come alive. This is unusual but this kind of involvement still requires support from the school, if only through encouragement and the provision of space. This project now has a real chance of continuing when this pupil leaves because learning support staff have supported him and infected other pupils with his enthusiasm. When this boy leaves the school other pupils and staff will be able to ensure that the project continues. However, a similar scheme led by younger children would probably need more adult commitment and support which could come from staff, parents, grandparents or external experts such as members of a local allotment society.

CASE STUDY

The involvement of learning support staff has been vital to this project's success. While learning support staff were probably not recruited to support school grounds work, it helps if staff show an enthusiasm and willingness to work outdoors. This also applies to other adults who could get involved including those working with very young children, those supervising break and lunch times, teaching assistants, science technicians or those employed directly by the school to maintain the site.

The allotment project also succeeded because of community involvement. Support from local stores and the Royal Marines enabled the school's minimal resources to be stretched. Many schools follow this example by finding volunteer labour and gifts in kind which help them to spread the resources and money they have. An SBM could well have good contacts with local businesses and school suppliers, who might be approached to fund and support a school grounds project. At Exmouth some funding for the school grounds project came from the school's own budget. Applications can also be made for grants and awards. An SBM's financial experience and expertise can be very valuable in co-ordinating such applications for grants and also for overseeing budgets.

This Exmouth project has become self-sustaining. Pupils maintain the allotment and the funds raised through sales of fruit and vegetables are invested in the project. This will not always be the case with projects in school grounds. All school grounds projects have maintenance implications, some of which can be allocated to volunteers, but very few school grounds projects will bring income into the school. Some maintenance changes reduce contract costs but many add to these costs and this needs to be considered at the design stage of a project's development. The SBM will be responsible for managing contracts and will need to be aware of the cost implications of the new and existing aspects of maintenance that these contracts cover and how changes to these contracts might be negotiated.

SBM Toolkit – SEM:3

Health and Safety is an essential consideration for school grounds developments. It is as important to consider the impact of not only the features that are to be created on the site, but also any development work. There will be issues to consider if contractors or volunteers are employed. Risk assessment will highlight some of these and insurance policies should be checked to see if these refer specifically to work done outside school buildings.

Even if an SBM is not part of a school's senior management team they can be called upon to support a school grounds project at different stages in its progression, thereby giving significant input. If this is the case the SBM should try to make the senior management team aware of the different ways they can, and should, be involved in any school grounds projects so that these have the best chance of success by using the varied skills and knowledge of members of the school community to their full potential.

SUSTAINABLE ENERGY AND WATER USE IN SCHOOLS

In the coming years of the twenty first century, energy and water costs are likely to rise in real terms. If a school's budget only rises to match inflation, then utility costs will take an increasing proportion of that budget, leaving progressively less for core educational activities. The increasing use of ICT in classrooms and offices, and the extended opening hours of schools, will further exacerbate energy costs and the resulting budgetary stress.

Traditionally, the management of energy and water has not been a school function, so the delegation of responsibility to schools for these can be a challenge to SBMs. However, the process of management often entails bringing together and coordinating the expertise of others to achieve desired outcomes, rather than the SBM having to work in isolation and know everything about the management of energy and water. As the role of SBMs has evolved over the last decade, so new areas of responsibility have been successfully assimilated into their role and their expertise has developed. Why should the oversight of utilities be any different? Indeed, denying or abrogating responsibility for these or failing to discharge oversight are likely to result in some of a school's precious finances being wasted.

It is a common perception, in both educational and engineering circles, that school personnel lack the knowledge and expertise to manage utilities, and therefore they are ill-prepared to shoulder this new role. It is true that most school staff would neither recognise a three-way motorised valve nor know what it does. But such devices are the concern of plumbers, electricians, technicians and building service engineers rather than managers. Most members of the school community are familiar with some of the basics of the management of energy and water management because:

- adults will have some experience of energy and water management from running their own homes;
- some teachers have greater knowledge of the wise use of water and energy as part of the national curriculum;
- many pupils will have picked up knowledge of energy and water use independently of the school.

Table 7.1   The role of different personnel in raising the profile of environmental engineering and demonstrating its relevance to every day school life

Personnel	Role and benefits
Governors	Proper discharge of their legal and environmental obligations. Better control of costs so that maximum funding can be directed to core educational activities.
SBMs and/or site managers	Spreading responsibility for the good management of resources in the school, thereby reducing the mistreatment of utility fittings.
Teachers	Additional ways of delivering the required knowledge, understanding and skills in many subjects (from English, to Science, to Citizenship). A cost-effective way of making links between classroom theory and real situations which pupils are already familiar with and which affect their comfort.
Engineers	Additional partners in getting the best performance from the systems that they have fitted.
Whole-school	Translating generalised concerns for the environment into specific sustainable actions.

All too often, school personnel neither recognise that they have relevant knowledge of water and energy use nor appreciate that what they know can be applied beneficially to the running of their school.

SBM Toolkit – SEM: 4

It may be necessary for teachers or SBMs to spell out the benefits of using a school's utility systems as educational resources.

In some cases, teachers are keen to exploit the school environment as an educational resource but are unsure of whether this is practical or permitted, and so they fail to start. The SBM or site manager may see the benefits of involving pupils in caring for the school, but could be hesitant to initiate this strategy, (as the Exmouth case study illustrates) because it is not part of their traditional remit. The engineers that supervise school water and energy systems may be looking for opportunities to spread knowledge and understanding of these systems, but are reticent because of their uncertainty about how their suggestions might be received. For one or more groups, a change in mind-set may be required as indicated in the Table 7.1 above.

GOVERNORS AND THE SENIOR MANAGEMENT TEAM

The members of the senior management team may be wary of acting in unfamiliar territory. They will need convincing that management of energy and water is a matter for them rather than just an additional task for the SBM, or a task that the local authority does without reference to them. The key argument is that, since most of the technical fixes that can be applied to water and energy systems have probably been implemented, preventing the escalation of energy and water costs requires the active participation of users in the school. This makes energy and water use a whole-school issue in which governors and senior managers must take a leading role.

SBMs, SITE MANAGERS AND THE CLEANING TEAM

It is important to convince the site management team that energy and water management consists of more than just checking that boiler controls are switched between summer and winter settings and ensuring that washers on leaking taps are replaced.

SBM Toolkit – SEM:5

In promoting an expanded view of site management, care should be taken by SBMs not to imply a criticism of the way this work has been done in the past. They should strive to involve the site team gradually in such things as formal energy walk-rounds and helping the cleaners work in ways that minimise energy and water use without compromising hygiene.

At some stage, the site manager will provide regular electricity, gas and water meter readings in a standard format. Some site managers have been carefully recording these readings for years, even though they have not been asked to do so and no one has used the data they have amassed. If these records are used to promote more efficient resource management, site managers will usually be delighted that their diligence has been recognised and will be put to good use.

Managing energy and water wisely is an important life skill for every member of the school community. Most teachers will be encouraged to see school buildings and their associated energy and water systems as additional learning resources that will help them to improve their teaching. However, as we saw earlier, SBMs have to be careful not to offend teachers by appearing to be interfering in the formal curriculum. This requires that teachers are assisted to:

- discover what is on site;
- find explanations of what each component of an energy and water system does and how it works;

- decide which aspects of energy and/or water management will support their teaching;
- develop appropriate schemes of work that support the national curriculum and also address ways in which the school can make more efficient use of energy and/or water.

Part of the SBM's role can be to help to bring teachers, educational advisors, the site manager and engineers together in situations that will encourage productive dialogues and actions. There is also a number of organisations that can help, such as local authority departments which include: Environment; Sustainability; Local Agenda 21; Estates; Architecture; Building Services; Technical Services; Utilities; Purchasing; Planning and the Chief Executive's department. Non-governmental organisations (NGOs) such as CREATE, Eco-Schools, Groundwork and Global Action Plan also play a part here and there are some energy supply, water and building service companies that will help schools.

ENGINEERS

Engineers often report on utility systems and consumption in terms that are difficult for non-engineers to understand. SBMs should try to persuade engineers to report in a language and with levels of detail that are meaningful and relevant to their school. This can take time as both sides have to become familiar with the differing needs, concerns and language of the other. A school's main concerns about energy and water use are likely to include:

- the monthly consumption of energy;
- comparisons of actual energy use with the energy use that would be expected for that month's actual weather;
- energy, water and sewage costs;
- predictions of maximum energy consumption and the costs arising, assuming that the weather is as cold as the worst experienced for those months in recent years, for the last three months of the financial year only;
- water consumption for the month/quarter/year;
- comparison of water consumption with previous, comparable periods.

SBMs should consider linking up with colleagues from other local schools in asking energy and water engineers to take a common, more layman-friendly, approach to discussing reports on energy and water use. SBMs will also need to try to encourage engineers to become involved with teachers, and perhaps pupils, in the development of educational resources based on the utility systems.

THE SBM

One problem with energy and water management is the large number of utility meters found in a typical school and the data that they provide. This is why spreadsheets are commonly used as a business management tool. Fortunately, setting up a utility spreadsheet only has to be done once, so it is worth getting it right first time. The local authority energy manager may be able to to give support by providing a ready-made spreadsheet or helping in some other way. Generating, updating and interpreting a school's energy building performance graph takes a little time. SBMs are becoming more adept at working with financial predictions and 'what if?' scenarios. A building performance graph is simply another financial prediction tool that uses energy units (kWh) instead of pound signs.

A new responsibility for the SBM is to liaise with those engineering professionals who have previously overseen the technical aspects of energy and water systems within their school, often without reference to the school's personnel. Many engineers are reluctant to approach school personnel because they are unsure about how they will be received.

Leaving management to a contractor or consultancy may appear the simplest way to discharge oversight and responsibility for energy or water management. However, outsourcing has two implications:

- Maintenance will only get equipment to the end of the contract period. This policy could store up major problems for the future that the school will have to fund.
- Knowledge of systems and the expertise on how to operate them best will be lost when the contractor's staff leave. The school and/or its new contractor will have to start all over again. This learning process can take one or two years, often wasting energy, water and money in the process.

Techniques for the management of water and energy are well established, and because consumption can be quantified improvements are readily identified and progress more easily tracked than in many social and organisational areas. This is why institutional practices such as energy and water use are ideal first steps towards creating a more sustainable school.

CONCLUSION

Sustainable development is an evolving set of competences rather than a mature discipline. Therefore, there is not and never will be a single, clear-cut, generally accepted method of being sustainable. Priorities and solutions will change with situations and contexts and will be decided in these situations and contexts. In these circumstances where outcomes cannot be prescribed, it is important that the development of sustainable schools is achieved through whole-school processes that prioritise participation and collaboration and link the formal and non-formal curricula. In this way everyone in school may play their part in deciding and implementing more sustainable ways of living.

What should be clear from this chapter is that everyone in a school has a part to play in making sustainable environmental management work in their school. If a whole-school approach is adopted, schools become better learning environments for pupils because there are tangible links between the formal curriculum and real environmental issues in the school and its local community. Pupils learn by doing things about real issues. Forging links between the five strands of whole-school approaches is shown to be good for SBMs because it leads to more sustainable management of a school's resources, whether these resources include school grounds, water, energy use or money.

Schools now have access to the Sustainable Schools Self-Assessment tool which uses the Ofsted self-evaluation headings to help schools to assess and monitor their development towards becoming more sustainable institutions. By adopting a whole-school approach, resource management becomes more efficient because everyone becomes a stakeholder in and observer of a school's environmental performance. This approach leads to both better management of resources and better learning. In short it leads to the development of the whole-school as a learning organisation in which educational and economic, social and enterprise matters become inextricably fused with each other.

REFERENCES

Adams, E. (1990) *Learning through Landscapes – A report on the Use, Design, Management and Development of School Grounds.* Winchester: Learning through Landscapes Trust.

Argyris, C. and Schon, D. A. (1996) *Organizational Learning II: Theory, Method, and Practice.* Reading, MA: Addison-Wesley.

Aspin, D. N. (1995) 'The conception of democracy: a philosophy of democratic education', in J. Chapman, I. Froumin and D. Aspin (eds), *Creating and Managing the Democratic School.* London and Bristol: Falmer.

Beane, J. A. and Apple, M. W. (1999) 'The case for democratic schools', in M. W. Apple and J. A. Beane (eds), *Democratic Schools: Lessons from the Chalk Face.* Buckingham: Open University Press.

Chawla, L. and Duffin, M. (2005) *Impacts of Place-based Education on Pupil Outcomes.* (Available at www.peecworks.org/PEEC/PEEC Research/S0032637E.)

Chillman, B. (2004) *Do school grounds have a Value as an Educational Resource in the Secondary Sector?* Winchester: Sussex University and Learning through Landscapes. (Also available at: www.ITI.org.uk.)

Clayton, A. M. H. and Radcliffe, N. J. (1996) *Sustainability: A Systems Approach.* London: Earthscan, World Wildlife Fund UK and The Institute for Policy Analysis.

Council of Europe (2000) *Everyone can Make a Difference: Council of Europe Pilot Project on Participation in and through School, Second Training Seminar for Teachers Report.* Strasbourg: Council of Europe.

Dyment, J. (2005) Gaining Ground: The Power and Potential of School Ground Greening in the Toronto District School Board**.** (Available at: www.evergeen.ca/eng/lg-resources.html.)

Education Development Center (EDC) and the Boston Schoolyard Funders Collaborative (2000) *Schoolyard Learning: The Impact of School Grounds.* (Available at: www.edc.org/GLG/schoolyard.pdf.)

Elliot, J. (1999) Sustainable society and environmental education: future perspectives and demands for the education system, *Cambridge Journal of Education,* 29 (3).

Fullan, M. (1999) *Change Forces: the Sequel.* London: Falmer.

Fullan, M. and Hargreaves, A. (1992) *What's Worth Fighting for in Your School?* Buckingham: Open University Press.

Henderson, K. and Tilbury, D. (2004) *Whole School Approaches to Sustainability: An International Review of Sustainable School Programs*: Australian Research Institute in Education for Sustainability (ARIES) for the Department of the Environment and Heritage, Canberra: Australian Government.

Jensen, B. B. (2002) Knowledge action and pro-environmental behaviour, *Environmental Education Research,* 8 (3).

Johnson, J. (2000) *Design for Learning: Values, Qualities and Processes of Enriching School Landscape.* American Society of Landscape Architects. (Available at: www.asla.org.)

Learning Through Landscapes Trust (LtL) (2003) *UK National School Grounds Survey.* Winchester: LtL. (Available at: www.ltl.org.uk.)

Malone, K. and Tranter, P. (2003) *School Grounds as Sites for Learning: Making the Most of Environmental Opportunities.* (Available at: www.educationarena.com.)

Nias, J., Southworth, G. and Yeomans, R. (1989) *Staff Relationships in the Primary School.* London: Cassell.

Ridley, M. (1996) *The Origins of Virtue.* London: Viking (Penguin).

Schnack, K. (1998) 'Why focus on conflicting interests in environmental education', in M. Ahlberg and W. Leal Filho (eds), *Environmental Education for Sustainability: Good Environment, Good Life.* Frankfurt am Main: Peter Lang.

Shallcross, T. (2003) *Education as Second Nature: Deep Ecology and School Development through Whole Institution Approaches to Sustainability Education.* Unpublished PhD thesis, Manchester: Manchester Metropolitan University.

Shallcross, T. and Moorcroft, R. (2004) *Report on the formative evaluation of the National College of School Leadership (NCSL) Certificate in School Business Management (CSBM): Creating a Better Environment in Our Schools.* Nottingham: NCSL.

Shallcross, T., Pace, P., Robinson, J. and Wals, A. (2006) *Creating a More Sustainable Environment in Our School.* Stoke-on-Trent: Trentham Books.

Smyth, J. and Hattam, R. (2002) Early school leaving and the cultural geography of high schools, *British Educational Research Journal,* 28 (3).

Summerson, T. and Shallcross, T. (2005) School Business Managers: essential profession or temporary political expedient? Paper presented at the *British Educational Leadership and Management (BELMAS) Symposium,* University of Manchester, February.

Titman, W. (1994) *Special Places: Special People.* Godalming: World Wildlife Fund and the Learning through Landscapes Trust.

UNESCO (2004) *United Nations Decade of Education for Sustainable Development 2005–2014: Draft International Implementation Scheme.* Paris: UNESCO.

Uzzell, D. (1999) Education for environmental action in the community: new roles and relationships, *Cambridge Journal of Education,* 29 (33).

Uzzell, D., Davallon, J., Fontes, P. J., Gottesdiener H., Jensen B. B., Kofoed J., Uhrenholdt, G. and Vognsen, C. (1994) *Children as Catalysts of Environmental Change.* Brussels: European Commission Directorate General for Science Research and Development.

Wildlife and Environment Society of South Africa (WEESA) (2004) *Schools and Sustainability: The Eco-Schools Programme in South Africa.* Howick: WEESA.

Section 2

Thinking Strategically

8

Strategic Management

David Brunton

INTRODUCTION

In the last three decades there have been unprecedented changes in the responsibilities that schools face, with a significant increase in the level of control that they may exercise over their future direction and strategic plans. This has implications for the way in which schools are led and managed. This chapter concentrates on the kinds of thinking and techniques needed, both by school business managers and the broader school leadership team, to understand strategic activities and make them work most effectively. Strategic processes require more divergent and exploratory attitudes to generate appropriate questions about how the future will be different from the present. This chapter, therefore, explores a number of different ways in which the strategic management of schools can be conceptualised, and seeks to draw conclusions about some of the implications for the work of school business managers.

The central framework for thinking about strategic management in schools in this chapter is drawn from the writing of Johnson and Scholes on understanding strategy development. They propose three 'lenses', or 'ways of seeing things', to enable the reader to think critically about strategic development in organisations. The three perspectives are: strategy as design, strategy as experience, and strategy as ideas.

This chapter also draws on research by Mintzberg et al. which sought to produce an accessible overview of the field of strategic management. They describe their research as a safari to reveal the 'whole beast of strategic management, and explore its various aspects'. Mintzberg and his team described the different schools of thought about strategy in organisations, each of which illuminates different aspects of strategic management. They write, 'Each has a unique perspective that focuses … on one [of the] major aspects of the strategy-formation

Table 8.1

Perspective (Johnson and Scholes, 2002)	Related schools of thought (Mintzberg et al., 1998)	Key concepts
Strategy as design	The Planning School	Systems development
	The Positional School	Rational decision making
Strategy as experience	The Incremental School	Logical incrementalism
	The Collective School	Strategic intent
Strategy as idea	The Visionary School	Strategic leadership
	The Learning School	Organisational learning
		Core competencies

process. Each of these perspectives is, in one sense, narrow and overstated. Yet in another sense, each is also interesting and insightful' (1998: 4).

They identify ten schools of thought, some of which merged into others over time. They cluster them into three categories: those that are essentially prescriptive, telling us how we should lead and manage strategic processes; those that are descriptive, providing insights into how organisations actually approach strategic management in practice; and those that are integrative, seeking to bring the various approaches together and make sense of the totality of strategic process in organisations.

There is a direct link between these schools of thought and the three lenses (or perspectives) described by Johnson and Scholes. This chapter explores the three perspectives in turn and the related schools of thought that seem to me to be particularly relevant to thinking about the strategic direction of schools today. In each case, the central tenets of the perspective are described, together with a brief summary of its major limitations and criticisms. This is followed by an analysis of some of the implications for our thinking about strategy in schools. The perspectives and schools of thought emerged at different times in recent history, each with its own trajectory of insight and influence. It is important to note that even those which have been overtaken by other approaches, and have declined in influence, still have important things to say about how we should conceptualise, plan, lead and manage strategic processes in school settings.

STRATEGY AS DESIGN

This is fundamentally a rational approach to planning (Glover, 1997). Johnson and Scholes state the perspective is based on 'the view that strategy development can be a logical process in which forces and constraints on the organisation are weighed carefully through analytical and evaluative techniques to establish clear strategic direction and in turn carefully planned in its implementation. (Johnson and Scholes, 2002, reproduced in Preedy et al., 2003: 142).

The planning school emerged in business settings in the 1970s and asserted the importance of strategic formal planning in organisations. That is, it argued that the process of strategic management was a distinctive area that should be approached systematically and organised as a sequence of distinct activities.

The underlying premises of this approach are that:

- strategic management should be a conscious and controlled process of formal planning;
- it is something separate from the daily operational life of the organisation, a distinctive set of activities;
- responsibility overall lies with the chief executive of the organisation, although others will inform the plan;
- strategies should be articulated and made explicit, and then implemented through detailed action planning (adapted from Mintzberg et al., 1998: 58).

Many different models of strategic management have emerged over time, and they have tended to increase in complexity and sophistication. A good recent example was provided by Hunger and Wheelen in 2003. They define the field as follows:

> Strategic management is that set of managerial decisions and actions that determines the long-run performance of a corporation. It includes environmental scanning (both external and internal) strategy formulation (strategic planning) strategic implementation, and evaluation and control. (Hunger and Wheelen, 2003: 2)

They describe their model of strategic management as consisting of four basic elements:

- *Environmental scanning* 'monitoring, evaluating and disseminating information from the external and internal environments ... the external environment consists of variables (opportunities and threats) that are outside the organisation ... The internal environment consists of variables (strengths and weaknesses) that are within the organisation'.
- *Strategy formulation* 'the development of long-range plans for the effective management of environmental opportunities and threats, in light of corporate strengths and weaknesses'.
- *Strategy implementation* 'the process by which strategies and policies are put into the development of programs, budgets and procedures. This process might involve changes within the overall culture, structure, or management system of the entire organization ...'.
- *Evaluation and control* 'the process by which corporate activities and performance results are monitored so that actual performance can be compared with desired performance' (Hunger and Wheelen, 2003: 10).

Environmental scanning: looking out and looking in

Evaluation and control: monitoring progress, evaluating impact, reviewing lessons learned

Processess

Strategy formulation: long-range vision and course of action

Strategic implementation: planning for action, managing projects and leading change

Figure 8.1 Processes of Strategic management

SBM Toolkit – SM:1

Using the proforma below, check with the SMT Senior management team) which of these four activities have been undertaken by whom and when:

Activity	Done	By Whom	When
Environmental scanning			
Strategy formulatsion			
Strategy implementation			
Evaluation and control			

The results should help you decide:

a   If your strategic plan has been based on logic planning.
b   Which activity you can contribute to.

The key criticisms of the planning school have been summarised very clearly by Johnson and Scholes (2002, reproduced in Preedy et al., 2003). From this critique, five key points can be highlighted:

- Strategic planning can become an intellectual exercise removed from the realities of the life and work of the organisation.
- The process of planning may become so complex and technical that individuals and groups may only make a limited contribution and not understand its significance.
- Strategy may become equated with the production of a plan, so that processes of implementation and review (and the real work of strategic development) become marginalised.

- The search for and commitment to the 'right plan' may promote inflexibility and a refusal to accept the limitations of the plan or to adapt according to changing circumstances.
- The very rational model of planning may result in a stifling of creative ideas and innovative capacity (adapted from Johnson and Scholes, 2002: 146–7).

Despite these criticisms, the rational model of strategic planning still has great significance for the work of schools. Perhaps the most important message from 'the planning school' for schools today is simply that the strategic direction of the school is important and is something that needs to be led, managed and organised in a systematic way. In terms of thinking, the literature on strategic planning in schools has evolved rapidly to provide a sophisticated understanding of the key concepts and techniques of leadership and management. However, in practice school leaders have different levels of awareness of the complexity of strategic planning and schools vary in the degree to which strategic planning processes have been embedded in their organisation.

In 1998 the Chief Inspector of Schools commented in his annual report that

> development planning is good or very good in only three schools in ten, and is unsatisfactory or poor in over a third. The development plan has a key role in the translation of aims and values into practice and gives the school a clear sense of direction and purpose ... Where development planning is weak it is often over-ambitious, unprioritised and poorly co-ordinated and implementation is inevitably sporadic. More commonly, there are weaknesses in the extent to which plans build upon thorough evaluation and provide for monitoring of their effectiveness. (Ofsted, 1998: 9)

Certainly some progress had been made by 2003, when HMI (Her Majesty's Inspectorate) conducted a survey of leadership and management in 150 schools and reported that:

> The quality of strategic and operational planning was a significant strength in the majority of the schools. They established clear priorities based on rigorous self-review ... Staff were generally involved in identifying priorities and planning for improvement; their views were listened to and taken into account where possible. Managers were mostly skilled at convincing staff of the need for change even when there were initially signs of reluctance.
>
> Where less effective practice was observed, managers failed to seek evidence of the impact of their management strategies. In these schools, there was a limited understanding of how monitoring and evaluating the quality of leadership and management could be used to inform planning for change designed to improve provision and raise achievement. (Ofsted, 2003: 30–1)

Increasingly complex and sophisticated models of strategic planning for school improvement have been formulated as time has passed. From a comparatively simple model of school development planning based on an annual cycle of

Table 8.2 Characteristics of four types of school development plans (Source: MacGilchrist et al., 1996)

Rhetorical plan	Singular plan	Co-operative plan	Corporate plan
No clear ownership	Owned by headteacher only	Partial ownership by staff, with willingness to participate	Shared ownership and involvement of all teacher staff and others
Lack of clarity of purpose efficiency	Used as management tool by the headteacher	Intended to improve efficiency and effectiveness	Shared sense of purpose to improve effectiveness
Poor leadership and management of process	Limited leadership and management of the process	Led by headteacher with involvement of some teaching staff	Shared leadership and management by all teaching staff
Nsegative impact	Limited impact	Positive impact across the school and in classrooms	Significant impact on school development, teacher performance and pupil learning

activities, more recent models have emphasised the need for medium- and long-term planning strategies; the most influential of these has been the sustained (2003) research by Davies and his colleagues to design, on the basis of experience, more elaborate models which enable school leaders to steer their schools purposefully in a context of global change and uncertainty. This research has advocated a shift away from sole reliance on 'the planning school' and the adoption of a broader range of strategy approaches. This work is discussed in more depth below (Davies and Ellison, 2003). Davies et al. (2005), however, have set out recently what they see as the potential value of the rational model of strategic planning. They write:

> The strategic plan is concerned with broad areas of development over the medium term. It focuses on key activities that underpin all of the school's activities. Strategic plans can be of use where schools seek to move beyond predictable events into a sustained and determined focus upon important areas of improvement. (Davies et al., 2005: 44)

It is perhaps still useful to emphasise some of the more basic characteristics of effective strategic planning for school improvement. It is informative in this respect to consider the research conducted in 1995 by MacGilchrist and others. They used case-study research to evaluate the quality and effectiveness of school development plans in primary schools. Their findings substantiated a typology of four different approaches to school development planning, as summarised in the Table above.

They concluded that 'a key finding of this study is that SDPs make a difference, but the nature of that difference is determined by the type of plan in use. Development planning can be used as a school improvement strategy but not all development plans lead to improvement' (1995: 237). The most effective plans (here the corporate plan) displayed the following key characteristics:

- A focus on teaching and learning, especially on improvements in the quality of pupils' learning.
- Clear control over the process of strategic planning and its key phases and activities.
- School-wide targets for improvement, supported by clear action plans.
- Strong sense of shared ownership and involvement by staff.
- Widespread confidence that the process would lead to improvements.
- The written plan seen as an open and working document.
- Financial resources and staff development linked directly to the plan.
- Sound arrangements for monitoring progress and evaluating outcomes. (adapted from MacGilchrist et al., 1995: 236).

This typology suggests some important tasks for school business managers. The first of these relates to their potential contribution in working with others to map the process of strategic planning in a school, and to translate this process into a series of well-ordered events, documents, deadlines, outcomes and discussions. The school business manager can play a key role in monitoring the process of strategic planning and can ensure that its implementation stays on track (Blandford, 1997). This potentially enables a school to develop school improvement strategies that are underpinned by a clear business plan that makes a direct link between strategic direction and resource management.

Glover (1997) provides useful guidance on the effective alignment of strategic decision making and efficient resource management. He sees this as a cyclical process which involves sequential activities related to auditing, planning, prioritising, implementation and evaluation. These processes taken together are designed to ensure that a school has an annual budget that (in the words of the National Audit Office 2000a):

- is realistic and affordable in relation to available resources and cash flow;
- is approved by governors on a timely basis;
- reflects the school development plan (SDP);
- is consistent with any longer-term financial plans for recovering deficits or saving up for future developments.

The National Audit Office emphasises the importance of the close alignment of a school's strategic plans for different aspects of their resource management, particularly curriculum, staffing and premises:

Curriculum development plans need to be drawn up following an analysis of the school's strengths and areas where improvements are needed. They should be costed to give short-term and long-term estimates of the resources needed to bring about the required development. **Staffing plans** will usually be heavily influenced by curriculum plans and again need to estimate the resource needs of the school in providing the planned staffing levels. **Premises plans** need to record both maintenance and development costs and, again, these are likely to be influenced by the school's curriculum plans, pupil numbers and the organisation of classes. (National Audit Office, 2000b: 10)

From this business planning perspective, it is possible to identify a series of key services that the school business manager can provide, to ensure that strategic planning is underpinned by secure financial data. Such services would include:

- comparing the school's financial performance with that of similar schools, identifying reasons for differences and taking action where necessary;
- investigating the school's position in the educational marketplace, and potential implications for the future finances of the school;
- producing estimates of likely funding levels and resourcing requirements for the next three years;
- costing action plans for school improvement and leading colleagues through systematic approaches to options appraisal;
- ensuring that all potential sources of funding have been identified and that income is maximized in appropriate ways;
- designing and managing systems for monitoring spending and evaluating cost-effectiveness.

Finally, Glover (1997) also emphasises the need for informed decision making and argues that those responsible for cost centres should be actively involved in the processes of budget-making, monitoring and evaluation. This suggests that school business managers should work closely with other staff in setting budgets and making spending decisions, so that calculation of costs is undertaken at the level of detail required to enable informed decision making about priorities, programmes and alternatives. This engagement of other members of staff in planning and budget setting is important to deepen their level of understanding of the rationale for strategic choices, and of the need for efficient resource management to support school improvement planning.

STRATEGY AS EXPERIENCE

The concept of strategy as experience is based on 'the view that future strategies of organisations are based on an adaptation of past strategies influenced by the experience of managers and others in the organisation, and are taken-for-granted assumptions and ways of doing things embedded in the cultural processes of organisations' (Johnson and Scholes, 2002; reproduced in Preedy et al., 2003: 142).

This perspective provides a clear challenge to rational models of strategic development as a discrete, analytical process in organisations. It suggests that in practice strategic planning may be less about directing and controlling and more about reflecting on experience, seeking consensus and shaping coherence. There is a link between this perspective and the 'incremental' and 'collective' schools of thought.

The 'incremental school' of strategic thinking draws upon 'the science of muddling through'. Researchers who were looking at strategic processes in organisations began to question the validity of thinking about strategy as a wholly deliberate, conscious and rational process that was completely separate from other aspects of organisational life. Instead, they suggest that in reality strategic decisions emerge from the working life and professional responses of members of an organisation that are then crystallised into shared understandings of what is best for the future of that organisation. This is linked to that organisation's capacity to the experiment and to learn from the experience. This strategic process was labelled 'logical incrementalism' (Quinn, 1980, cited by Mintzberg et al., 1998: 181) to describe the way in which 'internal decisions and external events flow together to create a new, widely shared consensus'.

This way of thinking about strategy would seem to be pertinent for schools for a number of reasons. For me, this starts from two fundamental ideas: the first, is that the school may not always understand clearly what it needs to do and how to do it. It recognises that an area of development is important, but is not quite sure how to proceed in the longer term. The second idea is that change involves the awareness and engagement of staff across a school if it is to be successful. These ideas are central to the concept of 'strategic intent'.

In the 1990s Prahalad and Hamel conceptualised strategic management in organisations as a collective learning process. Much of this learning concerned the core competencies of an organisation, that unique set of abilities that could be applied to the development of a range of products or services and would give that organisation its competitive advantage in the marketplace.

Given that nurturing and developing these core competencies is at the heart of an organisation, its strategic development and commercial success lie in its ability to identify ways in which these competencies might be further developed in the future or applied to different settings. That is, strategic thinking needs to focus on the future and to anticipate what the future might look like and how that organisation could best work towards it. This kind of thinking is called 'strategic intent' and it 'envisions a desired leadership position and establishes the criterion the organization will use to chart its progress …' (Hamel and Prahalad, 1989: 6, cited in Mintzberg et al., 1998: 219).

Educational writers such as Davies emphasise that it is important to see the building of strategic intent alongside traditional strategic planning. They argue that, while the latter can cope with those activities that are predictable, the former is concerned with focussing on the development of improved understanding of complex or uncertain challenges facing the school in the medium term. The key purpose of activity related to selected 'strategic intents' is to deepen a school's capability to understand these challenges and to prepare to make more informed decisions in the future.

Therefore, action plans in relation to the strategic intentions identified by a school often take the form of small-scale pilot projects. They are likely to involve research and development activities, perhaps seeking out best practice elsewhere. This enables a school to return to a key issue or challenge at a later stage, hopefully with an increased and shared understanding of what is involved and how best to proceed. This is an example of emergent strategy that builds on the experience of researching and leading innovation in relation to an important aspect of school improvement.

The concept of strategy as experience raises some interesting dilemmas for the work of the school business manager. Emergent strategy is seen as something that is particularly important within professional organisations, where a key group of talented employees with a broadly shared identity and academic background are relatively powerful in determining the strategic direction of their organisation (Mintzberg et al., 1998: 192). This approach recognises the resistance of some professional groups/individuals to changes in their professional practice and the importance of securing the commitment of all to the key values and strategic choices of the organisation.

SBM Toolkit – SM:2

Set up a risk analysis of each change programme based on your estimate of resistance to change in individuals. At least there'll be no surprises when you hit a wall with somebody!

Some professional organisations (notably universities) have been characterised as organised anarchies where intelligent, strong-willed professionals pursue local goals and values that may be disconnected from the official mission statement and strategic priorities. In such organisations strategic decisions may be formed by administrative fiat, collective choice or individual professional judgement. The incremental school suggests that strategic planning may be most effective when it is based on consensus and builds on experience.

This is a cyclical approach to strategic development, in which strategic goals and actions are reviewed regularly, so that further decisions are shaped by reflection and discussion of the experience of innovation and the analysis of its impact. From this perspective, strategy is created through retrospective sense-making: a process of imposing sense on past experience. It has been called a 'grassroots model of strategy-making' (Mintzberg et al., 1998: 196).

In a school setting, such an approach has important implications for the roles of headteacher, chair of governors and the senior leadership team, as even a grassroots model of strategic development needs to be shaped, guided, led and managed. The leaders of an organisation can promote the development of an emergent awareness of a strategy amongst staff and stakeholders by sponsoring and disseminating specific initiatives that fit with its central tenets. This can also be linked to the professional judgement of a school in deciding when is the right time to make an important strategic change, and what is the right way to carry it out. Davies and his colleagues call this 'determining effective strategic intervention points' (Davies et al., 2005: 64). It is fundamentally about deciding when and how to make key changes; they suggest that it involves taking into account individual readiness, organisational requirementss and external conditions.

This is a useful point at which to reflect on recent changes in the characteristics of schools as professional organisations. In the past, schools were mainly populated and dominated by one professional group – that of qualified teachers. However, over the last decade schools have changed in two important respects: the first example is in the number of staff other than teachers who now work in schools. In *Time for Standards* (2002), the DfES reported that between 1997 and 2002, the number of administrative and support staff in school increased from under 140,000 to over 210,000 and projected a further rise to almost 300,000 by 2005. It can also be argued that the roles of administrative and support staff have also become more specialised and complex. Two key examples can be provided: the first relates to the role of school business managers themselves, who as part of the remodelling agenda, have increasingly taken on the intermediate and advanced levels of responsibility as defined by the DfES (see *Looking for a Bursar?*, 2003). The second example is that of higher level teaching assistants, who are taking on more complex tasks and deeper responsibilities to support the learning of pupils. In both cases, new career trajectories are being developed, new specialised roles are being defined and new working relationships are being established.

The increased specialisation of staff in schools means that key decisions can only be made on an informed basis if staff reflecting those different specialisms are able to make a contribution to the strategic direction of their school. The use of ICT to support teaching and learning provides a good example, where fundamental questions about curriculum and pedagogy need to be considered alongside issues and options that relate to technical capacity, network security, child protection, procurement options, assessment management, risk assessment, software licenses, maintenance contracts … and so on.

This suggests that increasingly strategic choices in schools require the application of different sets of specialist expertise and technical knowledge, and that this is likely to be dispersed across the school as an organisation. It has been suggested that school business management is a rising profession, but one that is also contested in some settings. This reflects the growing capability of school business managers, and the new and distinctive sets of knowledge and expertise that they bring to the schools in which they work.

However, the effective application of these new kinds of knowledge and expertise is dependent upon the tact and diplomacy of the school business manager, to ensure that their potential contribution is heard in a constructive and challenging rather than a negative and threatening manner. The school business manager may find themselves engaged in a medium-term change strategy, to persuade others of their potential contribution to the life and work of the school. This is a structural change, in which the predominance of one kind of educational knowledge is being questioned and new kinds of complementary knowledge are needed to secure the future of the school.

Given the importance of collaborative and corporate approaches to school improvement planning, it is vital that all of the different groups of staff across that school are engaged in the strategic direction of that school. With more complex and diverse staffing structures, consideration needs to be given to the way in which each group of staff contributes to the key values and vision for learning of the school, and is consulted over decisions affecting the future of the school. The third approach to thinking about strategy emphasises the complexity of organisations and provides some pointers for the engagement of all staff in processes of strategic direction and school improvement.

STRATEGY AS IDEA

This approach to strategic direction emphasises innovation and the characteristics of organisations that are able to innovate. It argues that there is a need for the continual challenge of what is taken-for-granted within an organisation and for a climate that will enable competing ideas to be discussed openly. From this perspective, the role of strategic leadership is not so much to control the development of the organisation, but to sponsor a climate in which others care about the organisation and wish to contribute to its future direction (Johnson and Scholes, 2002: 152). The central task of the senior leaders within a school is to define, through consultation, the core values of their organisation and its overall vision or mission.

SBM Toolkit – SM:3

The SBM is better placed to provide a realistic picture of the commitment of *all* staff to the core values of their school. Staff who are not teachers can often provide a more powerful image for parents than the work that goes on in the classroom (for example, litter in the playground).

Make it part of your role to at least find out if they *know* about core values!

Mintzberg and his colleagues identify two key schools of thought that relate to the notion of strategy as idea. First, the entrepreneurial or visionary school emphasises the importance of a vision that 'serves as both an inspiration and a sense of what needs to be done ... deliberate in its broad lines and sense of direction, emergent in its details so that these can be adapted en route' (Mintzberg et al., 1998: 124–5). In a school setting, this emphasis upon vision can be related to both the moral imperative behind the strategic direction of the school, and the need for futures thinking that focusses upon the long-term development of a school and the environment in which it operates. Second, Mintzberg's learning school of thought emphasises that organisations need to think consciously about their capacity for change and to seek to become 'learning organisations'.

Denton describes the three primary characteristics of a learning organisation: these are a learning strategy, flexible structure and blame-free culture. In his view, a series of other characteristics flow from these (including vision, awareness, and team working), but these three establish the organisational framework in which others may exist to a lesser or greater extent. The first characteristic, a learning strategy, requires a corporate strategy that embraces both learning and innovation as specific goals, and views strategic development fundamentally as a learning process (Denton, 1998: 92).

Denton's second characteristic is a flexible structure. At one level, he is concerned with what has been called 'strategic human resource management', and the need to ensure that staffing levels and structures are aligned to the emerging requirements and resource levels of an organisation. But in terms of strategic management itself, Denton is more concerned about the flexibility required to enable an organisation to analyse its needs, set out priorities and target energies accordingly. This requires the formation of teams who need to work together in purposeful ways to take forward the strategic management of school, at each stage of the processes of strategy formulation, implementation and review. Denton argues for the creation of small, autonomous centres responsible for specific areas of provision. He also advocates cross-functional working through the creation of multi-professional project teams and suggests that it is the role of the senior leaders to facilitate and encourage such enterprises.

This echoes Handy's task culture, in which the staff of an organisation are seen as a network of talented individuals. He says 'this culture seeks to bring together the appropriate resources, the right people at the right level ... and to let them get on with it' (Handy, 1993: 188). The creation of teams involves bringing together those individuals who collectively have the different knowledge and skills (or potential) to address a specific task. This is a problem-centred approach to school improvement: one that targets areas of need and aspiration, and then focusses energies on these. Flexibility is required because school improvement is fundamentally a moving target, and an organisation must be responsive to change and challenge. Within the terms of existing job descriptions, specific areas of importance may emerge at a given time and may well be reflected in the performance objectives set for an individual within their appraisal cycle, as well as in the action plans for school improvement.

Denton's third key characteristic of a learning organisation is a blame-free culture, in which employees are encouraged to innovate and to learn from experience. The core values of an organisation play an important role, in 'providing a framework for behaviour and performance' and ensure that any innovation or experimentation is shaped by the organisation's over-riding mission; a values-based approach to risk management (Denton, 1998: 93).

The concept of the learning organisation draws upon and integrates many of the ideas and approaches which have been discussed previously in this chapter. It could be argued that organisational learning should be at the heart of any school and its strategic direction. However, in 1993, Michael Fullan felt that he had to conclude on the basis of his researches that:

> The school is not now a learning organisation. Irregular waves of change, fragmentation of effort, and a grinding overload is the lot of most schools. (1993: 42)

Twelve years on, it could be suggested that such pressures on schools still exist, but they have generally grown in their sophistication of thinking about strategic development and improvement planning and have much greater understanding of the importance of vision, values, innovation and collaboration.

One approach to strategic development in schools which is fundamentally about learning emphasises the need to develop the strategic capabilities of a school. This is about making investments in how the school community as a whole conceptualises, leads and manages its strategic development. Davies et al. identify these strategic capabilities as follows:

- a fundamental understanding of teaching and learning;
- a high level of trust and communication;
- the use of assessment for learning;
- a creative and innovative culture;
- a positive team approach to problem solving;
- a learning and reflective school community. (Davies et al., 2005: 65)

For the school business manager, and their potential contribution to the development of a school as a learning organisation, it is useful to reflect upon commercial settings and the distinctive characteristics of the 'learning company'. Pedler et al. (1997) set out what they saw as the key characteristics of a learning company:

- *A learning approach to strategy*: where policy and strategy formation are consciously structured for learning, for example, by sponsoring projects that create feedback to inform further decisions.

- *Participative policy making*: where all members of the organisation and its stakeholders have a voice in making policy and defining strategy.
- *Empowering front-line staff*: where staff are empowered to act on their own initiative within the core values.
- *Formative accounting and control*: where systems of budgeting, reporting and accounting are set up in such a way that staff understand how resources can be used wisely.
- *Internal exchange*: where there is staff awareness of the distinct contribution of each division and team within the organisation (supply chain), and a commitment to providing high standards of service to internal customers.
- *Reward flexibility*: where there are more flexible and creative rewards for the individual contribution and innovation of staff.
- *Enabling structures*: where roles, structures, processes and procedures can be changed easily to meet new needs and circumstances.
- *Boundary workers as environmental scanners*: where the observations and experiences of those who work directly with key clients and stakeholders are listened to.
- *Inter-company learning*: where the organisation works with others as part of a series of networks and alliances.
- *Facilitating learning and self-development*: where there is an emphasis on staff development and training. (Adapted from Pedler et al., 1997: 16)

This checklist of organisational characteristics provides a potential lens through which the policies and practices of a school can be evaluated, and whereby proposals for development can be identified. Senge states that 'the organisations that will truly excel in the future will be the organisations that discover how to tap people's commitment and capacity to learn at all levels in an organisation' (Senge, 1990: 4).

CONCLUSION

This chapter has aimed to review the different perspectives in thinking about the strategic direction of organisations, and to draw some implications for schools and for school business managers. However, one model of strategic development has not been discussed as yet, and this is of central importance for a school. This model is called 'imposed strategy' and concerns situations where leaders face the imposition of strategy by government agencies or other external forces. It could be argued that using the sorts of thinking and techniques described above is likely to make a school more effective in terms of how it interprets and responds to external imperatives to change.

REFERENCES

Blandford, S. (1997) *Resource Management in Schools: Effective and practical strategies for the self-managing school*. London: Pearson Education.

Davies, B. and Ellison, L. (1999) *Strategic Direction and Development of the School*. London: Routledge.

Davies, B., Davies, B. and Ellison, L. (2005) *Success and Sustainability: Developing the strategically-focused school*. Nottingham: National College for School Leadership.

Department for Education and Skills (DfES) (2002) *Time for Standards: reforming the school workforce*. London: DfES.

Department for Education and Skills (DfES) (2003) *Looking for a Bursar?* London: DfES.

Denton, J. (1998) *Organisational Learning and Effectiveness*. London: Routledge.

Fullan, M. (1993) *Change Forces: Probing the Depths of Educational Reform*. London: Falmer.

Glover, D. (1997) Resourcing Education: linking budgeting to educational objectives. In Preedy, M., Glatter, R. and Levacic, R. (eds) (1997) *Educational Management: Strategy, Quality and Resources*. Buckingham: Open University Press.

Handy, C. (1994) *Understanding Organizations*. (4th edn) London: Penguin Books.

Hunger, J. and Wheelen, T. (2003) *Essentials of Strategic Management*. New Jersey: Pearson Education.

Johnson, G. and Scholes, K. (2002) Exploring Corporate Strategy. Harlow: FT Prentice Hall. Reproduced in Preedy, M., Glatter, R., and Wise, C. (eds) (2003) *Strategic Leadership and Educational Improvement*. London: Paul Chapman Publishing.

MacGilchrist, B., Mortimore, P., Savage, J. and Beresford, C. (1997) The Impact of Development Planning in Primary School. In Preedy, M., Glatter, R. and Levacic, R. (1997) *Educational Management: Strategy, Quality and Resources*. Buckingham: Open University Press.

Mintzberg, H., Ahlstrand, B. and Lampel, J. (1998) *Strategy Safari: The complete guide through the wilds of strategic management*. Harlow: FT Prentice Hall.

National Audit Office (2000) *Keeping Your Balance: Standards for Financial Management in Schools*. London: OFSTED.

National Audit Office (2000) *Getting the Best from your Budget: A guide to the effective management of school resources*. London: OFSTED.

Office for Standards in Education (OFSTED) (1998) *Annual Report of her Majesty's Chief Inspector of Schools – Standards and Quality in Education 1996/7*. London: OFSTED.

Office for Standards in Education (OFSTED) (2003) *Leadership and Management: Managing the School Workforce*. London: OFSTED.

Pedler, M., Burgoyne, A. and Boydell, D. (1997) *The Learning Company*. London: McGraw-Hill.

Preedy, M., Glatter, R. and Wise, C. (eds) (2003) *Strategic Leadership and Educational Improverment*. London: Paul Chapman Publishing.

Quinn, J. B. (1980) *Strategies for Change: Logical incrementalism*. Homewood, IL: Irwin.

Senge, P. (1990) *The Fifth Discipline: the art and practice of the learning organisation*. New York: Doubleday.

Managing School Improvement and Performance

Dave Grewer and Peter Taylor

INTRODUCTION

Education, worldwide, is experiencing a time of frenetic innovation where it can often be felt that values have been replaced by measures. Many schools complain of initiative overload; they have become subject to a series of fragmented and episodic changes that have resulted in school leadership being increasingly less focussed upon its key function of leading learning. School leaders, including business managers, must therefore regain ownership of vision and seize the initiative or they will become mere functionaries in a system and not leaders of people and shapers of hearts and minds.

This is a time to re-affirm our values; it is a time when new approaches to leadership and managing school improvement are crucial. Changing lives and shaping the future make up our role but this has implications: children's lives will change in many, many ways, colleagues lives will change, your own life will change. This is the profound nature of school improvement and performance management. This chapter urges SBMs to become involved in these two processes, and to consider the difference they can make to children's lives.

Hullo, I am Angelica. I am five years old. I really don't have much of a past. In fact, I am the future. You need to understand what I am learning to believe, how I think about my future, what my world view is. You and I both want to be a success in the world which I will enter as an adult and which I will be responsible for. In future days I will admire you for being able to look forward with me and to help me define what I need to learn. My world is already very different from the one you have grown up in. (Beare, 2001)

SCHOOL IMPROVEMENT

Effective school improvement is best managed when the leaders in a school are those people who walk ahead and are genuinely committed to deep change in themselves as well as in their organisations. They lead through developing new skills, capabilities and understandings. They come from many places within the organisation.

Too often schools make quick decisions which can be fatal and surely the essence of a learning and intelligent school is knowing when to think and act quickly and knowing when to think and act slowly. Schools must become learning communities to survive and to manage school improvement effectively and they need to consider how to cultivate and sustain learning under conditions of complex and rapid change. When considering the management of school improvement there is a pivotal need to develop a new mind set. Why is this so important? One of the issues that affects teacher morale and possibly de-motivates them from time to time is that they do not feel a sense of control and an ability to shape their work. Real educational change depends on what teachers do and think – it is as simple and as complex as that. Davies and Ellison (1999) identify three approaches to school improvement and development:

- Tactical   – one year operational planning.
- Strategic   – three year planning.
- Building Capacity   – leadership dispersed at all levels creating coherence and sustainability.

CAPACITY BUILDING

It is in this area of building capacity that effective school improvement strategies lie. The three intelligences of leadership are integral to the effective management of school improvement: IQ (analytical thinking); SQ (Vision and Values); and EQ (Effective Relationships). The latter two, SQ and EQ, are of specific significance when considering the third-level approach to school improvement – that of building capacity for sustained success. There are several key questions to reflect upon when determining your school's present position as you move towards this upper level of school improvement.

SBM Toolkit – MSI:1

Ask yourself, how do you think your school would respond to these key questions: Does my school ...

- Acknowledge the need to consider and plan for new ways of doing things in the short and long term?
- Ensure that the learning vision is focussed upon learning at all levels: pupils, teachers, support staff and the school as an organisation?
- Provide a range of opportunities for teachers and assistants to become more expert in pupil learning – sharing the responsibility for organising the learning experiences?
- Ensure that people see that their abilities, responsibilities and worth are recognised?
- Adapt the curriculum, amend roles and responsibilities and aspects of the school, including the use of meetings, to facilitate and coordinate school development?
- Empower others to lead including those without formal roles?
- Develop a sense of collective responsibility for change?

Times change and so what works for leaders will change. Senge (1996) states 'We are coming to believe that leaders are those people who walk ahead, people who are genuinely committed to deep change in themselves and in their organisations. They lead through developing new skills, capabilities and understandings. They come from many places within the organisation'. So where do you think your school is operating strategic or capacity building? What evidence is there of rethinking roles and changing leadership as Senge suggests? What are the barriers?

One of the fundamental pre-requisites to effective capacity building and sustained school improvement is the foundations within a school and how solid they are. HayMcBer identified six key dimensions of a context for school improvement, each of which can contribute significantly to an overall level of high performance: 'The perception of staff about the environment of the school. It is the "atmosphere of the workplace", which influences individual and group patterns of behaviour. It is, in effect, staff's perceptions of the "way we do things here"'.

Flexibility

- Bureaucracy minimised.
- Innovation.

These incorporate the perception staff have about their freedom to act in the school (bureaucracy!) and the degree to which they perceive that there are unnecessary rules, procedures, systems of administration (including meetings, paperwork and policies) and practices that interfere with task accomplishment. New ideas are easy to get accepted.

Responsibility

- Autonomy.
- Risk taking.

These incorporate the perception that staff have a lot of authority delegated to them and the degree to which they can run their jobs without having to check everything with their team leader and feel fully accountable for the outcome.

Clarity

- Purpose.
- Vision.

These incorporate the perception that the staff understand the big picture, know what is expected of them in their jobs and understand how these expectations relate to the bigger goals and objectives of the school.

Standards

- A drive for improvement.
- Challenge and support.

These incorporate the emphasis that staff perceive the senior team puts on improving performance and doing one's best, including the degree to which staff perceive that challenging but attainable goals are set for the school, its staff and its pupils, and that mediocrity is not tolerated.

Rewards

- Recognition.
- Differentiation in terms of recognition.

These incorporate the degree to which staff perceive that they are being recognised and rewarded for good work, that such recognition is directly and differentially related to levels of performance, and that staff know where they stand in terms of their performance.

Team commitment

- The level of discretionary effort.
- Providing extra effort when required.

These incorporate the perception that staff are proud to belong to the school, will provide extra effort when needed, and trust that everyone is working towards a common objective.

The challenge for every school to consider is the extent to which these dimensions are effectively addressed within schools. Only then will they be able to manage school improvement in such a way that real *impact* is made. Fullan (2001) emphasises the need for real coherence by stating that this will only be achieved when we address these key areas which are so crucial to sustained and effective school improvement:

Schools are very good at:

- Initiation
- Implementation

However, schools are less effective at

- Institutionalisation of change – which leads to significant
- *impact*.

The climate and foundations within our schools are obviously key elements, but how do we develop competence within a school to seriously confront the rapid pace of change and all its implications?

IMPROVING THE PEOPLE AND THE PLACE

David Hopkins, Louise Stoll, Michael Fullan and Andy Hargreaves promote a distinct model for building capacity which has been adopted by the UK's NCSL (National College for School Leadership), providing a distinct model for building capacity for sustained school improvement which addresses the development of three essential capacities:

- Personal.
- Interpersonal.
- Organisational.

We are focussing specifically upon the area of organisational capacity and Hargreaves (1991) sees it like this:

It is the knowledge and skills we build and use to enhance teaching and learning.

The primary function of the head is to ensure that as many people as possible have been given leadership opportunities to increase and mobilise the school's capacity.

Ideally the school's management structures should reflect the optimal distribution of these opportunities to contribute to its overall effectiveness.

So, what more do we need to do in our schools?

Similarly, real effective schools develop the key capacities of effective leadership:

- Vision and values.
- Understanding change.
- Creating and sharing knowledge.
- Effective relationships.
- Creating coherence.

I once heard a headteacher encapsulating the real meaning of what we are trying to achieve as we move towards the third, high level of approach to managing school improvement. He said:

Trust, confidence, a supportive atmosphere, and support for risk taking – a culture that says you can take a risk – you can go and do it. If it doesn't work, we learn from it. I think there's a range of cultural issues that support distributed leadership and create a climate; high levels of communication; willingness to change and to challenge; a climate that recognises and values everybody's opinion.

THE LEARNING SCHOOL

Once you have considered these crucial questions and issues we can then begin to consider how the emerging concepts of a learning school and learning centred leadership can enable all schools to move nearer the approach to school improvement which focusses upon building capacity and moves beyond the strategic perspective.

These concepts enable schools to explore the way they function and the extent to which their individual organisation is focussed upon addressing improvements that are going to have a real impact upon learning and pupil achievement. The importance of this is best illustrated in this statement by Fullan (1993): 'The school is not now a learning organisation. Irregular waves of change, episodic projects, fragmentation of effort and grinding overload is the lot of most schools'.

To be a learning school we need to develop an insight into:

- the concept of a learning school as a creative framework for thinking;
- the kind of learning that is needed;

- the importance of learning-centred leadership and our ability to lead learning;
- self-evaluative tools to assess where we are;
- process tools that will provide an impetus to the creation of a learning organisation.

So why do we need to address school improvement from this perspective? Consider this perspective in turn as a possible response (Stoll and Fink, 1996): 'Internal capacity in a school is the power to engage in and sustain the continuous learning of teachers and the school itself for the purpose of enhancing pupil learning'.

THE SBM AND SCHOOL IMPROVEMENT

As we begin to reflect upon these essential new concepts what do these key questions mean for you as a school business manager: How do we

- Regain control of our own agenda?
- Become agents of change rather than victims?
- Re-establish confidence in our own professional skills?
- Take responsibility for our own learning and leadership?
- Be a school that in itself can learn?
- Be more than a sum of its parts?
- Recognise the importance of leadership at all levels in enhancing organisational learning?

Organisations function in many different ways but only a few move on to greatness. These organisations are able to embed leadership at all levels so as to manage school improvement as a whole and in a way which creates an essential synergy. Ofsted's framework for inspection is specifically focussed upon these very issues and the extent to which leadership is embedded throughout the school. Morgan (1998) identified these possible profiles:

- *Machines*: interlocking parts – defined roles.
- *Organisms*: living rather than mechanical beings – adapting to change.
- *Brains*: able to process information – develop frameworks for learning.
- *Cultures*: emphasis upon values and ideas.
- *Political*: different sets of interests, power struggles, conflicts.
- *Psychic prisons*: people trapped within their own thoughts – alternatives not seen.
- *Flux*: chaos and complexity – flows of positive and negative feedback.
- *Domination*: using people for their own ends.

Schools operate at three levels of consciousness – surviving, adapting and sustaining – and our objective should be to move towards sustaining. When an organisation is operating at the level of surviving then they employ many established habits and processes to carry out basic tasks. They tend to be responsive and reactive and there is a lack of overall clarity of purpose with no real context for change. In terms of an organisation which is adaptive, they tend to make the necessary changes to adapt to what will be needed and respond to trends and developments. Strategic planning and operational target setting are evident but this is not necessarily the case with strategic thinking. Sustaining organisations create as well as respond to their context. There is a futures thinking perspective and there are places where there is a commitment to the development of internal capacity, where people are proactive rather than reactive and there is confidence in owning professional judgements.

School leadership of all types is ultimately concerned with learning, but too often we do not follow this logic in reality. Pressing issues lead to a management and task-driven situation for leaders and schools. Urgent takes over from important, *but* we must not lose sight of the big picture (SQ) for school leadership at all levels must focus upon re-emphasising the quality of teaching and learning as well as establishing schools as learning communities. This is where the role of the school business manager sits when considering your place in managing effective and sustained school improvement.

SBM Toolkit – MSI:2

The NCSL has produced some very good research into what it is effective leaders do in school which makes an impact upon the essential purpose of pupil learning. This is now available as the NCSL's Learning-Centred Leadership Toolkit. It will provide a useful framework for you as shool business manager and then as a member of the senior leadership team to evaluate how effective leadership is in the school. This approach will undoubtedly enable it to function at the higher level of sustained school improvement.

There are key questions and indicators by which a school can really establish its strengths and weaknesses in managing whole-school improvement in the twenty first century. The key aspects of research using the NCSL's Learning–Centred Leadership Toolkit are:

- *Aims, values and cultures* Do they provide a focus upon learning for all?
- *Impact upon learning* How do leaders make an impact?
- *Knowledge* How does a school build its knowledge about effective teaching and learning?
- *Professional dialogue* How does this play a part in influencing classroom practice?

- *Systems and processes* What do we use to improve learning and teaching?
- *Involvement* How does a school engage the wider community as partners in learning and teaching?

In conclusion, leadership of schools is changing rapidly. It is about new mind sets that will enable us to face new initiatives and develop improvement plans so as to be proactive in our management of change. Your role as school business managers is pivotal to this process.

PERFORMANCE MANAGEMENT AND SCHOOL IMPROVEMENT: THE LINK

An ancient Chinese proverb tells that 'a journey of a thousand miles begins with a single step': the journey of school improvement begins with a single step also but the trick is to ensure that that first step is taken in the right direction!

Once you have developed the mind set and capacities needed to engage in school improvement, you may wonder what is the mechanism that will ensure school improvement takes place? This is the sort of business-like question a good business manager will ask. Ideas and philosophy are essential but they are not much use if they are not translated into day-to-day terms. They are also not much use unless they actually make the lives of the pupils/students and adults in your organisation better. An effective performance management process can help you understand your organisation and people so you know what the issues are, what people think and how effective they are, where you want to get to and how to get there. This is the essence of school improvement and performance management is the key management tool to help move your organisation and people in the desired direction.

CASE STUDY

When Liz arrived at Worth Primary School in Cheshire, she expected to work as the school secretary; she had no idea that eventually she would end up on the leadership team. Now Liz is fully involved in the school's improvement and performance management process.

After several years at the school it became clear to the school leaders that Liz was a very able school secretary, fast at typing, used shorthand, was organised and had ideas of her own – but she was content in her role. After some time Liz was encouraged to take on more responsibility and support the classroom staff in as many ways as possible, in terms of administrative and resource support. As a result of her expanded role she was regarded and worked as an administrative officer for some time, but she was never an administrator by nature.

CASE STUDY (CONTINUED)

Liz had ideas about how to improve the office and she had no problem in letting other staff know her ideas and views. After some encouragement from the headteacher and chair of governors, Liz decided to undertake the Certificate of School Business Management (CSBM) with Manchester Metropolitan University; a National College of School Leadership programme.

Upon completion of the CSBM, Liz was again encouraged to redesign her workload, and that of Sally the school's part-time secretary, and of course she was asked to re-assess the pay grades of both Sally and herself. Liz now serves on the senior leadership team (SLT) and leads her own team, which is the resource and finance team. She appraises Sally and Tony the maintenance officer.

She knows the needs of the school in terms of curriculum and personnel/human resource issues and she is able to align the talent and work of her team with school resources to help meet those needs. The role Liz now has is key in the effectiveness of the school; her efforts support the classroom staff in their efforts to support the learning and well-being of the main clients of the school – the pupils.

Performance management should help you align the potential, aspirations and talents of your staff with the vision and direction of your organisation. This is the development of a 'Personal mastery [which] is a set of practices that support people – children and adults – in keeping their dreams whole while cultivating an awareness of the current reality around them' (Senge, 1994).

SBM Toolkit – MSI:3

Ask yourself if the review and appraisal processes in your organisation are coherent and integrated, or fragmented, with weak linkages between school development planning, the appraisal meeting, target setting, data analysis, work observation and professional development. If this is the case then maybe the performance management process in your organisation is not linked to school improvement sufficiently well.

EFFECTIVE PERFORMANCE MANAGEMENT

The first step that needs to be taken in ensuring performance management is effective, in your context, is to examine your own motives, intentions and leadership qualities. An effective performance management process will use detailed observation and performance data relating to the individuals in your team. These are sharp instruments, ones that should be used professionally, wisely and with compassion. Sharp instruments can be used to heal or damage and must be used with care.

If you are unclear as to why and how the process is to run, what chance is there of motivated but busy staff buying into it? If performance management is seen as a bolt-on process and yet another task designed to take staff away from the core tasks in their job, then it is destined to fail. If performance management is to be effective in your organisation you must be confident of both the purposes of the process and of your motives, hopefully seeking to align and develop the aspirations and talents of your staff and not to monitor and control.

As the process becomes more effective, aligned, attuned and integrated, your organisation will hold the gathering and analysis of data and information as key. This data and information then inform the cycle of planning, monitoring and review, which in turn informs the improvement/development plan. As your skills and capabilities in relation to performance management become more proficient the process will move from being a once-a-year event to being the key process in understanding the organisation, both co-ordinating and maximising the talents and aspirations of staff and impacting powerfully on the organisation's climate, culture and results.

A well-organised performance process can become transformational for you, for your team and for the organisation; a process that literally enables people to examine the needs of their organisation and themselves. This can lead to deep change if handled well by a skilled team leader.

> Typical leadership actions associated with transformational models include; coaching and mentoring designed to support individuals and increase leadership capacity generally; visible dispersals of leadership responsibility throughout the staff group whose members are trusted to initiate and complete tasks; and group decision-making that is highly participatory, open and democratic. (Gold et al., 2003)
> And as observed by Hammer and Champy:
> Managers change-from supervisors to coaches … Process teams, consisting of one person or more, don't need bosses; they need coaches. Teams ask coaches for advice. Coaches help teams solve problems. Coaches are not in the action, but close enough to it so they can assist the team in its work. (Hammer and Champy, 1994: 74–5)

This is not to be taken lightly; know the potential of the process and use it wisely.

CREATING THE CULTURE

You will know from experience that it is not easy to get someone to change their behaviour or habits, such is the way of human nature. If you accept the fact that except in extreme circumstances 'adults change themselves, especially regarding sustainable behavioural change. In other words adults decide what or how they will change' (Boyatzis, 1998: 4). You have to take the first step in creating a culture and climate in which your team can develop themselves, not a climate of control where you think you are making people change. If you want a plant to grow you must place it in fertile soil, feed it, water it, protect it from the extremes of the elements – and then it will grow on its own. This is the mind set that will help an effective culture and climate grow in your context.

In a practical sense, how do you as a leader gain enough respect from your people for the performance management process to be of benefit? Clearly, it helps if you are good at your job, if your skills and knowledge are sufficient and if you are experienced and professional. However, for the performance management process to be really valued and transformational your deeper motives and competencies need to be evident to the staff. If staff are to talk to you about their weaknesses, their concerns, their aspirations and their vision then trust must be in place.

> Trust is the essential link between leader and led, vital to people's job, status functions and loyalty, vital to fellowship. It is doubly important when organisations are reaching rapid movement, which requires exceptional effort and competence, and doubly so again in organisations like schools that offer few motivators. (Evans, 1998)

These deeper and more personal competencies or qualities are often referred to as 'emotional intelligence'. Without a sufficient degree of understanding of yourself and your team as people no formal training in team leadership or performance management is going to make you effective; you need to understand your team and yourself.

> When an organisation [and team] has developed sufficiently well a less hands on style of leadership will need to be adopted, one which empowers and develops other leaders in the organisation. The process of letting go of the reins of control can be very painful for leaders who prefer the hands on approach. (Rowan and Taylor, 2002: 12)

Once your team is starting to become effective you need to allow them to lead also; you may set limits and delegate carefully but you cannot control a highly effective team and if you do they will only ever move at your pace and think with one perspective. This urge to control must be addressed and you will need to accept that you are no longer at the forefront of every development; in this aspect your team will be able to develop a degree of flair and self-motivation. 'Common commitment of this kind requires a conception of leadership that is neither linked to status nor embodied in the actions of any single individual, but rather dispersed or shared throughout the school and, as such, is available to everyone' (Gold et al., 2003).

THE SCHOOL BUSINESS MANAGER AS TEAM LEADER

If you lead a large department or office you may have quite a few people who report to you or your managers; if this is the case you may need to develop other team leaders within your department. The advice is that it is best if a team leader is responsible for the performance management of no more than four colleagues, although it is possible to work with more. It is quite common for SBMs to be working in small offices and possibly alone in terms of administrative tasks.

There is no one context that is common so you will need to make arrangements that fit your particular situation. In some schools the SBM appraises the caretaker as well as other office staff. Some SBMs appraise and manage other support staff such as technicians and classroom support staff, especially those that have a more practical support role rather than staff such as higher level teaching assistants. There are no hard and fast rules or regulations in this matter; it is for you, your school leaders and your staff to design a process and structure that works in your context. The key thing is that you know your team and their work. Another ancient Chinese proverb says, 'It doesn't matter what colour the cat is so long as it catches mice'. Design your system to match your context.

SBM Toolkit – MSI:4

The performance management process outlined here goes beyond the concept of line management; the role suggested is more that of a coach, suitable for a professional context where staff are regarded as colleagues. In this professional setting you are likely to have staff who want to engage; if you have staff that are causing problems or are incompetent, then the performance management process should be suspended and other procedures brought into place (disciplinary and competency procedures for example).

With colleagues who are professional in their approach you will be able act as coach in the performance management process. You will be able to work with your team to help them develop their own strategies to move themselves and their work forward. You will not be at the centre of all developments and you will not be the source of all knowledge and power.

> Good coaches don't solve a team's problems; they help individuals solve their own problems. Coaches manage through questioning rather than dictating. Instead of effective coaches issuing orders they ask, 'What do you need to accomplish?' or 'What alternatives have you considered?' or 'Have you thought how? ... Effective and

empowering leaders encourage other leaders and members to solve problems on their own. They coach for success before the team member's action, not after the failure. Coaching for success increases the likelihood of success, which in turn builds confidence. (Wellins et al., 1991: 175)

THE APPRAISAL/REVIEW MEETING

Unless your organisation or your professional regulations dictate the timing and format of the appraisal/review meeting, it is best designed to suit your staff and the context of your organisation. It is common for there to be one appraisal meeting per year where performance to date is reviewed and recorded; this may involve a review of targets or objectives. Within the same meeting there will usually be a discussion about the future work, aspirations and needs of the individual, again with the key elements of this being recorded during the meeting. The final phase should address strategies to move the individual on (which may be recorded as targets or objectives); it is quite possible for all this to take no more than 60 to 75 minutes. This meeting is best held in quality time and in a quiet and comfortable room.

Egan (2002: 26) suggests it is useful for managers (and team leaders) to hold a model in mind when coaching. His model is simple and effective; he asks the coachee to consider the issues in stages:

- *Stage 1*: 'What is going on?' (Current scenario)
- *Stage 2*: 'What solutions make sense for me?' (Preferred scenario)
- *Stage 3*: 'How do I get what I need or want?' (Action strategies)

After a review of the progress made in the previous year, this model can be used in this order to coach the appraisee/coachee in a practical yet empowering sense. In fact this model can be used when a colleague asks questions that you think they should be able to answer themselves. Try it, it works.

SBM Toolkit – MSI:5

It is common for the records of the appraisal meeting to be completed and signed by both parties during the session. It is also useful if the appraisee can add a comment in relation to their agreement (or not) with the results of the meeting.

Whilst the coaching method attempts to engage and motivate staff to take the lead role in their own appraisal it needs to be recognised that there will be a time when the appraiser and appraisee disagree; in such a case you may have to stand your ground and if necessary refer the appraisee to the appeals procedure.

Research undertaken by Reading (2003: 17) found that the teachers questioned thought the following about performance management and their appraisal meetings:

- They valued a personal professional dialogue.
- 'We can "prove" we have hit our targets.'
- The school is moving in the same direction.
- If the headteacher reveals their school targets it becomes easier for us to shape our classroom targets.
- There is a value in formalising the process, ensuring it happens and having resources/training to support objectives.
- Performance management plugs the gaps.
- Classroom observation has been a boost to morale.
- People are more focussed and reflective and there is more joined up thinking at school level now.

When they were asked what was still problematic, teachers said:

- The process is still too cosy between some team leaders and teachers.
- There are timetable problems – people leaving their classes to conduct meetings and observations.
- It is difficult getting quality supply cover.
- There are delays in the cycle due to illness, maternity leaves, Ofsted.
- There is still significant paper work; which no one will see because the process is largely confidential, between the teacher and team leader.
- It is difficult ensuring equity in meeting staff development aspirations.
- Not everyone will get additional financial incentives.
- If performance management is handled badly staff may feel they are doing a less than adequate job.

Even though this research relates to teacher performance management in England, you can learn from its findings to ensure your appraisal/review meeting is as effective as it can be.

THE EVIDENCE BASE

Garratt (1990: 45) states coaches engage in 'monitoring but not intervening in the reality – the eyes on hands off approach'. You need to know your team and their work without seeking to control too tightly or interfere; this is no easy task.

For your performance management and school improvement processes to be effective you will need to hold the gathering and analysis of data, information and work/task observation as key. Reflection on such objective data forms the basis of good management information which in turn forms the basis of knowledge relating to an organisation and the individuals within it. Quality data, information and knowledge underpin and inform the appraisal interview which in turn informs professional development, coaching and support of individuals and teams. The cycle of planning, monitoring and review informs the development plan and various action plans; this is the basis of an integrated performance management process.

> Through these integrally linked processes of observation and analysis, we come to see clearly the discrepancies, incongruities, and failure to reach intentions. The problem begins to emerge more clearly, and we begin to see our own role in the problem more clearly. (Osterman and Kottkamp, 1994)

To have an effective performance management and improvement process you may also need to gather what some may refer to as 'softer' data and information relating to the informal systems and relationships; what some refer to as the shadow side of the organisation.

> Managing the informal systems is not usually part of a manager's job description. But perhaps it should be, because the arrangements conducted under the informal system can either enhance or limit the productivity of the organization ... Heightened awareness, what we might call a working psychology of people, is the starting point for managing all forms of the shadow side of individuals. (Egan, 2002: 59)

Quite simply, the effective use of hard and soft but valid data motivates staff if used properly as part of a structured professional dialogue designed to help them in their core tasks. The process needs to be professional, logical, intelligent, sustainable, unbureaucratic and integrated with the other processes of the organisation.

Experienced colleagues are unlikely to be motivated to change unless you move away from opinion and towards offering evidence that identifies behaviours and outcome information that is accepted by the appraisee. If 'a journey of a thousand miles begins with a single step', then it seems logical and professional to ensure that we must first know where we are, that the first step is taken in the right direction, that we have an appropriate destination in mind, that we know where we are when we arrive and that we can offer the evidence to prove it!

PERFORMANCE MANAGEMENT AND PROFESSIONAL DEVELOPMENT

If you use the performance management process to gather quality management information you will see the process is not separate or in addition to the core function of an organisation, its teams and individuals, but a flexible yet systematic professional process that enables and supports continuous improvement through professional development. The organisational learning that takes place as a result of performance management should be clear with a direct linkage between appraisal/review, professional development, action plans and the development/improvement plan; one informs the other in a cycle of growth and development.

You will have already accepted that 'learning does not occur in any enduring fashion unless it is sparked by the learner's own ardent interest and curiosity – which in turn means that learners need to see where they want to go and to assess where they are' (Senge, 1994). In this process the professional development of staff is not a series of events taking place off site, but clearly identified strategies owned by the appraisee and linked to their needs and aspirations. Much of this development may take the form of in-house coaching and support which often proves to be very cost effective if done well.

If undertaken properly, and as a result of review and reflection, this integrated approach to coaching and training which is tailored to the needs of the organisation, teams and the individual can lead to deep and systemic change that goes well beyond the quick fix of some off-site courses.

> The fix it model is a form of single loop learning: A solution is developed to correct the presenting problem, but the underlying causes of the problem are neither recognized nor addressed. Single loop learning is largely ineffective in contributing to long term solutions to problems because the underlying assumptions that reinforce the ineffective behaviours are never examined. Double loop learning, on the other hand, holds the potential for real change because it examines these underlying assumptions, or theories-in-use, as part of the problem solving process. (Osterman and Kottkamp, 1994)

Professional development becomes very focussed and specific to the needs of individuals and teams so they can function effectively, with motivation, in order to help their organisation serve its clients.

KAIZEN: KEEPING IT SHARP

Kaizen is the Japanese term for 'continuous improvement by small steps'; if you like, it is evolution not revolution. 'School leaders who take seriously their instructional role are concerned to promote and develop their schools as learning systems or professional learning communities' (Gold et al., 2003).

SBM Toolkit – MSI: 6

Once the performance management system is in place, and proving effective, you need to ensure that it is kept 'sharp' by regular review and improvement. To keep the process sharp and effective, ask your team what they think of the process at least annually. You may ask, 'what went well?' (WWW) and let staff comment that it could be 'even better if' (EBI) we did this or that as an improvement (EBI).

This need not be a complex task, it may not even involve a staff meeting to formally review the process. In a mature organisation you could put a flip chart sheet in a prominent place in the office and divide it into two vertical columns, one headed with WWW and the other with EBI.

CASE STUDY

So now Liz meets with Sally and Tony to review their targets and their professional development annually. She attempts to align the work of her team with that of the rest of the organisation. She meets with them mid-year to review progress and hear about any issues they have. Now she is growing into the role of coach for her team, but this does not come easily to Liz as she has been very hands on and personally efficient for many years.

As school business manager she now has so many tasks to manage she can no longer undertake them all in person, so the process of delegation and coaching is being developed. This is not an easy process for somebody who is relatively new to the coaching aspect of performance management and leadership, but she is finding it rewarding and effective.

Once your staff get used to this kaizen process it can be used by you to review all sorts of processes. In this way your performance management process will continue to be linked to school improvement and valued by those involved as practical, sustainable and relevant.

CONCLUSION

Any organisation in any context, nation or continent will be exposed to change. Change is one of the constants in life and unless our organisations and people can constantly adapt and improve these organisations will not thrive or even survive; we must accept this.

To hold the concept of school/organisational improvement at the heart of leadership is essential. Performance management is simply a superb mechanism that helps us translate aspirations, plans and human desires into reality. This is not difficult if approached with optimism and an open heart. With these concepts, capacities and processes at hand we can transform our own organisations from within.

No longer will there be the need to act as a functionary of imposed external/ political change; we will be involved in evolutionary and internal change and not revolutionary change imposed by external pressure. When business managers and other school leaders think in this way they will be leaders of hearts and minds and leaders of their communities: professional people worthy of autonomy and respect.

REFERENCES

Argyris, C. (1978) 'A Leadership Dilemma: Skilled incompetence', in C. Argyris and D. Schon (eds), *Organisational Learning: A Theory of Action Perspective*. London: Addison Wesley.

Argyris, C. and Schon, D. (1974) *Theory in Practice: Increasing Professional Effectiveness*. San Francisco, CA: Jossey-Bass.

Beare, H. (2001) *Creating the Future School*. London: RoutledgeFalmer.

Boyatzis, R. (1998) 'Self-Directed Change and Learning as a Necessary Meta-Competency for Success and Effectiveness in the Twenty-first Century,' in R. Sims and J. Veres (eds), *Keys to Employee Success in Coming Decades*. Westport, CN: Quorum.

Caldwell, B. and Spinks, J. (1992) *Leading the Self Managing School*. London: Falmer.

Cockman, P., Evans, B. and Reynolds, P. (1999) *Consulting for Real People*. New York: McGraw Hill.

Covey, S. (1989) *The Seven Habits of Highly Effective People*. London: Simon & Schuster.

Davies, B. and Ellison, L. (1999) *Strategic Direction and Development of the School*. London: Routledge.

Egan, G. (2002) *The Skilled Helper, a Problem-Management and Opportunity-Development Approach to Helping*. (7th edn). Brooks/cole: Thomas Learning.

Evans, R. (1998) *The Human Side of School Change*. San Francisco, CA: Jossey-Bass.

Fullan, M. (1993) *Change Forces: Probing the Depths of Educational Change*. London: Falmer.

Fullan, M. (2001) *Leading in a Culture of Change*. San Francisco, CA: Jossey-Bass.

Garratt, B. (1990) *Creating a Learning Organisation*. London: Director Books/ Fitzwilliam Publishing.

Gold, A., Evans, J., Early, P., Halpin, D. and Collarbone, P. (2003) *Principled Principals?* London: Sage.

Goleman, D. (1998) *Working With Emotional Intelligence*. London: Bloomsbury.

Goleman, D. (2003) *Destructive Emotions and How We Can Overcome Them*. London: Bloomsbury.

Hammer, M. and Champy, J. (1994) *Re-engineering the Corporation*. London: Brealey.

Hargreaves, D. (1991) *The Empowered School: The management and practice of development planning*. London: Cassell.

HayMcBer/TTA (1998) *Leadership Programme for Serving Headteachers*. London: TTA.

Morgan, G. (1998) *Images of Organizations*. London: Sage.

Nonaka, I. and Takeuchi, H. (1995) *The Knowledge Creating Company: How Japaneses companies create the dynamic of innovation*. New York: Oxford University Press.

Ofsted (1995) *Framework for the Inspection of Nursery, Primary, Middle, Secondary and Special Schools*. London: HMSO.

Osterman, K. and Kottkamp, R. (1994) 'Rethinking Professional Development', in N. Bennett, R. Glatter and R. Levacic (eds), *Improving Educational Management through Research and Consultancy*. London: Paul Chapman Publishing/Open University.

Parkin, M. (2001) *Coaching and Storytelling*. London: Kogan Page.

Reading, M. (2003) Still on the Cycle, *Management in Education,* 16, (5).

Rowan, J. and Taylor, P. (2002) 'Leading the Autonomous School', in J. Heywood and P. Taylor (eds), *School Autonomy.* European Forum on Educational Administration, Bulletin 2.

Schein, E. H. (1984) Coming to a new awareness of organisational culture, *Sloan Management Review.*

Schein, E. H. (1985) *Organizational Culture and Leadership.* San Francisco, CA: Jossey-Bass.

Senge, P. (1994) *The Fifth Discipline Field book.* London: Brealey.

Senge, P., Cambron-McCabe, N. H., Lucas, T., Smith, B., Dutton, J. and Kleiner, A. (2000) *Schools That Learn.* London: Brealey.

Stoll, L. and Fink, D. (1996) *Changing Our Schools. Linking School Effectiveness and School Improvement.* Buckingham: Open University Press.

Wellins, R., Byham, W. and Wilson, J. (1991) *Empowered Teams.* San Francisco, CA: Jossey-Bass.

10

Change Management

Joy Coulbeck

The final chapter in this section draws together and builds on what has gone before. In the previous chapters the need for change and growth has been explored but it is in this chapter that how and why change can be managed are addressed. It is predicated on the view that significant change in schools is not easy, and requires skilful and patient managers who understand the stages through which the change events need to move.

INTRODUCTION

> If anything is certain, it is that change is certain. The world we are planning for today will not exist in this form tomorrow. Philip Crosby, 1999

'We are changemakers!' was the prime minister's declaration at the UK Labour Party's conference in 2005, but nobody in the English education sector was surprised. After two decades of intense educational reform and innovation the pace and complexity of change has not slackened. Managing rapid change has become a familiar challenge for schools and colleges across the country as they seek to be ever more successful in this highly-pressured and global society. Evidence internationally (Hargreaves and Fink, 2001; Fullan, 2004) indicates this is a widespread factor to be faced by twenty first century schools, creating pressure on school leadership to manage change processes well.

However, it is the nature of these pressures and reforms to be ambiguous and out of step with one another, competing for schools' precious resources: time, money and the greatest resource of all – human effort. Pressure is felt both by those who deliver the education for pupils and by those who administer the systems to support teaching and learning. The school business manager (SBM) experiences the impact of this no less than any other member of the school community; indeed, the SBM is at the hub – a crucial focal point in the implementation and management of change – where systems meet, interact, connect or at times collide.

This chapter seeks to explore some ideas about the theory of change management and to identify key factors in successfully accomplishing change in schools, particularly from the SBM's point of view – for there is no doubt about the impact that an effective school business manager has upon a school. If change is to happen, it can succeed or fail at many points. The SBM is in a unique position to exert leadership skills to ensure that implementation is smooth and that the systems to deliver the required outcomes are securely in place. They achieve this through understanding the change management process, the systems that are involved and through effective management of people.

The context of educational change will serve to set the scene within which the profession of school business manager is quickly forming. Understanding the environment and culture of schools fuels good leadership decisions and the SBM is well placed to reflect on the complex nature of twenty first century schools and their ever-changing activities.

THE CONTEXT AND CHALLENGE OF EDUCATIONAL CHANGE

A long history of reform and innovation over the last quarter of a century has resulted in what commentators call 'innovation overload'. This is particularly so for England, although perhaps less so for Scotland, Wales and Northern Ireland where regional legislation has, for example, abolished the publication of league tables for certain age groups and significantly reduced some element of competition. In North America, Fullan (2001) comments that:

> the biggest problem facing schools is fragmentation and overload. It is worse for schools than for business firms. Both are facing turbulent uncertain environments but only schools are suffering the additional burden of having a torrent of unwanted, uncoordinated policies raining down on them from hierarchical bureaucracies. (Fullan, 2001: 23)

Change is perhaps most frequently seen as being imposed directly by the government or indirectly through local authorities (LAs) and that schools are seen as long-suffering under this onslaught. The frequency of these directives and requirements is at times rapid, leading to the notion of the 'torrent' mentioned above. How well school leaders can respond effectively to new legislation or new LA policies will determine the overall success of a school. This inevitably means revising or installing new systems, policies, processes or practice. This means change.

In educational settings, though, change is not always easily understood – meanings are ambiguous, the implications of change unclear. Here lies one of the fundamental truths about all management of change in organisations: that only by effective management of people through change can the outcome be achieved. People in general distrust change and are often resistant to it, especially if they do not understand the reasoning behind such change. Changes imposed from outside the school are very often greeted with antipathy for this reason. The staffroom comment 'Why change? We've always done it this way' is evidence of this recognisable viewpoint and provides us with a good example of the type of challenge facing the manager who is trying to change the attitudes, perceptions and points of view of people at the point of change.

This is not the whole picture, however. Change is not always externally driven, although at times it may seem so. Schools and colleges are seeking to improve all the time. They have no choice given the demands of inspection and the glare of public accountability, but as the world changes so schools seek to do also in order to provide the most up-to-date education for their pupils. New ways of teaching and learning, new technologies, new approaches to the curriculum are being devised as much by schools, in many cases, as by external agencies. Schools are now experiencing more opportunities for school-based innovation than they have had since the 1960s and 70s.

Nowhere is this more evident than in the School Business Manager programme, which in England has seen a phenomenal rise in the leadership activity of school business managers, making a huge difference to their schools through innovative and entrepreneurial projects, by securing funding or saving vital resources (see the website at: www.ncsl.org.uk), and in working alongside teachers to achieve projects to improve the experience of children in schools. Kirstie Croote's personal evidence below of studying change management while on the DSBM programme provides a good example of how the SBM is uniquely positioned to lead well in implementing change.

CASE STUDY

The Change Management module allowed me to consider how to effectively manage a change process. The area I chose for my project was the implementation of performance management (PM) for support staff. This is a key area for schools and making such a change needs to be planned and implemented with great care. Being responsible for three members of staff whose reaction to PM was varied, showed that as a manager I had to encourage, listen and support the team.

I have learnt to consider what makes a successful team and how different values can contribute. The effects of change can be made a better experience for people by keeping them fully informed, by making sure that the proposed changes are communicated as good for all concerned and beneficial to the school and that ideas are welcomed and people's opinions are valued in decision making. Guiding and supporting team members throughout a change process are key to its success.

I have recognised the need for change to enable schools to improve and accept external changes and link these with internal developments. External changes are very much outside the control of a school, however, the way in which these are managed are paramount to their success. Internal changes should be managed and planned with care, recognising the impact on individuals whilst considering views and opinions.

As a school business manager, it became evident that I play a vital role in any change process. Being able to take on many different roles in a team became apparent and I feel that my ability to communicate with colleagues will aid all new developments. A successful SBM would need to be able to take on the role of administrator, manager or leader in many aspects of their work.

The Change Management module has further enhanced my professional development and I am now confident and keen to oversee future changes. Studying how people react to change has further developed my listening and communication skills.

Kirstie has highlighted the key points of this chapter: the importance of the SBM's role and of handling people well, and understanding the nature of the changes that face a school whether they are generated from within or imposed from outside.

THE FUTURE DEMANDS A NEW APPROACH

However constant a school's circumstances would seem to be, it would be unwise to be lulled into a false sense of security. Reputation is crucial when it comes to attracting new pupils and in the twenty first century this depends not just on improving results, but on the holistic provision for the child as outlined, for example, by the *Every Child Matters: Change for Children* agenda (DfES, 2006). This is a new approach in the UK to ensure the well-being of children and young people from birth to age 19 where the government's aim is for every child whatever their background or their circumstances to have the support they need – to be healthy, stay safe, enjoy and achieve, make a positive contribution, achieve economic well being:

> This means that the organisations involved with providing services to children – from hospitals and schools, to police and voluntary groups – will be teaming up in new

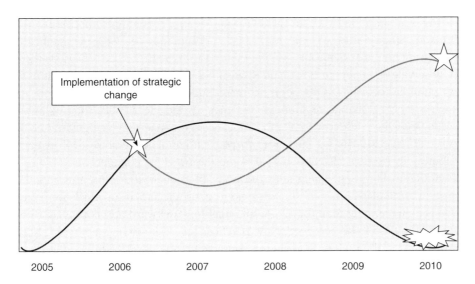

Figure 10.1 Sigmoid Curve: The choice for change for School A (Source: Handy, 1999)

ways, sharing information and working together, to protect children and young people from harm and help them achieve what they want in life.

The change factor in this case has therefore now multiplied, as schools look towards radically different ways of working and embrace new partners while dissolving traditional boundaries. With falling rolls being the norm in many areas of Europe, each school needs to reappraise its capacity, its future and its ability to adapt. Failure to do so leads to decline. This is a classic situation, repeated in all aspects of human experience – the fact that everything has a natural life span.

Consider School A with a new headteacher, aiming and planning to be the best. The initial growth of the organisation is strong, but reaches a levelling-out at its peak. Having improved and improved, having been inspected and commended as achieving at the very highest level, where else is there for the school to go? Staff will comment 'This is the way we do things to get these results.' But few schools, no matter how highly achieving, can maintain their peak position without change. What if the headteacher, or other key personnel, were to leave? Catastrophic downturns have been known. This is exemplified by Figure 10.1 above, which demonstrates how an organisation can survive by renewing itself, re-inventing its purpose or product, creating some new feature which challenges the downward trend.

This is a simplified view to make a point. Without looking to the future and thinking strategically schools may miss the moment to make a significant change. When, say, School B in competition locally with School A markets their new service or facility, it is too late to wish that School A had thought of it first. As numbers on roll (NOR) begin to drop, suddenly the scale of the price of such a lack of change awareness becomes all too clear. With their skills of strategic analysis added to a depth of knowledge concerning budget and NOR forecasts, the SBM has a clear role to play at senior leadership level in contributing to strategic discussions, assessing the need for change.

Notice in Figure 10.1 that after the point of change, the initial few months are not particularly smooth. It takes time to get back into an upward curve and this is a challenging time for all. People may feel awkward and confused. New ideas take time to be accepted. New practices take time to be embedded. New systems have their teething problems. But eventually, effort and expenditure in the new direction pay off, and the decline is averted. To even the most impartial observer it is clear to see in which organisation it would be preferable to be in the year 2010!

SBM Toolkit – CM:1

Whether externally imposed or internally driven, it is suggested that managing change in educational organisations boils down to the same basic principles:

- Ensure that you and your staff understand the change being proposed.
- Immediately seek to appraise the impact on the systems involved, especially if these are accredited (ISO 9000 (International Standard Organization), IiP (Investors in People), and so on) and impact on the people affected.
- Think and plan strategically. What will this mean for the school? Let your staff know this.
- Select and implement effective change management strategies.
- Understand the dynamics and lessons of change – particularly allowing for the unexpected.

This is similar to the 'Seven Ss' approach also known as the McKinsey Model designed by Peters and WaterMan (1982). http://www.themanager.org/models/7s%20Model.htm

- Strategy: key tasks and who will perform them.
- Structure: the most effective way to divide up the work involved.
- System: monitoring, among other aspects.

- Staff: recruitment (if applicable), motivation, morale.
- Skills: develop people's competencies to complete the work successfully.
- Style: how to lead and how to delegate in the best way.
- Shared Values: common beliefs that will help a team to reach its goals.

This advice enables us to uncover key elements of effective change management but does not necessarily illustrate the whole picture. Change is highly complex and unpredictable, so before the manager approaches this with assumptions about logic and rational approaches, there is a need to stop and consider what change really means.

Michael Fullan (1993) is a guru on change management and widely recognised as the world's leading expert. Here he offers his Eight Basic Lessons of the New Paradigm of Change, which offer insight into the pitfalls and perversity of change, interpreted as follows:

Lesson 1 – You can't force change: The more complex the change, the less you can force it. Educational change involves people taking on new beliefs, skills and understanding, which takes time.

Lesson 2 – Change is a journey, not a blueprint: Change is non-linear, loaded with uncertainty and can be unpredictable.

Lesson 3 – Problems are our friends: Problems are inevitable, but we can't learn or be successful without them. The way problems are handled is vital to the success or failure of the change.

Lesson 4 – Vision and strategic planning come later: Premature visions and too-rigid planning can be counter productive.

Lesson 5 – Individualism and collectivism must have equal power: Both individual issues and teamwork count.

Lesson 6 – Neither centralisation nor decentralisation works: 'Change flourishes in a sandwich; when there is census above and pressure below, things happen'. This would be the outcome of effective distributed leadership.

Lesson 7 – Connection with the wide environment is critical: The best organisations learn externally as well as internally.

Lesson 8 – Every person is a change agent: 'Change is too important to leave to the experts'. (pp. 21–21)

Perhaps, the most powerful of these lessons is that change must be owned by the people involved, or it will not work very well.

UNDERSTANDING ORGANISATIONS

Although the human race is programmed to face up to changing circumstances and to adapt in order to survive, it has to be said that managing change is, in fact, far from being a simple process. Organisations are complex forms of society and not all respond well to change. Some organisations are said to be stuck, in fact, hardly able to modify a simple process, whereas others are dynamic, forward looking and definitely on the move. School business managers are often most aware of what category of organisation applies to their schools.

The school or college is an organisation like any other. Handy (1999) paints a clear picture about them, explaining why the subject of change is a difficult one for many:

> Organisations are not machines, even though some of those running them would dearly like them to be so. They are communities of people, and therefore behave just like other communities. They compete amongst themselves for power and resources, there are differences of opinion and of values, conflicts of priorities and of goals. There are those who want to change things and those who would willingly settle for a quiet life. There are pressure groups … clashes of personalities and bonds of alliance … *The challenge for the manager is to harness the energy and thrust of the differences so that the organisation does not disintegrate but develops.* (Handy, 1999: 201. Original emphasis)

Clearly the possibility of disintegration is one to be avoided! The methods to achieve what Handy recommends here must be identified and grasped if the SBM, along with other school leaders, is to manage effective change. But exactly how the energy and thrust of people's differences can be harnessed cannot depend on the action of the single leader. The way an organisation works, lives, breathes even (for it is organic in nature) will help or hinder such harnessing. Organisations today depend upon effective distributed leadership so that there is shared ownership of the strategy that needs to be put in place and with it the effective management of people. They also depend on the effective management of systems. The school business manager has a key leadership role in both aspects of this new vision for schools.

For although organisations are not machines, there are still machine-like qualities to them. A smoothly running organisation can be said to be like a well-oiled machine. Quite apart from fully functioning employees, what lies behind this picture is the idea of systems. Schools, like engines, have component parts and systems that work in conjunction with one another. As has been mentioned in the previous chapter, the work of Senge (1990) is helpful here.

It has been suggested that school business managers generally understand and manage systems far better than academic staff, since the effective handling of systems comes with the territory. But even systems have personalities – stubborn, worn out, cantankerous, problematic – and they are often taken for granted until something goes wrong. What is important here is to separate systems from people. As we have seen, managing change pushes the boundaries of people's familiar working practices often causing conflict. The SBM can reduce the blame culture when problems occur by keeping a clear picture of where systems may be at fault and where human error is to blame.

The following words of warning show how attached people tend to be to well-worn systems and just how difficult changing them can be:

> There is nothing more difficult to plan, more doubtful of success, nor more danger-ous to manage than the creation of a new system. For the initiator has the enmity of all who would profit by the preservation of the old system and merely lukewarm defenders in those who would gain by the new one. (Machiavelli, 1513)

This also shows that the problem is not new!

THE RELATIONSHIP BETWEEN CULTURE AND CHANGE

The culture of a school is often explained in terms of what people repeatedly say and do and this has a significant effect upon how change is managed. Culture is said to be 'the way we do things around here' so that if changes are announced, for example, but not followed through then people may tend not to take them seriously. If there is a divisive culture, where different groups of people concentrate on furthering their own interests, then there will be an overall lack of cooperation within a school.

In the Strategic Management module (DSBM) much has been written about the importance of vision. So if a school's vision is published in the prospectus, pinned on the wall but never discussed openly within the school community, then the vision may not be embedded in reality and people will not feel as if it is anything to do with them. Therefore the vision will not be evident in the school culture, inevitably hindering the progress of a school towards the real-isation of its aims.

SBM Toolkit – CM:2

Ask support staff to undertake a 'vision audit' for a week. Ask them to note incidents/events/stories which illustrate or deny the vision, *in their view*. This is a good 'snapshot' of how the school 'lives' its vision.

Throughout the School Business Manager Development programme there is the theme of the rising profession of SBM. School culture can accelerate this process or bring it to a halt depending on the circumstances. Since SBMs have a pivotal role within a school community it is important to address this issue.

Angela's story below demonstrates clearly what potential there is in the role and she has also identified what she feels are essential factors necessary to be able to manage change well. Her keen observation also sheds light on the impact that cultural differences can have on the SBM.

THE IMPORTANCE OF CLARITY, CULTURE AND CHANGE

Angela Sorby is a DSBM candidate in the north west of England and works in the secondary sector.

What is important to a School Business Manager is getting rid of the grey area not only when managing change but in the SBM's role in general, for what is needed is clarity. In the SBM's role you need something very specific – clear guidelines, strong support and guidance from school leaders so that the SBM knows exactly what she is empowered to do. It is no good making decisions, recommending courses of action only to find that it is beyond the remit of the SBM's role to go that far.

Therefore I feel that there needs to be clear guidelines as to the level of authority that an SBM has, so that in managing change she knows exactly where her input is required and does not find herself coming up against a brick wall! A good relationship with both the governing body and the senior leadership team of the school is essential so that communication facilitates clear understanding.

The rise of the SBM involves empowerment to fulfil potential of this role, which is still an unknown quantity for some and even 'frowned upon' in some schools. This is where the culture of a school plays such a big part where my role is concerned. Teachers may look at the SBM in surprise when she is being involved in 'their domain' for the first time, as if to say, 'Why are you involved?'

It is a continuing problem that school culture still admits to the notion of *non-teaching staff*. I find that insulting for I am not 'non' anything. It's true that I am not a teacher and don't stand up in front of classes, but I am fully informed about the 14–19 agenda, have attended all the conferences and know what a contribution I can make to the progress the school is making towards implementing the changes. I can see clearly just how much teachers need an empowered SBM to be involved in some cases since they themselves are so focused on teaching and learning and totally absorbed in what they have to do.

When I have to implement a change I know that some people may be surprised at my involvement, and that there may be some resistance. It is so important that I get the support that I need from the senior leadership team. People need to know how I am involved right from the start – teachers need to have clear communication that I am involved in managing a change and that I need their support and cooperation. I then concentrate on clarity and on getting the direction and the strategy right. After that I operate an open door policy, so that anyone with questions or queries can come to discuss them.

What Angela is making a case for is central to this chapter – that without clarity roles are unclear, without consistency systems function below the optimum and without good communication the culture that can help or hinder is unlikely to be altered.

UNDERSTANDING CHANGE IN EDUCATIONAL ORGANISATIONS

In order to understand the key factors in managing change, we need to look at the theory of effective schools, as these organisations have clearly mastered change processes to get where they are. Research undertaken by Stoll and Fink (1996) concluded that there were some common features regularly seen in effective schools:

- shared goals;
- responsibility for success;
- collegiality;
- continuous improvement;
- lifelong learning;
- risk taking;
- support;
- mutual respect;
- openness;
- celebration and humour. (Stoll and Fink, 1996 pp. 92–8)

These are features that apply across the whole-school community, that create the fundamental culture which enables learning and facilitates effective change. Shared goals indicate clarity of vision and strategic direction which need to be communicated openly within a collegial atmosphere. Angela's views above indicate the impact of how this operates on someone like herself when coping with a 'grey area'. The idea of continuous improvement is covered in Chapter 9 but should be mentioned here, since change is not worth undertaking if it does not improve the experience of children and students in a school.

We have the term 'lifelong learning' and we shall demonstrate later that the idea of everybody being a learner, including those at the very top, enhances change management on a wide scale because it gives people permission to take risks, to undertake new ideas and, occasionally, to make mistakes. It is not the making of the mistake that is important here, it is what happens when people make a mistake that matters. In a learning organisation mistakes are treated as learning opportunities! If people feel that it is too dangerous to take risks then growth will ultimately be stunted.

The last four items on Stoll and Fink's list centre on those features of a healthy organisation that enable people to be at ease – for if they make a mistake there is support, if they need to know something there is openness, they understand their role and they are respected as they respect others in their roles, and not least there is celebration and humour – all of which make for an organisation ready to take on tough challenges and important changes.

We wanted to obtain detailed information of how an SBM manages change in practice and the following story provides evidence across many fronts – the rising profile of the SBM, the pace of change and how even small alterations can have a significant effect on a school. Margaret's account records an interview with the researcher for this chapter.

The experience of managing change – a school business manager's view

Margaret Beaumont is a DSBM candidate in the north west of England and works in the secondary sector.

What has the pace of change been like for you in your job?

The pace of change has been quite rapid at my school, as we are in between headteachers at the moment and do not expect to be appointing one for a further twelve months. During this period the acting head has put me on the senior leadership team (SLT) and that has made a big difference to my role as school business manager. We are coping with many initiatives right now – the Teaching and Learning Review (TLR) Remodelling the Workforce, Extended Schools, Specialist Sports College status (and subsequent redesignation), raising achievement at Key Stage 4, Self-Evaluation for Ofsted and so on.

Now that I am on the SLT I feel that people recognise my worth – especially through the workforce remodelling strategy – teachers realise that they are not expected to perform administrative tasks and for the most part they value someone who can get things done on their behalf. They also appreciate that somebody is needed to manage the growing numbers of support staff.

Is that the term that is usually used – support staff? Do teachers sometimes refer to 'non-teaching staff'?

Sometimes they do, but when we were bidding to have Sports College status we came across AOTTs – Adults Other Than Teachers, and we use that a lot.

How do you feel about being on the SLT now? Have you been able to manage change more effectively?

CASE STUDY

CASE STUDY (CONTINUED)

I feel more empowered to manage change, yes, definitely. For instance I have just introduced a Performance Management (PM) scheme for support staff. Previously there had not been anything in place for them. The SLT (with me included) decided on the line of management and I am implementing the policy whereby PM is cascaded down. I delivered the process to three leaders who then delivered it to their own teams. What I learnt from this process was that there were two types of workers:
1) those who see their job as a career and want to do better, and who are keen to learn and improve in order to develop their career, and
2) those who see their job as a job and not a career at all and are therefore much less interested in career development and less motivated to change.

Have you a specific example of managing change?

Yes I have. As a result of the new PM process I ascertained that the site supervisor had a problem that prevented him from performing his role as he wanted to, and the problem was that teachers very often failed to communicate their needs for his work at a time or in a way that allowed him to see that the required jobs were done. Teachers would either forget to ask him for his help or would ask him at an inopportune time, when he was unable to attend to the request. Together we devised a form that will now be used for all requests regarding facilities, with room for the site supervisor to comment on the actions required.

I feel a real sense of achievement here, for although the change is only a small one, it makes the life of the site supervisor so much better and will have a knock-on effect on the teaching and learning activities in the school. For instance the next event will be an exam, and exam tables will need to be in place at the right time – tying up the loopholes in the request procedure will mean that teachers are not scurrying round trying to get them put out at the last minute. Everyone will benefit.

I firmly believe that all aspects of school life have an effect on teaching and learning and therefore all staff contribute to the raising of standards. We are all important cogs in the wheel of education.

Margaret's account is good evidence of the two aspects we have been considering – the role that systems have to play and how people can be managed. Margaret's evidence shows that systems can resolve the blame culture relatively easily and that change, well handled, raises self-esteem and the sense of achievement.

PEOPLE AND CHANGE

The human spirit does not adapt immediately to change. Mikhail Gorbachev

Change by definition means learning something new or different, and one model that helps us understand this process is called the Conscious Competence model, which has four stages:

1 Unconscious incompetence: 'I don't know that I don't know'.
2 Conscious incompetence: 'I know I don't know and I'm going to do something about it'.
3 Conscious competence: 'Now I know what to do'.
4 Unconscious competence: 'I naturally accomplish what I have to do without thinking about it'.

Stage 2 indicates the pain barrier element of human response to change: going into unfamiliar territory or leaving familiar, well-worn practice behind: 'out of the comfort zone'. Supporting people as they navigate through this territory is vital, as without support, reinforcement and encouragement some people are likely to flounder instead of flourish. If everyone engages in the learning culture, individual experiences of success and failure can be easily absorbed. Einstein was known to have said 'The more I learn, the more I realise I don't know', which suggests a constant loop of learning. Some schools are striving to become learning organisations, where leaders uphold learning as valuable to everybody and school is a place where learning is an activity that occurs at every level and in every sector.

How do people react towards change? Blanchard (1992) suggests that there are seven Dynamics of Change:

1 People will feel awkward, ill-at-ease and self-conscious.
2 People initially focus on what they have to give up.
3 People will feel alone even if everyone else is going through the same change.
4 People can handle only so much change.
5 People are at different levels of readiness for change.
6 People will be concerned that they don't have enough resources.
7 If you take the pressure off, people will revert to their old behaviour.

Let's look at these factors in more detail:

1 *People will feel awkward, ill-at-ease and self-conscious.* In all types of change processes there are certain patterns of response that occur again and again. It is important that the SBM understands some of these patterns, since they are normal occurrences. Understanding them enables the SBM to avoid over-reacting to the way people behave, people who, at times, seem to be behaving in uncharacteristic ways.

2 *People initially focus on what they have to give up.* People often find change threatening precisely because of this factor. They feel awkward or

uncomfortable as they get to grips with the new regime or ways of working. People do not want to be seen to be incompetent, therefore it is an uncomfortable place to be. Hence they would prefer not to have to give up what they used to do well.

3 *People will feel alone even if everyone else is going through the same change.* This feeling of isolation is very common, as everyone sees things from their own point of view, and under pressure tends to focus on their own experience. People feel that their situation is unique, requiring special understanding. It is important that the SBM shows empathy and understanding for those in this situation, while remaining proactive and focussed on the overall goal. Try to be emotionally intelligent and patient as you guide people through the pain barrier.

4 *People can handle only so much change.* It must be remembered that people who have to go through too much change within too short a time may become stressed leading to performance being impaired. If possible it is wise to avoid multiple changes happening simultaneously, or in quick succession. If you know that you are going to introduce changes (that are under your control), it may be a good idea to address how people are feeling right from the outset.

5 *People are at different levels of readiness for change.* Some people thrive on new ideas and changes in practice because of the excitement that this represents for them. Many others don't relish the prospect of change as we have seen, because they view it as threatening to them. Change can be very divisive in this way and even long-established working teams can split over this issue. In time those who resist initially will adapt and change, usually more quickly under the encouragement of those who readily embrace the change. Keeping channels of communication open will enable this process to be effective.

6 *People will be concerned that they don't have enough resources.* Change does consume resources, and where people are concerned this involves not just their time but also what Handy terms 'e factors' such as energy, effort and enthusiasm. People need time in order to learn, and without quality time, normal work may be impaired. It is important for an SBM to realise that this may occur, and to offer practical support if possible.

7 *If you take the pressure off, people will revert to their old behaviour.* If people suspect that the change event is weak, badly administered and not monitored regularly then they are very likely to revert to their old ways of doing things either openly or covertly. It is a function of leadership to keep people focussed on the new course.

Since managing change involves managing people, it is worth considering one view of the way in which people may experience change and the stages they may encounter as they pass out of their comfort zone into a zone of discomfort, ambiguity and what some many view as just plain threatening. The following figure is intended to shed light on specific phases of reaction.

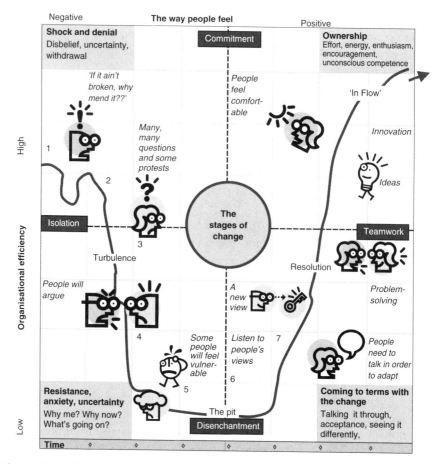

Figure 10.2 The stages of change (Coulbeck) adapted from the People's Network Change Management Toolkit
www.mla.gov.uk.website/programmes/peoples_network/advisory_groups/change/

By integrating Blanchard's stages into this model we can see that there is still a long way to go by Stage 7. We have only just turned the corner and if we get Stage 7 wrong then people will, as he says, revert to their old practices and behaviour. The key question is, if we accept this model as one that can help us understand how we handle people through the stages of change, *how* do we move people out of the negative into the positive, if that is what we are facing?

The key to this process is language and communication. It involves the information that is presented, how it is presented, when it is presented and to whom. How people speak to one another, whether anyone listens and what the outcomes are of consultation and discussion all determine whether people can be facilitated through the change stages. Sometimes implementing change can fall at the first hurdle, simply by getting the announcement wrong, or not giving people the right time and space to consider the news.

Managing people through change requires different leadership approaches at different times as described in Fig 10.3 below, all of which have different approaches to communication. There are occasions on which to be forceful and directing, there are other times when it is necessary to coach, demonstrate and be supportive, until ultimately the leader can delegate the system and its operation to the person in charge. It is worth noticing that the curve of leadership support and intervention is the exact opposite to that of people's experience in Fig 10.2, so that high intervention and support are required when people are going through the most challenging and unsettling phase of change.

The school business manager employs these different tactics with new staff members, for example, or those members undertaking a new system. Being aware of the fact that it is a good idea to adopt different roles while people are changing is liberating. Some managers remain stuck in the first quadrant, believing that unless they direct people nothing will get done. This is an example of the X-style of management that MacGregor (1960) described, and he went on to illustrate how a manager stuck in this mode ends up distrusting the workforce, believing that they will only work if they are under not only direction but the threat of punishment too.

His theory naturally suggests an alternative – a theory Y of management where the manager pulls people along, encouraging and motivating them, believing all the while that they are interested in their jobs and want to do well. As with most theories it soon becomes clear, as in Fig 10.3, that a blend of approaches is the most successful for the school business manager, the main point being that they must be acutely aware of what style they are employing and why!

However, nothing is ever quite as simple as this illustration might suggest although the strategy it portrays is certainly an important one. Remember that Fullan said that change was non-linear? This means that change operates on multi-levels, working at different speeds, sometimes going round in loops, sometimes doubling back on itself. Working in partnership with a team that functions well means that the many fronts of the change process can be tackled in a concerted way. It also means that the complexity of change can be shared – with the responsibility shouldered in a purposeful way – in theory. In order to illuminate this process further, Kotter's (1995) work may enable an SBM to put practical steps into place to ensure progress from *difficulty* to *delivery*.

KOTTER'S EIGHT-STAGE PROCESS OF CREATING MAJOR CHANGE

Each stage acknowledges a key principle identified by Kotter (1996) relating to people's response and approach to change, in which people *see, feel* and then *change*. Kotter's eight step change model can be summarised as:

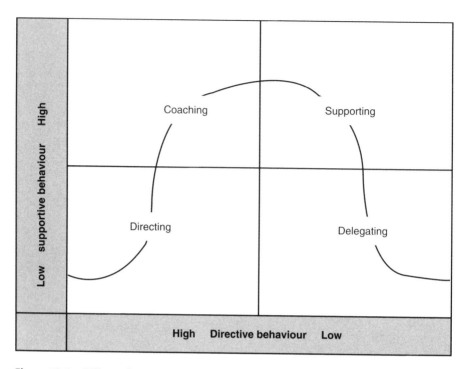

Figure 10.3 Different leadership approaches to the management of people through change. Adapted from Blanchard et al. (1994)

1 *Establish a sense of urgency* Inspire people to move, make objectives real and relevant. Identify and discuss crises, potential crises or major opportunities (Strategic Management analysis tools are helpful at this stage).

2 *Create a good team* Get the right people in place with the right emotional commitment, and the right mix of skills and levels. If this is not a practical proposition focus on putting together a group with enough power to lead the change and – most importantly – get the group to work together like a team.

3 *Develop a vision and strategy* Get the team to establish a simple vision and strategy and focus on emotional and creative aspects necessary to drive service and efficiency. Create a vision to help direct the change effort and develop strategies for achieving that vision.

4 *Communicate the change vision* Involve as many people as possible and communicate the key elements while responding to people's needs. Keep communications simple – make technology work for rather than against you. Use every means possible to communicate the new vision and strategies.

5 *Empower action* Remove obstacles and enable constructive feedback and lots of support from leaders – reward and recognise progress and achievements. Get rid of obstacles. Change systems or structures that undermine

the change vision. This step also recommends encouraging risk taking and non-traditional ideas, activities and actions, but it recognises that this may not be possible in all cases.

6 *Create short-term wins* Set aims that are easy to achieve – in bite-size chunks. Finish current stages before starting new ones. Plan for visible improvements in performance, or 'wins'. Recognise and reward people who made the wins possible.

7 *Don't let up* Foster and encourage determination and persistence, encourage ongoing progress reporting and highlight achieved and future milestones. Consolidate the gains.

8 *Make change stick* Reinforce the value of successful change via recruitment, promotion and new change leaders. Weave change into the culture. Create better performance through the embracing of quality systems and provide a quality client-centred culture, better leadership and more effective management. Identify and celebrate the connections between new behaviours and organisational success.

Finally, Bacal (2005), in summarsing Kotter's work, emphasises how important it is for leaders to anticipate and respond to people's concerns and feelings and that keeping a record of people's reactions will enable managers to identify the kinds of reactions and questions that have come up and, more importantly, how the manager responded.

Remember that the success of any change rests with the ability of the leaders to address both the emotional and practical issues, in that order. (Bacal, 2005, www.work911.ccm)

The school business manager manages change

The following insight is from a primary SBM who feels that studying on both CSBM and DSBM awards has empowered her to implement change.

Tracey Morrison is a DSBM graduate in the north west of England and works in the primary sector.

Being in primary is different from being in secondary as far as the school business manager is concerned. The culture in the primary sector views my role as 'only admin'! But gaining the CSBM and DSBM awards has enabled me to implement new ideas. Recent projects that I have done have been on remodelling the workforce (Change Management) and improving attendance (Managing School Improvement) and both have involved managing change.

It has been very pleasing to see how everything in my project on improving attendance has been put into place and has had an impact on the statistics that the government uses as indicators. These are real results.

People are listening to me now and they can see the difference in me – I feel that the knowledge I have gained on the programme has empowered me to be able to manage change well. For example, having implemented the new staffing structure under the Remodelling of the Workforce policy and appointed new support staff I now have a managerial role with all support staff and they automatically look to me now for guidance and management which is certainly new! My job has evolved significantly!

CONCLUSION

What this chapter has set out to consider are effective methods that the school business manager can put into place to manage change. This has meant seeing educational institutions as organisations which are much more than the mechanical systems they contain. The culture of a school has been seen as an important factor in helping or hindering change management, as it impacts on the way people see both themselves and others and also on the way they view innovation and change.

Finally we have explored the human factor of change, since without getting people on board change is unlikely to be successful. Understanding how people see things, view things and understand themselves is all paramount to achieving success. Opinions are fickle and what is a widely-held conviction one term can be easily outmoded the next, or as Crosby (1998) remarked: 'After all, not too long ago tomatoes were considered poisonous. (Available at: http://www. philipcrosby.com/pca/C.Articles/articles/year.1998/article98_10.htm).

Perhaps the last word should focus on the occasionally bizarre nature of educational change, which could and should provoke humour. Thus we return to the last element of Stoll and Fink's (1996) features of effective schools, namely *celebration* and *humour*, without which it is firmly suggested change would be a tough challenge indeed.

REFERENCES

Bacal, R. (2005) *Understanding the seven dynanmics of change*, http://www.work911. com/cgi-bin/links/jump.cgi? ID=256.

Blanchard, K. (1992) Available at: www.work911.com (accessed 25 September 2005).

Blanchard, K. and Johnson, S. (2000) *The One Minute Manager*. New York: HarperCollinsBusiness.

Blanchard, K., Zirgami, P. and Zirgami, D. (1994) *Leadership and the one minute manager: Increasing effectiveness through situational leadership.* London: HarperCollinsBusiness.

Businessballs (2005) Available at: www.businessballs.com.

Crosby, P. (1998) http://www.philipcrosby.com/pca/C.Articles/articles/year.1998/article98_10htm.

Crosby, P. (1999) Available at: http://www.philipcrosby.com/pca/C.Articles/articles/year.1999/article99_07.htm.

DfES (2006) *Every Child Matters*, http://www.everychildmatters.gov.uk/aims.

Everard, K. B. and Morris, G. (1996) *Effective School Management* (3rd edn). London: Paul Chapman Publishing.

Fullan, M. (1993) *Changing Forces: Probing the Depths of Educational Reform.* London: Falmer.

Fullan, M. (2001) *Leading in a Culture of Change.* San Francisco, CA: Jossey-Bass.

Fullan, M. (2004) *System Thinkers in Action: Moving beyond the standards plateau.* http://www/michaelfullan.ca/Articles04systemThinkers.pdf.

Garratt, B. (2000) *The Learning Organisation: Developing democracy at work.* London: HarperCollinsBusiness.

Handy, C. (1999) *Understanding Organisations* (4th edn). London: Penguin.

Hargreaves, A. and Fink, D. (2001) *Educational reform and school leadership in 3-D perspective.* http://www.hcsl.org.uk/media/415/E5/educational-reform-and-school-leadership-in-3d-perspective.pdf

Johnson, S. (1999) *Who Moved My Cheese? An amazing way to deal with change in your work and in your life.* New York: Vermillion.

Kotter, J. P. (1995) 'Why transformation efforts fail', *Harvard Business Review,* 61.

Kotter, J. P. (1996) *Leading Change.* Boston, MA: Harvard Business School Press.

Law, S. and Glover, D. (2000) *Educational Leadership and Learning: Practice, policy and research.* Buckingham: Open University Press.

MacGregor, D. (1960) *The Human Side of Enterprise.* London: New York: McGraw-Hill.

Machiavelli, N. (1513) *The Prince* cited in Poole, B.J. (2001) *Education for an Information Age: teaching in the computerized classroom* (3rd edn). http//www.pitt.edu/poole/InfoAgeTutorials/Intro.pdf (Accessed 31.05.06).

National College for School Leadership (NCSL) (2002) *Leading the Management of Change: Building capacity for school development.* Available at: http://www.ncsl.org.uk/media/F7B/92/randd-building-capacity.pdf.

Senge, P. (1990) *The Fifth Discipline.* London: Brealey.

Stoll, L. and Fink, D. (1996) *Changing our Schools.* Buckingham: Open University Press.

Section 3

Reflection and Analysis

11

Impact in, and on, Schools

Clive Opie and Angela Harnett

INTRODUCTION

As O'Sullivan et al. (2000) note 'a key aspect of delivering effective learning is the efficient management of resources' and that for this to occur the 'recon-ceptualising of the role of the school bursar into the educational resource manager' (2000: ix) is paramount. It is then by no accident that the term 'bursar' has now largely been superseded by 'school business manager' (SBM).

The critical importance of the SBM, especially as schools take increasing autonomy over their affairs, was recognised by O'Sullivan and arguably it was through his call – for the formal recognition of the need for professional train-ing for bursars to enable them to meet the challenges such autonomy would give rise to – that the Bursar Development Programme (BDP) became a real-ity. Rightly the growth, development and exceptional success of the BDP (NCSL, 2005) should be laid at the door of those tasked with its delivery, but its overall achievement highlights one of the very real success stories regard-ing integration of theory and practice in the educational arena.

The backgrounds of those attending the BDP (school secretaries, LEA (local education authority) employees, employees from private sectors, for example accountants) inevitably resulted in tutors invariably being faced with a range of expertise and skills, with the only common denominator often being a very sound knowledge of financial matters. Knowledge and expertise in Human Resource Management, Risk Analysis, Facilities Management (other elements of the BDP) varied, as did active involvement in, rather than passive representation on, the senior management team (SMT) of respective schools. In fact the many relationships of SBMs with others in their schools (teachers, SMT, TA [Teaching Assistants], HLTA [Higher level Teaching Assistants] and other support staff) only

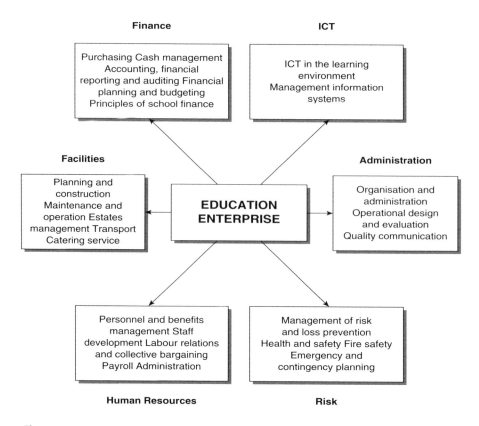

Figure 11.1

adds to the complexity and importance of the role. As Steve Munby, chief executive of the National College for School Leadership (NCSL) notes in his Foreword to the *BDP Impact and Evaluation Report* for 2005 (NCSL, 2005)

> SBMs have a key role to play in school. They can ensure better use of resources and facilities and enable teaching staff to find greater satisfaction in their work through a renewed focus on teaching and learning. They also have an important leadership role in which the mastery of finance and resource management disciplines are valued as vital and important skills. We know that effective school leadership is a prerequisite to improved performance in schools. (Munby, 2005, NCSL report)

O'Sullivan et al. similarly recognised this position, providing a comprehensive overview of such in their text (2000: 24–6). Interestingly though, and quite often, participants had a more limited (and often less positive) view of themselves at the commencement of their BDP, indicating that they 'initially perceive the role (through the diagnostic) as one of administration, with some management activities' (Moorcroft and Summerson, 2004: 4).

The pivotal role of the SBM is however no longer (if ever this was the case by those actually undertaking the role) in question. The formal education of this vital group of managers through the BDP, aimed at building up the prestige and professional recognition of their role, is now an integral part of the tapestry of overall educational leadership programmes issuing from the NCSL. The previous chapters detail the elements of the BDP and highlight the significance that each has in ensuring a coherency and legitimacy to an SBM in their critically crucial and varied role.

Figure 11.1. based on that from O'Sullivan et al. (2000: 30), clearly reflects the link between their research evidence and the practical implications of the BDP.

Having successfully achieved the linkage between theory and practice (as we have no doubt our co-writers have done) what we aim this chapter to do is to look at the evidence for the impact of the BDP on the working practices of SBMs. For example, what impact has the BDP had on raising the confidence of its participants, that is, enabling them to realise they have the wherewithal to make a difference not only to resources management but also in the whole operation of their schools? Has it helped in networking with other SBMs? Has it given them additional self-belief in their problem-solving ability? Has it assisted them in improving their presentation skills – often a key concern, especially when presenting to a less than accepting SMT or governing body? What are participants' views on the impact that the BDP has had on their own professional development?

Evidence for the impact that the BDP has had (for this certainly is visible) has been taken from the *Impact and Evaluation Reports* 2003/04 and 2004/05 of the BDP (NCSL, 2004; 2005), from candidates' responses during the programme and a case study group of 20 early graduate SBMs. It is also perhaps worth noting that as the BDP is still in its infancy, and although evidence suggests it has to date been highly successful in meeting its objectives, it is probably the case that the real impact that its participants will undoubtedly have in schools might not be seen for a number of years yet.

IMPACT AND EVALUATION REPORTS 2003/04 AND 2004/05

These reports (NCSL, 2004; 2005) provide a comprehensive overview of the background to the BDP and its launch nationally in 2003. This overview puts in no doubt the need for skilled and competent SBMs but in the context of this chapter it is the comments from those who have participated in the BDP which reveal the range of impacts that it has had upon them and their schools.

Comments from the reports such as:

> I have learned a great deal, not only about the role of the SBM but also about myself and how my role in education in York can benefit the learning of children in our city. (NCSL, 2004: 26)

> My knowledge, confidence and capabilities have increased enormously and as a direct result, so has my role in school. (NCSL, 2004: 28)

> Over time, I have taken a lead role in project management, particularly related to the ICT infrastructure, and I happily take responsibility for overseeing school finances,

> ensuring that we achieve the best possible value for money. I also have responsibility for line-managing some of the support staff. (NCSL, 2005: 26)

> I cannot speak highly enough of the programme. It has equipped me with so much knowledge and has filled me with the confidence I needed to share that knowledge in so many ways. (NCSL, 2005: 27)

are indicative of the way that participants on the BDP have felt that it has positively impacted not only on their own personal confidence but on their role in their schools. It is worth noting at this point that undertaking the BDP can result in the achievement of two awards: the Certificate in School Business Management (CSBM – Year 1) and the Diploma in School Business Management (DSBM – Year 2). In the most recent NCSL *Evaluation Report* (NCSL, 2005) 92 per cent of CSBM graduates and 92.3 per cent of DSBM graduates reported that the BDP had had an impact on their ability to operate as a leader in their schools (p. 34).

It is not however just by enhancing personal confidence that the BDP has heralded an impact. Sharing ideas with others is seen as an important aspect of an SBM's role and over the time of the BDP, recognition of the importance of networking can be seen to have increased.

> I have had informal discussions with headteachers about the SBM role and how it can help headteachers shed some of the administrative burden so they can concentrate on teaching and learning. (NCSL, 2004: 26)

> The opportunity to be involved in the CSBM was an important step in defining my professional status as a school business manager. It helped not only to raise the profile of my role in the school, but I have also used the opportunity to raise the profile across my LEA. As a result several colleagues are now on the course including my senior administrative officer. The opportunity to meet with and share knowledge with other bursar professionals has also been significant for me and I am sure for many of my colleagues. (NCSL, 2004: 30)

> I am a peripatetic school business manager in three primary schools. As a result of experience on the programmes, I have subsequently been involved with many building projects in all three schools including lift installation, classroom expansion, toilet refurbishment, improved accessibility in all schools and am currently engaged in a large project to expand one of my schools' intake from 75 to 90, having driven this by putting a strategy to governors and following through with the LEA school organisation team. (NCSL, 2005: 29)

This leads to a key point which is the crucial importance of the full support of the headteacher in maximising and helping develop the role of the SBM:

> My headteacher, who is very supportive of the programme, encourages me to share my CSBM experiences with groups of headteachers. This is really important as headteachers play such a crucial role in empowering school business managers. (NCSL, 2005: 26)

The development of problem-solving skills factors highly in the BDP programme materials and this has been recognised by participants:

> The materials are exceptional. There have been so many times I have thought 'I know that' but when you start reading on you think 'Or maybe I don't'. I don't think anybody in the group thinks they know everything, no matter how long they've been in the job. (NCSL, 2004: 27)

> The headteacher has much more time to focus on teaching and learning and is convinced that the best-ever Key Stage 2 SAT results are entirely due to the workload I have removed from him and the improvements I make, such as getting better value for money through a clear plan for using budgets, for example devolved capital, effectively. Furthermore, governors have a very clear picture of what is happening, what will ha pen, how this will be resourced and the impact and benefits for the school. (NCSL, 2005: 29)

All the knowledge acquired through the BDP, or indeed any programme, is of little value if the presentation of its application is flawed. Our personal experience as BDP tutors would suggest that having inadequate presentation skills is by far the greatest concern of participants with many, had they the chance (which they don't), willing to opt out of exercises set to improve them. Although we are not convinced that the presentation skills of many of the participants were as poor as they supposed them to be (and this is supported from the evaluation analysis shown), after being on the BDP there was a 78 per cent and 76 per cent increase in participants' self-evaluation of their ability in oral and written communication respectively.

Perhaps the most important objective of the BDP is to enhance the professional and career development of the participants.

> The opportunity to be involved in the CSBM was an important step in defining my professional status as a school business manager. It helped not only to raise the profile of my role in the school, but I have also used the opportunity to raise the profile across my LEA. As a result several colleagues are now on the course. (NCSL, 2004: 29)

> I learnt a lot, not just about the theories and strategies of leadership and management, but also about myself. (NCSL, 2005: 28)

> This course challenged my thinking and enabled me to see how I could be more effective in a leadership role. As I completed the course, I saw I had developed from being someone who reacted to being proactive – from managing to leading. (NCSL, 2005: 30)

Additionally, our anecdotal evidence gleaned from participants only supports the comments above and indicates that in many cases the training received on the BDP has heightened their professional standing amongst their colleagues (both teaching and non-teaching) and, if not in financial terms, has resulted in a recognition that their role is crucial to the smooth and effective running of the school. Continued career development is also seen as important by many SBMs which is why the Institute of Education at Manchester Metropolitan University has launched the first BA in SBM to cater for those wishing to progress further, having successfully completed the CSBM and DSBM. This is gratifying as it addresses both a concern of ours and is also aptly expressed by O'Sullivan et al. (2000), re-echoing the comments of a primary school bursar in 1997,

The job … doesn't seem to have any career development … I can't progress any further … I could go to a bigger school and do the same job or stay in the school and develop in more education management areas than pure finance. (p. 57)

It is the case, however, that despite the positive accolades above there are still an unacceptable number of cases where schools or other stakeholders have not wholly embraced the concept of SBM, and where candidates report resistance from management and teaching personnel.

I am still frustrated at not being part of the SM team. (Harnett, 2004: 1)

Barriers to change are not difficult to recognise and revolve around

- *Attitudes* a change in the notion that school business managers have a leadership role to take within schools.
- *Competencies* the need for a greater understanding of the competencies of an SBM.
- *External factors* the tight centralised control of educational processes.

The final word in this section should be positive (as the evaluations of the BDP strongly suggest) and this goes to a CSBM/DSBM graduate who notes that her opportunity for professional development should continue and be extended to others:

As a profession, bursars/business managers have a tremendous range of skills to support effective school management. Raising their professional standing within education can only bring major benefits for education as a whole. The CSBM and DSBM are having a significant impact and I hope the impetus for change linked to training and development of all support staff in schools continues. (NCSL, 2004: 30)

SBM Toolkit – Imp1

To find out more about the Bursar Development Programme, access details on the following NCSL website where you will also find PDF files on the Impact and Evaluation Reports: http://www.ncsl.org.uk/managing_your_school/bursar_development/managing-bursar-development.cfm.

If you are an SBM who has not been on the BDP, contact your LEA to find other SBMs who have done so and solicit their personal views about it.

As a headteacher, are you aware of the significant impact that a professionally trained SBM could have in the management of your school? If not try and talk with peers who have embraced the skills of their SBM and see what a difference this has made to their schools.

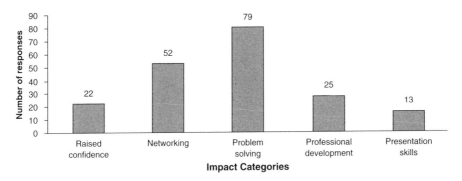

Figure 11.2   Responses reflecting personal impact of the BDP on its participants

EVIDENCE FROM CANDIDATES' RESPONSES DURING THE PROGRAMME

The self-evaluation forms from a total of 56 SBM participants from across five regions of one provider of the BDP were analysed. Although the evaluations were not aimed at directly addressing the issue of impact of the BDP on their practice, they were nevertheless analysed in terms of the impact that they felt the BDP had had on their personal development. The analysis resulted in 191 responses being linked to impact which could be categorised into five areas (see Figure 11.2), namely

- raised confidence;
- networking (covering team working and working with other SBMs);
- problem solving;
- presentation skills;
- professional development (including personal role).

From the total number of responses, 79 specified that the programme had had an impact on the development of their problem-solving skills. This is encouraging as improving problem solving was one of the main objectives of the BDP. Fifty two responses felt that one specific impact of the programme was improved networking, that is, that participants valued being able to talk to other SBMs on the course, sharing ideas and thoughts on various issues.

Twenty two responses specifically noted that the BDP had helped raise their confidence and that this, although still early days, was also impacting on their role back at school. This outcome matched the 25 responses which felt that the BDP had given them a greater understanding of the role of the SBM and that this had impacted on their own perception of the role. The BDP had also given candidates a better view of how to develop their role within their own organisation and felt it would impact on how they viewed their own professional development.

The fact that only 13 responses specifically mentioned that presentation skills had improved during the course perhaps needs some clarification. The participants, at the time of completing the evaluation, had had little practice to use such skills in a wider arena and therefore it could be that this response just reflected this. We are also not convinced that their presentation skills were as poor as the participants suggested they were and so this figure merely reflects this position. However, given that after the BDP there was a 78 per cent and 76 per cent increase in participants' self-evaluation of their ability in oral and written communication respectively, this is probably a much better indication of the impact that the BDP had actually had upon participants' presentation skills.

The above responses are from 56 respondents' evaluations taken from across five regions of one BDP provider and as such can be considered to offer acceptable validity. What is of additional interest, although whilst arguably offering less objective findings, is that when another cohort of 17 participants in one region were asked to give a personal evaluation of the impact of their BDP programme, their responses were not too dissimilar from the those of the larger group.

Seven said that the BDP had increased their skills and knowledge (problem solving) and improved their confidence (raised confidence, presentation skills, networking), providing statements such as: 'I now have more knowledge in lots of areas but more importantly I know where to look to get the information I need'; 'I have changed my way of thinking – I now tend to look at a wider picture'; 'Huge increase in confidence: more knowledge, different perception of self and role'; 'more assertive'; 'Information from the websites has been invaluable'; 'Increased confidence in expressing my opinion'.

Similarly, five reported that there had been a change in perceptions/attitudes to the role of the SBM (professional development) stating: 'My school has changed its perception of the role of the school administrator'; 'A gradual recognition by the headteacher that CSBM is very worthwhile'; 'Taking part in the course is like putting on a new suit'.

What was most encouraging was the very positive response from three of the participants that significant changes within their job had taken place. 'The course I feel did contribute to me obtaining a new position as a bursar'; 'I have gained a far more positive relationship with my Head – I now feel more part of the team and have gained a rise in salary'; 'My job has changed – the ICT co-ordinator now thinks of me as someone with enough knowledge to be involved in curriculum ICT decisions'; 'I am now contributing to leadership/planning issues'.

We would argue that all the above responses are in fact indicative of the positive impact the BDP has had on its participants. As we have noted there is still no room for complacency but it is clear that the significant difference that an

SBM, having undergone the BDP, can have on school efficiency and effectiveness is not in doubt. Without wishing to appear critical perhaps headteachers who do not already work closely with their SBM might be wise to consider more carefully the professional capabilities that a trained SBM has and how these can help them in the management of their school, and in so doing give appropriate recognition and remuneration for these skills.

SBM Toolkit – Imp2

As one SBM noted due to lack of funding in their school 'The headteacher is worried I will apply for other jobs when I have finished the course'.

If you are a headteacher in such a position, and given what you have read so far, can you afford to lose your trained SBM?

As a headteacher are you making the best use of your SBM? Are they on the SMT in a proactive role where they could, from the evidence provided here, make a significant impact on the efficient working of your school? If not – have you asked yourself why?

CASE STUDY: GROUP RESPONSE TO IMPACT ON THE ORGANISATION

Having ascertained views from participants actually on the programme, it seemed important to also ascertain from those who had completed the CSBM and/or DSBM their views in order to solicit the slightly longer-term implications of the impact of the BDP. To achieve this, 16 successful participants of the CSBM and three from the CSBM/DSBM were consulted via a questionnaire and follow-up telephone interviews as to how they saw the BDP impacting upon their roles as SBMs.

Analysis of the questionnaire indicated that the areas that BDP participants felt had had most impact on their role within their organisation were in the areas of Human Resource Management (HRM) and Change Management. Given the changes in these areas that government initiatives over the last few years have generated, for example the National Agreement on Raising Standards and Tackling Workload (NRT, 2003), Every Child Matters (DfES, 2005a), TA and HLTA development (TDA [Teacher Development Agency], 2005a) and Extended Schools (DfES, 2005b), this is perhaps not a surprising find (see the TDA, 2005b publication, *Building the School Team,* for a comprehensive overview of developments to date of training for support staff). It is extremely encouraging that the BDP has helped, not least the SBM participants in this group, to more successfully manage these changes in their schools.

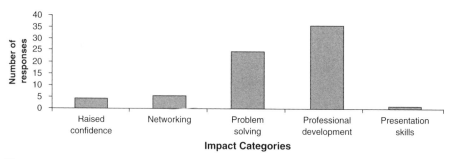

Figure 11.3 Personal impact – case study

Although respondents felt that the BDP had had a positive impact on most of its other core areas of study (for example, financial management, risk analysis, ICT and facilities management) and collectively had helped with school improvement, impact in the area of administration was seen as more limited. That this was the case was thought to be attributed to the fact that participants already had expertise in this area and so came to view its impact as less significant. However, on further exploration it became clear that although in terms of administration per se the BDP had had less impact, what was clear is that the participants had become more involved in the higher leadership/ management level of administration, for example links with LAs (local authorities), additional responsibility for support staff and their allocation and appraisal, and that overall the BDP had had a positive impact on this.

The implications of this and other findings presented here are that the BDP has helped SBMs enormously in dealing with the significant changes their organisations are experiencing. In addition the SBMs in this case study were able to comment on a number of positive impacts that the BDP had made to the recognition of their skills and capabilities: 'I am treated with more respect'; 'My status in school has been raised'; 'I am consulted about decision making'; 'Have joined SMT meeting'; 'SMT interested in my ideas'; 'It has given me the confidence to write policies'; 'I have joined the working party on remodelling'.

What is less encouraging is that it is still the case that too many organisations are not embracing the skills of its trained SBMs, with such comments as 'Little or no impact'; 'Reluctant to accept that the administrative staff working with the SBM are capable of some of the roles now done by SMT' and 'Management points are still being offered to teaching staff for what are basically administrative not teaching roles'.

Finally, we thought it would be useful to try and draw some correlation with the evaluations presented earlier on the regional view of the impact of the BDP. As such, the participants in the case study (see Figure 11.3 above.) were asked to comment on similar impact categories. Apart from professional development (including personal role), the results indicate a remarkable similarity in views and this is satisfying. Perhaps even more rewarding though is to see that more than one year on, participants in the BDP felt that their professional development had significantly increased, as we would argue that it is this area that is likely to have the most impact on candidates and therefore their schools and fares well for the successful implementation of the government reforms around *Every Child Matters* (DfES, 2005a).

CONCLUSION

The BDP is still in its infancy. However, having been launched in 2003 with the original pledge to train 1,000 bursars by 2006 – 'The programme has already awarded 140 certificates, 1,025 candidates commenced training in 2003 and we anticipate at least a further 1,300 commencing their training during 2004 (NCSL, 2004: 8)' – it has already surpassed this target.

Its success in supporting SBMs in realising their crucial role in managing schools is, on the basis of the findings in this chapter, not in question. Where the skills and knowledge of an SBM having undergone the BDP are embraced, schools have seen a significant improvement in the efficiency and effectiveness of the management of resources (HRM, ICT, facilities, administration and so on), and a positive impact on their teaching and learning environment and the workload practices of all staff. As one headteacher noted at a recent SBM Ceremony:

> Audrey used to tell people she was 'only' a school secretary. This was not her own view of the role yet she despaired that others thought of it as a nice little term-time job with a bit of typing, filing and answering the telephone. I know how important, complex and demanding the role has become but frustratingly this is not understood even by school colleagues, school governors and the LEA … she has done much research and has used the knowledge and skills the CSBM has developed for the benefit of her school. She discusses national education initiatives with renewed confidence … and her enthusiasm is motivating others.

This comment would appear to echo a word of caution to those headteachers who are not yet fully cognisant with the role of SBM, as the evidence here suggests they are missing out on using the skills of a key figure to help in the management of their schools. Our advice for those still in this position is to check this out with those peers who have done so on how they have embraced the skills of the SBM and the impact this has made to the effective and efficient running of their schools.

Finally the role of the SBM will, and should, take on more significance and continued and advanced training, through avenues such as the BA in SBM, will ensure this happens. From evidence presented here the success of the BDP is not in doubt. The import of the skills of the SBM, where embraced, in achieving significant improvement in school management is also not in question. The task is to educate those SMTs still unconvinced of the critical importance the SBM has in the management of their schools, so that they realise what a key player they have in their midst who is not employed to their full capacity in helping to meet the Every Child Matters agenda.

REFERENCES

Department for Education and Skills (DfES) (2005a) *Every Child Matters: Change for children.* Available at: http://www.everychildmatters.gov.uk/publications/ (accessed December 2005).

Department for Education and Skills (DfES) (2005b) *Extended Schools: Access to opportunities and services for all.* Available at: http://www.teachernet.gov.uk/_doc/8509/Extended-schools per cent20prospectus.pdf (accessed December 2005).

Harnett, A. E. (2004) *CSBM Impact.* Unpublished research. Manchester Metropolitan University.

Moorcroft, R. and Summerson, T. (2004) *Leaders backing Leaders: A programme of school business management.* IPDA Conference Paper, 22–23 October, Birmingham, UK.

Munby, S. (2005) Available at: http://www.ncsl.org.uk/managing_your_school/bursar_development/managing-bursar-munby.cfm (accessed December 2005).

National College for School Leadership (NCSL) (2004) *Bursar Development Programme: Impact and evaluation report 2003/04.* Nottingham.

National College for School Leadership (NCSL) (2005) *Bursar Development Programme: Impact and evaluation report 2004/05.* Nottingham.

National Remodelling Team (NRT) (2003) *National Agreement on Raising Standards and Tackling Workload.* Available at: http://www.remodelling.org/programmes/na.php (accessed December 2005).

O'Sullivan, F., Thody, A. and Wood, E. (2000) *From Bursar to School Business Manager.* London: Pearson Education.

Teacher Development Agency (TDA) (2005a) *Higher Level Teaching Assistants.* Available at: http://www.tda.gov.uk/support/hlta.aspx (accessed December 2005).

Teacher Development Agency (TDA) (2005b) *Building the School Team.* Available at: http://www.tda.gov.uk/upload/resources/pdf/s/swdb-1yp.pdf (accessed December 2005).

12

Future Developments

Irene Naftalin

INTRODUCTION

Recently I was supervising a mature student, who I was to debrief after her visit to a large secondary school where she was conducting a consultancy. The consultancy focus was 'The development of a management structure for administrative staff'. My student is a teacher engaged on a part-time Master's degree programme in educational leadership and management. She had found her visit somewhat mystifying and distressing. She had spent the whole day in the office, exposed to an array of staff tensions, that neither engaged her understanding nor her empathy. Her only venture out of the office was to meet the kitchen staff.

There was nothing familiar about the environment in which she found herself and she felt no sense of the school that she was visiting. It was just a day at the office. She was scathing about the fact she had not seen one child for the entire day, that no-one had thought to show her round the school, nor introduce her to the teaching staff or the headteacher.

In her obvious distress at being so completely transported out of her own world, she had missed the message. The office staff had not been unwelcoming or dismissive of her. They had, in fact, shown her their world. This was 'school' as they knew it. They had introduced her to 'their people'. In their world, they had little contact with children or with teachers. It would not have occurred to them that showing my student round the school would be of interest to her or that it had any relevance to what she was there to do. In her distress she had not allowed herself to experience or to learn from this exposure to a parallel universe that co-exists with her own, inhabits the same space, uses the same facilities and is employed to contribute to the same endeavour. The significance of the way in which these two worlds fail to connect with each other was evidenced as much by her distress and her lack of comprehension about the meaning of her experience, as by the content of her story.

This story painfully illustrates the gulf that separates teaching staff and support staff. They know little of each other's worlds and they do not necessarily see themselves as part of a shared endeavour to which they both contribute in different ways. In my experience of the bursar development programme, as a tutor and as an assessor, this is a familiar theme particularly exemplified in the struggle that some participants experience when required to reflect on their contribution to their school's vision for teaching and learning. For many participants this question comes from a distant and alien planet. They often ask, 'What has this got to do with me?'

This chapter is dedicated to creating an understanding that is intended to do much more than build bridges to connect the two worlds, but aims to create a sense of a single community working together towards a single defining purpose. It therefore has an unapologetically strong educational focus, in order to locate the context of school business management firmly within the vision for education and to help aspiring school business managers make sense of the ways in which they will make an increasingly significant contribution to the vision for teaching and learning.

This chapter is about progression. It is about future developments. Paradoxically the way to think about the future is first to understand the past and the journey that brings us to the point of envisioning the future from our current vantage point. The chapter opens with context setting about the nature of futures thinking and it goes on to explore some of the futures thinking that has informed government and shaped educational legislation over the past decade.

A large part of the chapter is devoted to telling the story of education and showing how the creation of the bursar development programme came about, plus where this fits into the bigger picture. The significance for the development of a role for school business managers is explored as an integral part of that narrative, reflecting the increasingly integrated nature of the way in which future schools will work.

The chapter, having reviewed the journey that has brought us to where we are now, then looks at the various themes and trends that will continue to inform future developments for future schools and what these could mean for the future of school business managers. By happy good fortune, the proposals in the White Paper, *Higher Standards, Better Schools for All* (DfES, 2005) coincided with the end phase of writing this chapter, making it possible to witness the early stages in the unfolding of anticipated future developments.

We begin with some futures thinking about the opportunities that will open up for school business managers, and the professional development that will be available to support the development of school business management as a profession. This is entirely necessary because we need to know where we're going, if we don't want to finish up somewhere else!

This chapter intends to

- locate school business management on the educational map;
- help to make sense of the relationship between school business manage-ment and the vision for teaching and learning;
- generate understanding of the way in which the vision for teaching and learn-ing defines the single unifying purpose for the whole-school community.

FUTURES THINKING

In this world of rapid change how can we know what the future will be like in five or ten years time?

Changes are happening in every sphere of life; the world stage is re-shaping itself economically and politically. Technology has changed communication and travel in ways that that were the scoff of science fiction less than forty years ago.

These changes have made information and knowledge accessible on a global scale and as a result, the traditional power bases are shifting. In parallel comes the rapid spread of disease across the world, sometimes threatening the lives of millions of people. Climate change, large-scale natural disasters and the rapid depletion of the world's natural resources have brought issues of poverty, health, environment and sustainability closer to the top of the international agenda.

Change is not new; the world has always been a dynamic and changing place. It is the speed of change that is new. Rapid change means that often there is not enough time to understand, adapt, accommodate and address the implications of changes before the next one arrives. In such a world, how is it possible to make predictions about the future? Something new and unexpected always happens to take us by surprise. Not only do we not know or under-stand what the technological, environmental, political and economic shape of the landscape will be, far less do we understand what their implications might be. Yet unless we engage in a predictive process that enables us to plan and prepare for the future, the future will overtake us and leave us behind – inadequately prepared.

We talk of vision. We perceive vision, as an essential ingredient of leader-ship. It is no longer enough to be able to look after and manage an organisa-tion well, for today and for this year, and to expect that this will be sufficient to take us safely into the year after that. Such organisations are actually cruis-ing gently along, unaware that the tide and the currents underneath them are moving faster than they are. Within a very short space of time, such an organ-isation finds itself becalmed or drifting off-course.

We require leaders to take things forward, to be aware of the currents and tides and to stay ahead of them. For this they need a clear sense of direction and defined goals and they need to take anticipatory action to secure the future. In order to do that, leaders need a well-developed view of what the potential future scenarios could be, a clear sense of which scenario they think they should be heading towards and how to get there.

So, in our modern world, how do leaders develop the power of prophecy?

What a funny world this is – once upon a time we used to burn people at the stake for engaging in this kind of witchcraft. Nowadays, we're all expected to have visions and leaders who can't produce a convincing vision fail the first test of leadership.

SBM Toolkit – FD: 1

When thinking about your department or your school, try to remember to 'place' it in a wider context. There are national and international organisations dedicated to envisioning the potential futures and working out the likely possible scenarios that might emerge, such as Demos in Britain, the Institute for Future Studies International in Copenhagen, the OECD, UNESCO, the World Health Organisation. Such organisations provide us with well-researched global information about the world's mega-trends and potential scenarios that help us to engage with this process of envisioning.

If you are serious about your profession, this is not a luxury but a necessity. The real leadership skill is to connect one's own context, core beliefs and values imaginatively to the global context to generate a personal dream about a desired future. When that dream captures the imagination of others, connecting with their dreams, then the desired future is simply a matter of the time it takes to make it happen.

There are several aspects to developing one's vision for the future, but acquiring an understanding of the potential future landscapes across the six areas of the PESTLE model (Political, Economic, Social, Technological, Legal and Environmental) provides an important framework within which to work. It is obviously important to know who the gifted visionaries are and whose voices are the most influential and to listen carefully to what they say, but envisioning the future is also about imagination.

Clearly, this process of generating potential futures can never be an exact science. There will always be a range of possible futures and we cannot know for certain which will be realised. However, we do have choice as to which futures we plan for and those choices are largely shaped by our understanding of the PESTLE landscape. At any point in time, there are both personal and collective actions that affect the shape of the future and for which we are responsible. What we do today either opens up or closes down the possibilities for tomorrow and in that very real sense we are active players in the creation of our future.

To be a visionary one needs to think 'outside the box'. To do this is to break the mould, to challenge the current paradigm, to escape the 'group-think' and think for oneself. Before we do this, however, we need to know what the 'box' looks like and who built it – the answer lies in history.

WIDER GOVERNMENT POLICY AND STRATEGY

In the UK the government has, over a long period of time, developed a set of policies designed to create and maintain high standards of service in the public sector, with particular emphasis on education and health as these are seen as the keys to future success. The government has a set of policy principles and practices that has informed its thinking across all the public services. The culture of continuous quality improvement, raising standards, target setting, league tables, performance management, continuous professional development, stakeholder involvement in governance, high levels of accountability to a range of stakeholders and public transparency through audits and inspection frameworks pervades all the public services. Policy ideas such as internal markets, public–private partnerships, devolved budgets, competition between the different institutions whilst at the same having to find ways to collaborate and work together to create specialist centres of excellence, were imposed on all the public services. Education was no exception. The fact that these policies are not the product of one political party, tells us that they are the product of a shared understanding of the vision of the future.

In 1997 when Labour came into power they seamlessly continued to build on what the Conservatives had already put in place. Over the last eighteen years, since the 1988 Education Reform Act, education has been in the grip of a continuous rapid change dictated by governments of both colours, in successive legislative acts.

WHY EDUCATION?

Why so much focus on education? Education is seen as central to our future success as an international player in an increasingly competitive global market economy. The basic structure of our education system was designed to support the industrial society of the nineteenth and early twentieth century, to provide a basic education for all children and to create an orderly, obedient and compliant workforce destined for the factories.

The winds of change started to blow with the 1944 Education Act, when education became both a right and a requirement for all children, and again in the 1960s when many new universities were created, enabling many more young people to extend their education beyond school. There was a growing awareness of the wealth of untapped human potential that was being lost through lack of educational opportunity. With the raft of new universities, grant money became available, making it possible for those with ability but who lacked the financial means to access a university education.

This was just the beginning. It was the 1960s' version of widening participation, but by no stretch of the imagination could this be described as mass education. Schools hardly changed at all. The curriculum and the examinations systems remained in place. The industrial paradigm on which schools were founded went unquestioned and has continued to remain firmly in place right up the end of the twentieth century. It is only in very recent years that we have begun to become uncomfortably aware that there is need for a radical rethink, generating questions about the kind of education our children need for the twenty first century and about how learning in schools should be structured and organised to ensure the best possible educational outcomes for all children.

The UK is not alone in recognising the economic realities and demands that a healthier population with a longer life expectancy (coupled with global competition for goods and services) will place on a nation's economy. In the developed countries, politicians have come to realise the need for a well-educated, highly skilled, highly flexible, creative, self-sustaining workforce which is capable of being innovative and entrepreneurial, thus maintaining the wealth of the nation, its standard of living and quality of life. The West has realised it cannot compete with Asia, in particular with China and India in terms of capacity for mass production, and therefore we have to find a different kind of competitive edge through innovation, enterprise, entrepreneurism and the production and delivery of high quality, and possibly highly exclusive, goods and services.

Actually, the way forward for *all* countries is seen to be through the mass education of young people, continuous professional development for all at all levels of career progression, and an attitude of lifelong learning which will maintain the currency of people's skills and competence, giving them the flexibility to be able to change direction to keep pace with global change. Here the UK is a leader with mass education intended to take the general population to a higher level of education than has ever been previously offered or expected. The intention is to develop the nation's knowledge and skills, thinking and creativity, and to generate a national mindset that remains open to new learning, new ideas, new possibilities and new opportunities throughout life.

One such international voice has been the UNESCO Task Force on Education for the Twenty-first Century (Delors, 1996) that provides an inspirational and far-sighted exemplar of a curriculum model designed for the twenty first century which takes account of all these concerns, through the concept of Four Educational Pillars namely

● Learning to Know.
● Learning to Do.
● Learning to Live Together.
● Learning to Be.

None of this can be achieved through a system that is designed to develop mass obedience and compliance. A new paradigm is needed for education: an education system designed to nurture curiosity, a desire to learn, a willingness to take risks and to experiment. An education system that fosters courage, self-esteem and independence of thought and that offers the opportunities to develop skills to levels of excellence. An education system that facilitates not just the acquisition of knowledge but the opportunities to translate knowledge into personal meaning and understanding as the basis on which creativity, sound judgement and wisdom are developed

A CURRICULUM FOR THE NEW WORLD

Of course, there is more to the education system than the curriculum and shifting the paradigm involves much more than a new curriculum, but a new curriculum can provide the starting point.

The Delors curriculum does not designate its four pillars as knowledge, skills, citizenship and self-realisation. It is far more subtle, complex and demanding, whilst being conceptually deceptively simple. The Four Pillars all start with 'learning to', in recognition that this an active and infinitely continuous act on the part of the learner, recognising that there is always more to learn and that learning is integral to our life-journey – there is always more knowledge and understanding to seek, more skills to develop, more action to take in the world, more we can do to benefit society and be better neighbours, friends, national and world citizens and more we can do to develop ourselves, our individual gifts and talents and to realise our own potential.

The notion of 'learning to' implies that the emphasis in this curriculum is not so much on the knowledge that we need, but on the skill of acquiring that knowledge, so that we can continue to acquire it for ourselves throughout our lives. As we deconstruct the model we are immediately confronted with the notion of active and continuous learning on the part of the learner. This is a curriculum that demands a radical re-think of traditional teaching methods that has tended to require learner-passivity and to discourage individual, independent and active learning behaviours.

As this chapter develops, it will be important to keep these concepts in mind as we shall see how they have been woven into the fabric of the educational developments of the last decade.

THE UK'S EXAMPLE

In the last two decades in the UK, perhaps two of the most important visionary voices listened to have been Michael Barber and Tim Brighouse. In 1992
they set out their vision for the future of education in this country in their pam-
phlet *Partners in Change*. In 1996 Michael Barber published his extraordinary
book *The Learning Game*, in which he set out a truly shocking picture of how
badly our education system was failing our young people. He established the
imperative for major reform, and set out a radical new agenda for the transformation of education, including a new curriculum for the twenty first century,
which although written specifically for the UK's context, shares similar thinking with the international curriculum published in the same year by UNESCO
in the Delors report. Everything that is set out in this book has been and is still
being translated into government policy. The twenty first century's curriculum
has yet to be tackled, but piece by piece the structures are being put in place
that will make that transition possible.

THE DEVELOPMENT OF GOVERNMENT POLICY FOR EDUCATION

The dawning of a realisation that our schools were failing 40 per cent of our
children in terms of providing them with an adequate education, far less an
education that would equip them for the modern world, came slowly at first
throughout the 1980s when standards were both rising and falling at the same
time. In other words, the rates of those who were leaving school without qualifications and often without basic literacy and numeracy were rising, whilst for
those who remained at school taking the public examinations the results were
improving year on year, with the gap between these two groups of young
people ever-widening.

Michael Barber (1996, Chapter 3) refers to those 40 per cent of our young
people whom schools were failing as 'the disappointed, the disaffected and the
disappeared'. These are the young people for whom school offers nothing of
interest or relevance, failing to meet their individual educational needs and to
engage, motivate or inspire them, and their responses vary from sitting it out, to
disruptive behaviour, erratic attendance or dropping out of school altogether.

As the government began to understand the meaning of these statistics it
recognised that this situation was untenable and unacceptable. It was economically and socially non-viable, potentially dangerous and almost certainly
disastrous for the future, and so began a relentless programme of educational
legislation that has lasted nearly twenty years and shows little sign of abating
any time soon. The main objectives have been to reform and transform education, to raise educational standards for all and most ambitious of the lot was
'thinking the unthinkable' – that of consigning failing schools and school failure to history.

In the early 1990s the Conservative government began, in earnest, to address the reality of the failure of the education system and in this they were actively and enthusiastically supported by the then Labour opposition. Their aim was to deliver 'Successful Schools for All'. Michael Barber noted that this was the first time that this familiar political refrain actually became a serious political imperative, with a hard-hitting legislative programme to secure its implementation. He mapped the agenda that he envisaged would then need to follow to make it happen!

Firstly, we need a means of evaluating the quality of every school in the country in a climate of openness. Secondly, we need to know what defines a good school. Thirdly, we need to know what a school should do to improve itself. Fourthly, we need to decide how best to intervene when a school proves incapable of improving itself (Barber, 1996: 123).

Transparency and public accountability became the order of the day in the regime of the National Curriculum; a programme of national testing for all 7,11,14 and 16 year olds. This incorporated an intensive and relentless programme of inspections that graded teacher performance, management performance and quality of teaching and learning, against a set of criteria designated in the framework for inspection as informed by school effectiveness research (Sammons et al., 1995). League tables were published, failing schools were named and shamed and we were told that there were 15,000 poorly-performing teachers in our schools. Some schools were put on special measures, others were closed and re-opened in the Fresh Start initiative, some were taken over by expert teams. All schools were given targets and had action plans following on from inspection. Schools were provided with PANDAs (Pupil and National Data Analysis) that gave them comparative data with other similar schools so that benchmark standards could be generated. Disadvantage was no longer acceptable as a reason for poor educational standards and low expectations of children's potential.

Then came the National Strategies, first focussing on primary schools with the Literacy Strategy, followed shortly afterwards by the Numeracy Strategy, which were later merged to become the Primary Strategy. After that came the Key Stage Three Strategy and most recently the Five Year Strategy for Children and Learners (DfES, 2004) that sets out the government's plans for education right from birth through to higher education.

The government gradually took the business of raising standards out of the control of LEAs (local education authorities) and schools and turned it into a major political agenda in which they have dictated the pace and nature of change in schools for nearly two decades.

AND SO TO SCHOOL BUSINESS MANAGERS ...

School effectiveness research sowed the seeds of ideas about learning the business of management of schools from business management. It was at this point that Senge's (1990) work on learning organisations was seen to have relevance for schools, with the idea that the most effective teachers are those who are themselves actively engaged in learning. Gradually these ideas evolved to include everyone in a school community, including the governing body, the leadership teams, the teachers, the headteacher and the whole kaleidoscope of support staff, including teaching assistants, lunch-time organisers, caterings and administrative staff.

The move towards schools as learning organisations can be easily mapped through the training opportunities and developments of the last ten years, not least of which was the opening of the National College for School Leadership (NCSL) in 2000, which has overseen the advent of national programmes for qualifications and programmes for aspiring heads, new heads, long-serving heads, middle leaders, ICT leadership, bursars and most recently leaders for children's centres, as well as a raft of other programmes to support the strategic development of schools both from within the college and from the Teachers Training Agency (TTA), recently re-branded as the Teachers Development Agency (TDA), including the most recent National Remodelling and Higher Level Teaching Assistants (HLTA) training programme. The advent of the Bursar Development Programme (BDP) in 2003 and HLTA in 2004 serve as excellent indicators of the progress of this agenda because it signals that the focus is shifting to the growing population of support staff now employed in schools and their contribution to the raising standards agenda.

In his book, *The Learning Game* (1996), Michael Barber's primary focus is on the development of teachers for future schools in a learning society. Central to his thesis is that of the school as a learning organisation and Barber is convinced that the first step toward this has to be to change teachers' perception of their role. He saw teachers as active and continuous learners, actively engaged in professional dialogue with their colleagues at a local, national and international level. This is seen as the most critical step towards being more effective teachers and therefore being able to contribute significantly to raising standards and to participating in the development of a curriculum fit for twenty first century learners. He says that teachers' workload is too burdensome, they are far too busy and the nature of teaching too relentless to enable teachers to have sufficient time or mental energy to devote to their own development, or to engage in professional dialogue or to think strategically about the nature of the education they are providing.

This is no way to prepare a profession for the learning society. Timetables need to be freed up and made more flexible. Pupils need to spend more of the day learning, but less of it in traditionally timetabled lessons. They need to be grouped flexibly, sometimes according to ability, sometimes according to interest and at other times according to the nature of the activity. For example, if pupils are watching a film or a video there is no reason why the pupil:teacher ratio should not be 100:1 (Barber, 1996: 230–1).

He shows that by approaching the timetable flexibly, holistically and strategically, time for teachers can be created which should be used for their professional development. He goes on to point out that if this is developed simultaneously with an increase in the number of trained support staff, the potential and capacity for schools to make radical change would be enormous.

SBM Toolkit – FD: 2

At a headteachers' conference in 1994, I hazarded a guess that by the end of the century less than 50 per cent of staff in school would be fully qualified teachers. I thought this was bold, but a secondary head came to see me afterwards and told me that in his school that threshold had already been crossed (Barber, 1996: 232).

To help make your case, you might quote this, but more powerfully. Why not find out what your percentage comparison is? Even more challenging, why not benchmark this against other more/less successful schools in the area?

He also advocated more administrators, but essentially Barber's lens was focussed on teachers. He touches only briefly on development of support roles in his mapping of a vision for education, but it is from here that we can take up the story from the perspective of the development of the role of school business manager. Barber suggests that administrative tasks such as assessment recording, entries for public examinations and attendance could be done more effectively and efficiently by people trained and skilled in administration than by those trained for teaching. He suggests that as the number of people employed in school other than teachers increases, so the need for highly skilled and trained professional administrators and managers will become ever greater. In the last two years we have seen some of the seeds of these ideas coming to fruition, but not all of them as Barber envisaged it. He clearly identified teachers as the ones who would lead the advance into this unknown territory. But the future is always unpredictable; one can set the direction and choose the route, but can never be sure of what might happen along the way.

In 2001, Estelle Morris (the then Secretary of State for Education) announced that there would be 1,000 trained school bursars by the year 2006. This of itself took everyone by surprise, but nevertheless it made good strategic sense and was a natural progression from David Blunkett's policies in the preceding two years in cutting the bureaucratic burden on schools. The next surprise was the enthusiastic take-up of the Bursar Development Programme, such that Estelle Morris's target was met and exceeded a year early and still continues to go from strength to strength. This programme has been enthusiastically embraced by many headteachers and by school administrators across the country, who have shown themselves not only to be hungry for training and the development of their professional status and role, but have also proved themselves to be avid learners.

The Bursar Development Programme (BDP) has become a resounding success and the speed of its impact on schools has taken everyone by surprise. Administrators, through the opportunities provided by the Bursar Development Programme, are emerging as aspiring school business managers and have taken to the role with extraordinary aspiration, imagination and vision. They are in the vanguard of adult learners in schools that is so integral and essential to the concept of transforming schools into learning organisations. They are setting the pace for the transformation agenda. Within their schools they are showing the way. They are setting a superb example of how to use new knowledge, skills and understanding to forge ahead with the transformation process and are helping their schools to take control of creating and shaping the future. Emerging school business managers have become pivotal to the process of paradigm shifting.

These aspiring school business managers are generating new sources of funds for their schools. They are doing this by looking at more cost efficient and effective ways to manage the school. Perhaps more immediately, in terms of impact, they are relieving headteachers from some of the administrative and business functions of the school by taking more responsibility for managing health and safety and school security, buildings maintenance and development, catering contracts and many other aspects of resource management. Many graduates from the bursar development programme have already been recognised in their schools as making invaluable contributions to their school's strategic planning and in some forward-thinking schools they are being invited to join leadership teams or change management teams. The nature, quality and most of all the speed of the impact they are making in schools, has been astounding and impressive. Appendix 2 of the *Bursar Development Programme Impact and Evaluation Report* (2006) offers the comparative statistics of the changes post CSBM compared to pre-CSBM in the time allocated to tasks and the nature of the tasks undertaken, details of income generation for their schools, change of role and career progression.

In 2005 the remodelling agenda brought about changes in the way schools are structured and organised, re-configuring the balance of the teacher role away from administration and management back to managing teaching and learning.

A key concept in the remodelling agenda is the matching of skills and expertise to tasks, as this is seen as the best way to maximise effectiveness and efficiency. To ensure the best possible teaching and learning is happening in the classroom, teachers need to be free to focus on teaching and learning. The corollary to this is that headteachers also need to be free to take responsibility for the leadership of educational endeavour in their schools and communities. The maxim is that teachers should be responsible for the teaching, headteachers responsible for the educational vision and provision, administrators for the administration and business managers for the business management.

Headteachers, with school business managers, are finding themselves relieved of much that has been burdensome and time-consuming. They will increasingly find themselves with schools that are enriched and empowered and they will be liberated to re-shape and re-develop their own roles as learning-centred leaders and system-leaders of learning organisations, (Fullan, 2004) in which their primary focus is the nature and quality of the education that each young person in the school receives.

PERSONALISATION: THE IMPACT ON LEARNING AND THE SBM

The next policy initiative that we can expect is the development of the personalisation agenda and the main goal is now in sight. The ultimate purpose of all of this change is the transformation of the education system to meet the challenges of the twenty first century. It involves ensuring that all children receive an appropriate education tailored to meet their educational needs, but at the same time demanding of them their highest possible aspirations and their commitment to achievement.

This is where we will begin to see, in earnest, the active implementation of Gardner's (2000) work on multiple intelligences and much other related research on learning and learning styles, for example that of Barbara Prashnig (1998), whose insight on the development of creativity has already made an impact on the way we organise some of our primary classrooms. Neuroscience research on how the brain works and how we learn together with parallel educational developments in new learning methodologies have undergone huge leaps in knowledge in the last ten years, such that we are now at the point where we can capitalise on this knowledge.

With the personalisation agenda, not only will we begin to see more recognition and nurturing of the individual gifts and talents of individual children and the use of multiple intelligence research to help to identify where each child's strengths lie, but also the implementation of this strategy to develop self-esteem and self-confidence as a basis for extending their education outwards into other areas. It will enable us to become educationally intelligent in planning the education of our children, literally starting from where each child is and working from there.

The personalisation agenda is one of the few remaining bridges to cross to take us irreversibly towards the transformation of our schools. Once we embark on the personalisation agenda on a mass scale, our education system will finally have become unrecognisable as the nineteenth century entity that it was pre-1988. The remaining bridges to cross will necessarily involve the development of a new curriculum and its assessment framework, together with the necessary parallel development in the transformation of the programme for teacher training to prepare them for such a transformed role.

The personalisation agenda demands a different paradigm in the way we organise teaching and learning. It will require teachers to manage the learning of their students but not necessarily to be the deliverers of that education. Ultimately, the teaching role will bear no resemblance to the current model and we are already on our way towards this. The first shoots of the transformed role have already appeared: there are more adults in the classroom for teachers to manage; teachers are developing planning for others to teach; an embryonic form of individual learning plans is in place.

Teachers will become more akin to learning managers and directors of study, where they will plan the programmes of study with students and their parents; not only subject and content but also learning method. They will monitor progress and they will work with their students to set aspirational targets. They will also work with teams of adults consisting of: new and recently qualified teachers; teaching assistants; ICT support staff; special needs and language experts; people from the community with expert subject knowledge and skills and volunteers, all of whom will contribute in their various ways to the delivery of programmes of study. They will also link with other schools and workplaces, where their role will be to put the programmes of study in place and to ensure quality. It will involve intricate planning at a level of complexity that will probably require both the use of project management methods and supervisory management of the delivery.

Such a model of teaching and learning demands a different paradigm for the way in which we organise our schools in terms of student and teacher timetables, student groupings, the school day, the school year, and the way in which we design and arrange the learning spaces, as described in *The Learning Game* (Barber, 1996: 230–1).

In the context of the goals described here, the government's recent agendas – Workforce Remodelling, Every Child Matters, Extended Schools and the Building Schools for the Future – are significant responses. When considered alongside extensive national development programmes for leadership training at all levels throughout a school, with HLTA to develop the teaching skills of classroom assistants, then the bursar development programme can be seen as an active implementation of the strategic plan to realise the vision of the transformation of education, fit for the twenty first century.

These initiatives can be summed up as wraparound care for children, with integrated services of education, health and social care. Schools will become increasingly open to the community, both to provide for community need (for example offering parenting skills and educational provision for parents, particularly in basic skills) and also for schools to receive skills and expertise from the community, thus enabling schools to expand the scope and range of their educational offering. New learning environments are being built and developed to provide learning spaces purposefully designed to support a wide and varied menu of teaching and learning methodologies and the provision of a curriculum designed for the twenty first century.

In looking in some depth at the development of educational policy, we can see where the creation and development of a new profession of school business managers fit into the panoply of educational legislation and, even more importantly, where it sits strategically in the relentless drive toward the total transformation of education in the UK, from birth to age 21.

KEY THEMES

Underpinning the legislation and the initiatives are some key concepts that will remain constant and will continue to inform future development for some time to come.

Clearly the way forward is seen as the development of schools as learning organisations (Senge, 1990). The Senge framework translates into an organisation in which the focus is on learning and where everyone in that organisation is actively and continuously engaged in learning. When this happens in school, the boundaries between different 'tribes' start to blur. As everyone begins to open their minds to the opportunities for learning they start to recognise and value what others have to offer and what they are able to offer to others. By learning together each person learns for themselves, as a team, a group, a class, a department and as an organisation. Everyone, not just the pupils, becomes a learner and everyone becomes a teacher. When this shift happens, so the resource capacity for teaching and learning is immeasurably expanded. Professional dialogue, enquiry, collaboration and learning exchange become integral to the culture and infuse every part of it and all its activities.

Such organisations necessarily develop structures that enable everyone to participate in their development and in the shaping of both the present and the future. These are vibrant organisations that value the creative potential of their communities of learners and they seek to harness and use the knowledge, skills, ideas and understanding which are generated. In this way commitment, belonging and motivation are fully engaged.

WHO WILL DO THIS?

Capacity building is of critical importance to the transformation agenda. Capacity building means expansion of the available resources and usually refers particularly to the human resource. It is not just another way of talking about expanding the number of employees. Capacity building is about maximising the way we nurture, develop and harness the potential contained within the available resource, not just maximising the use of what exists but expanding its range and scope.

It involves individuals extending themselves as far as they can both in breadth and depth. It is about working together to create the synergy that generates more together than any individual can produce on their own. It is about the creation of networks for collaborative learning, sharing expertise and drawing upon people and their expertise from a wide range of sources beyond one's own institution. Most essentially it's about everybody becoming engaged in learning. It is also about finding creative ways to use time and other resources in order to become time and cost efficient. All of this will not only expand capacity, but the wider the network the more it will stabilise the sustainability of that expanded capacity.

One of the many reasons why the bursar development programme has been so successful may well be because all of these principles are integral to it. The description of a learning organisation and the strategies for capacity building will be very familiar to all those who have participated in the programme and they will recognise these as the critical factors that have empowered them to make a difference in their schools.

The concept of transformational leadership (Burns, 1978) informs thinking about capacity building whereby all employees are invited to step out of the limits of their role-defining boxes in order to participate in the development of their organisation by sharing more of what they have to offer, in terms of knowledge, skills and expertise. Current thinking is much influenced by the concept of distributed leadership (Leithwood, 2001) which is a way of organising schools so that they are leader-full but with a strong accountability structure that is defined by alignment with and commitment to a shared set of core values.

At the heart of all these concepts is a recognition of the need for continuous professional development, lifelong learning, learning new skills, developing a wider knowledge base and, most importantly, for collaborative learning with the development of professional dialogue and professional enquiry as core components of professional life, all of which comprise the engine that will drive the transformation agenda forward.

FUTURE SCHOOLS

The new shape of transformed schools is still in the process of creation. It is clear that there will be a shift away from centralised decision making about how schools should be organised and how education should be delivered. The concept of distributed leadership will apply at a national level. The key elements of accountability, a core curriculum, national testing, high educational standards, personalised education, extended schools, integrated provision of services for children and well-managed schools provide the common framework to which all schools must adhere, but how these are to be delivered will increasingly become the accountable responsibility of those with the role of delivering and implementing all this.

This will involve schools becoming increasingly responsible for how education is structured, what is offered and how it is delivered. It will necessitate working collaboratively with other schools and with other professions. Some schools may decide to work as a collective within a cluster in order to maximise provision, expand capacity and be more cost efficient. Others may opt for a campus style with a variety of phases and types of school on a single site, for example nursery, primary, secondary, with perhaps a sixth form or further education college attached. Another possibility might be a consortium of specialist college schools working co-operatively to provide wider availability of their facilities and expertise.

Campus schools, clusters and consortia may evolve over-arching or merged management structures. It will all involve partnership working and the development of inter-professional relationships.

SBM Toolkit – FD: 3

The future development of large-scale personalised learning will involve the management of learning spaces and in-school learning resources to maximise use, whilst at the same time providing for the varied diet of learning environments that it requires. It will involve developing wider networks of relationships with workplaces, community organisations and parents. Individual learning contracts with pupils and parents will need to be organised, scheduled, managed, audited and tracked. The management of growing numbers of support staff will become a bigger and more significant function.

Ask your headteacher about the schedule to introduce personalised learning, and then offer to produce a 'resources plan' to cover some of the implications.

All of this opens up enormous scope for the expanded role of school business manager.

The government's latest White Paper (DfES, 2005), was released just as the writing of this chapter was being finalised. In it we can see the progression of themes discussed in this chapter. The key principles at the heart of that document are the requirements for improved teaching and learning and the devolution of financial and educational control to schools (but with continued rigorous accountability largely with local authorities). The later will be responsible for ensuring quality and will have the strategic oversight of local educational provision to ensure choice, diversity and equitability.

Schools will be expected to deliver a high quality education for all their pupils and the focus of performance measurement will shift from global indicators of school performance to those that will measure the individual achievements of pupils. There will be greater and better choice for parents, improved disciplinary powers for teachers, and more opportunity for public–private partnerships. Schools are to be based on the model of new academies, somewhat akin to what had been grant-maintained schools. Independent schools, many of which had previously been grant-maintained, will be able to opt into the state sector.

The following quotes indicate that the current prime minister and the then secretary of state for education perceive this legislation as capable of finally securing the path towards transformation

> These pivotal and irreversible reforms will create independent state schools driven by the needs of pupils and parents. (Tony Blair, 25 October 2005)

> These reforms are the next essential step in changing forever the education system for the better ... our plans radically improve the education system, putting parents and the needs of children at the heart of our schools, freeing up schools to innovate and succeed, and bringing new dynamism and new providers ... we need an education system that is designed around the needs of the individual, with education tailored to the needs of each child and parents have a say in how the school is run ... More than anything it is a White Paper about aspiration. We must have the highest aspirations for every child whatever their talents and ability. And we must have a school system that can respond to those aspirations. Working together with our many partners in schools and communities we can achieve our aim of a world class education system, with every school a good school and every pupil achieving. (Ruth Kelly, 25 October 2005)

The reforms signalled by this White Paper do not have specific implications for school business managers beyond what has already been discussed. The White Paper underlines the main trends that dictate the need for change, inform the focus of the government's key objectives and determine the key concepts that shape policy development. It confirms what has been discussed here.

The relentless path towards transformation is continuing to be progressed step by step through an agenda of decentralised, distributed leadership at a whole-system and individual school level, creating space for innovation and creativity in the curriculum, in their delivery, and in the structure and organisation of learning in schools. This will be mediated through expanded collaboration and partnership with a range of stakeholders and new partners, with local communities, other professional disciplines and other institutions. Aspirational standards are to be set for schools and for children, and the focus is shifting towards individual education and individual achievement.

The scope and opportunities for school business managers afforded by this White Paper are now enormous and the door is wide open, but SBMs have to step up – and step through the door.

FUTURE DEVELOPMENTS

It is clear that we have entered the Knowledge Age. Most of us are not yet sure what this means, but we do know that it involves high levels of ICT competence and that it allows information to be transferred with ease and speed to and from anywhere in the world. We know that it facilitates the creation of learning communities at a local, national and international level and that it puts the world's knowledge resources in the hands of every literate person on the planet who has access to the internet. All of this enables us to create new knowledge and new understanding at a speed that we are almost incapable of comprehending. So fast and so huge is the development of knowledge that we cannot keep pace with it.

This is why collaborative learning, learning communities and expanded partnerships are now the only way forward. Teachers can no longer be the sole reservoir of expert knowledge from which children draw their learning. It is no longer possible for any individual teacher to fulfil this role sufficiently or adequately enough to meet the need or the demand. Knowledge can no longer be the source of the teachers' expertise. The source of teachers' expertise will be located in managing the quality of the education which children receive. Their expertise must reside in the knowledge and skills of learning and teaching.

WHAT DOES THIS MEAN FOR SCHOOL BUSINESS MANAGERS?

Effective systems of knowledge management will become a major part of what schools will need in order to provide the personalised learning pathways that will become the norm. Tracking down sources of knowledge and expertise and maintaining appropriate databases and relationships will be crucial. It also means that when there is strategic thinking and planning to do, when working groups need to be established, when professional interest groups want to develop, it is the knowledge manager who will play a crucial role in generating the best potential candidates for membership of such groups because of the knowledge they hold as to who has the relevant skills, expertise, knowledge and specific areas of interest. It is all about good networking, developing good inter-professional and inter-institutional relationships and good management of this tacit knowledge.

The increasing multi-culturalism and diversity of populations throughout the world have already presented new challenges to schools to provide for the needs of an increasingly diverse school population and this will continue to grow. It requires a new look at considerations of school ethos and the management of respect and understanding between the different communities. The wraparound care of the extended school will be very important in this. Inter-professional working and ensuing inter-professional dialogue will help everyone to learn together to ensure that children's educational and welfare needs are appropriately met in a properly coordinated way. There will be administrative, coordinating and financial implications that will become part of the remit of the school business manager. The role for school business managers in supporting this agenda will again come from good networks of relationships with community leaders and community members, learning about the linguistic cultural and religious requirements and ensuring that the facilities, resources and materials are in place to meet these needs.

THE SBM'S PROFESSIONAL DEVELOPMENT IN THE UK

In terms of the future for professional development for school business managers, the CSBM will continue to support the first level of training by creating a basic map of the territory that the role of school business manager covers. This territory is expanding very fast, partly because those emerging from the programme have already substantially grown and expanded the role, and partly because the pace of change in transforming education is of itself generating new needs and demands that inevitably will be integrated into the school business manager's role.

Despite the rapid expansion of territory, the CSBM is likely to remain the same size and the expansion will have to be coped with either by expanding the offer of choice within it or by making significant changes to the DSBM to accommodate new aspects of the role.

The DSBM, is currently, and possibly inappropriately, focussed on a strategic level of operation, with an entry eligibility requirement of membership of the senior leadership team. This is probably unrealistic for many and in consequence it prevents a mass take-up of the DSBM programme and as such has placed a significant barrier in the progression route for the majority of CSBM graduates. Given that many CSBM participants enter the programme as school secretaries or financial administrators, it is the exception rather than the rule that some manage to break into senior leadership teams within a year of starting the CSBM, thus denying eligibility to progress to the DSBM.

The DSBM was conceived before the full implications of the impact of the bursar development programme began to unfold. It had been designed to be the final stage in a two-step progression route and hence was targeted at the strategic level of school business management, thus intended to be for the relatively small number who would reach senior levels of management in their schools, but the way in which the CSBM has been embraced has changed the landscape much faster and more effectively than was anticipated. In these changed circumstances the current diploma is now awkwardly misaligned and in consequence the unanticipated development needs of the wider population of emerging school business managers are not being addressed.

Launching in 2006 will be a top-up undergraduate degree that will enable graduates from the CSBM/DSBM progression to complete the programme to degree level. With the current positioning of the DSBM, it is clearly going to be some time yet before there will be substantial numbers coming forward for degree level, but this does not remove or lessen the need.

The pressure for the development of a graduate profession capable of participating strategically is going to become both a demand and a requirement from headteachers who, in light of the White Paper proposals of October 2005, now have a huge educational challenge to meet. They and their teachers are going to have to make a paradigm leap into becoming what they need to be, in order to transform their schools into learning organisations. It means that they must put their energies and focus into addressing the really big educational questions about the development of a twenty first century curriculum, its delivery and its assessment, and into re-conceptualising their traditional role. These changes cannot be implemented effectively without the skills and expertise that school business managers can contribute, simultaneously to give teachers and headteachers the time and capacity to devote to the professional questions that they must now address and to participate actively in the strategic planning that will follow.

A NEW FORM OF LEADERSHIP IN LEARNING CENTRES

The task ahead is so enormous that headteachers will cope only by embracing principles of distributed leadership, which means that everyone in the school community is aligned with the vision and subscribes to the core values and can therefore be fully trusted with the leadership roles that will involve responsible and appropriate decision making and action in the best interests of the school and that move the school forward towards the achievement of its goals. To be able to participate effectively in this, school business managers capable of such levels of autonomous leadership and strategic participation will require deep understanding of the vision for education in their own schools, of what they are trying to achieve and how they are trying to get there and of the wider educational context – the national agenda in which it sits. This agenda demands integration. Professions are being brought together. Teaching and learning and administration will no longer inhabit separate worlds.

'What is your contribution to the school's vision for teaching and learning?' is a question to which everyone in school will know their own answer. It is what will define job roles, the relationship of jobs to an organisation's goals, the place of jobs in the organisational structure, the inter-personal and inter-professional relationships, and the professional ethos of the whole school community.

Not all school business managers are destined to become chief executives, just as not all teachers become headteachers. In the future we will see the development of a career pathway in which there will be roles of many kinds at various levels, all the way up to chief executive. Roles such as financial directors; human resource directors; knowledge and information managers; estates managers; learning space and learning resource managers; admissions, attendance and examinations officers; personal assistants; bid-writers; income generators and budget managers; these are just a few of the possibilities

The suite of programmes described here will ably support the professional development of school business managers and provide them with the knowledge and skills that they need to progress the role and develop careers in tandem with the unfolding of the transformation agenda and to develop a career path that runs parallel with their teacher colleagues. There is little doubt that the role will expand and develop and there will be a huge demand for the knowledge, skills and services that school business managers will be able to offer.

INTERNATIONAL MASTERS

Appropriate Masters programmes already exist but there will be an inevitable growth in this area, modelled along the lines of an MBA adapted to suit the educational context in which school business managers work. There is already significant international interest in the school business management developments taking place in the UK. In 2005 a UK team, under the auspices of the Institute of Education at Manchester Metropolitan University Cheshire, the NCSL and the Institute of Administrative Management, took the programme to South Africa to introduce it to aspiring school business managers and to train prospective tutors. Other countries are also expressing interest. There will be a growing need for international collaboration to develop the programme for the international market. There will also be an increasing demand for research to investigate the impact of school business management in schools and to look at the contributions they make to the transformation agenda. Masters students and graduates will be in a prime position to undertake this research and to progress it to doctorate level. They will be positioned to support these international developments and to become school business consultants, nationally and internationally to be the future deliverers of the development programmes, as well as being positioned to develop their school business management careers in schools right up to chief executive level, sharing school leadership in partnership with headteachers. The newly developing Masters programmes are being designed to reflect these aspirations.

When the whole framework of professional development is in place, the demand for the professional development for school administrators will grow exponentially and a swift transition to a graduate profession of school business manager will follow. The existence of school business managers with strategic competence, confidence and capability will be rapidly reflected in impact in schools right across the country. The trends indicate that the development of a workforce of this calibre and capability will prove to be one of the key factors that will determine the successful implementation of the transformation agenda.

CONCLUSION

This chapter focusses on progression towards future developments. The context for thinking about future development is set into an understanding of the nature of futures thinking; how it is informed by the past, by the futures thinking that informed the journey into the present, by the sense we make of the current landscape and by the ideas and information generated by organisations and people dedicated to the task of envisioning the future.

The identification of global mega trends is informing the shape and direction of the educational transformation. The way forward is seen in a paradigm shift that will create schools as learning organisations, in which the whole school community is continuously engaged in learning which is designed to meet their respective individual learning needs. The grand design of the legislation is mapped, showing how each piece of legislation puts in place another building block towards the construction of a transformed education system.

Learning and teaching are placed at the heart of the organisation and its central core that defines the why, the what, the who, the how and the where of every aspect of school life. The maxim is that teachers should be responsible for the teaching, headteachers responsible for the educational vision and provision, administrators for the administration and business managers for the business management.

The development of the role of school business manager is integral to the agenda for radical change and the path of its past and future evolution is woven into the transformation narrative, reflecting the essential agenda for the integration of the whole school community working together towards the same goals.

The task ahead for headteachers is so huge that principles of distributed leadership will become the norm. Changes of this magnitude will be implemented with greater success and effectiveness by enlisting the skills and expertise that school business managers offer. Effective deployment of school business managers and other support staff will provide teachers and headteachers with the time and capacity to devote to the professional questions that must now be addressed. Effective school business managers will become a huge asset and will quickly play such a vital role in the strategic planning that will follow that they will be increasingly seen to be in partnership with teachers and headteachers, all working together towards the same goal.

To be able to participate effectively in this, school business managers have to develop the competence, confidence and capability to enable them to participate in a strategic partnership that is focussed on the vision for teaching and learning and must be capable of assuming autonomous leadership roles.

The Bursar Development Programme as rolled out nationally in 2003 is itself founded on the principles of learning organisations. It was so enthusiastically embraced by school administrators that the government's targets for participant completion were met one year earlier than scheduled. Through the opportunities provided by the programme, school administrators are emerging as aspiring school business managers and are re-shaping the role in schools. They are making an immediate and impressive impact in schools and in so doing have accelerated the pace of the transformation agenda.

A suite of programmes from undergraduate certificate level through to doctorate level is anticipated, to support the professional career development of school business managers by addressing their needs as a developing profession that will work in tandem with the teaching profession to provide and support an education system designed for the twenty first century which is fit for purpose.

REFERENCES

Barber, M. (1996) *The Learning Game*. London: Victor Gollanz.
Barber, M. and Brighouse, T. (1992) *Partners in Change: Enhancing the Teaching Profession*. London: IPPR.
Burns, J.M. (1978) *Leadership*. London/New York: Harper and Row.
Delors, J. (1996) *The Treasure Within*. Geneva: UNESCO. Available at: http://www.unesco.org/delors/fourpil.htm.
Department for Education and Skills (DfES) (2003) *The Future of Higher Education*. London: The Stationery Office.
Department for Education and Skills (DfES) (2004) *Five Year Strategy for Children and Learners*. London: The Stationery Office.
Department for Education and Skills (DfES) (2005a) 14–19 *Education and Skills*. London: The Stationery Office.
Department for Education and Skills (DfES) (2005b) *Higher Standards, Better Schools For All, More Choice for Parent and Pupils*. London: The Stationery Office.
Fullan, M. (2004) *System Thinkers in Action – Moving beyond the standards plateau*. London: Innovations Unit/DfES Publications.
Gardner, H. (2000) *Intelligence Reframed: Multiple Intelligences for the 21st Century*. New York: Basic Books.
Harris, A. and Lambert, L. (2003) *Building Leadership Capacity for School Improvement*. Maidenhead: OU Press.
Hopkins, D. (2002) *Instructional Leadership and School Improvement*. Available at: http://www.ncsl.org. uk/media/F7B/52/kpool-evidence-hopkins.pdf.
Istance, D. (2002) *Schooling for the Future – trends, scenarios and lifelong learning*. Paris: OECD/CERI. Available at: http://www.oecd.org/dataoecd/50/46/1940163.pdf.
Leithwood, K., Jantzi, D. and Steinbach, R. (1999) *Changing Leadership for Changing Times*. Buckingham: OU Press.
Leithwood, K. (2001) School leadership in the context of accountability policies, *International Journal of Leadership in Education*, 4(3), 217–35.
NCSL (2006) *Bursor Development Progromme: Impact and Evaluation Report* 2004/05, Nottingham: National College for School Leadership.

OECD (2004) International Schooling for Tomorrow Forum, Toronto. Lead Country Paper: England. *Progress Report on Futuresight – England's Contribution to the Toolkit.*

OECD (2005) *Overview of the OECD schooling for tomorrow programme.* Available at: http://www.oecd.org/document/6/0,2340,en_2649_201185_31420934_1_1_1_1,00.html.

Prashnig, B. (1998) *The Power of Diversity.* New Zealand: David Bateman. Available at: http://www.creativelearningcentre.com/resources.asp?page=articles&sub=learn-ingstylesarticles&lang=&cs=NZ%24&cr=1&theme=main.

Sammons, P., Hillman, J. and Mortimore, P. (1995) *Key Characteristics of Effective Schools: A review of the school effectiveness research.* London: OFSTED and the Institute of Education, University of London.

Senge, P. (1990) *The Fifth Discipline: The art and practice of the learning organisation.* New York: Doubleday.

Williams, C. Horne, M., Mc Carthy, H., Creasy, J. Harris, S. (2004) *Progress of Futuresight.* Available at: http://www.oecd.org/dataoecd/41/58/32503581.PDF.

Index